Childhood Narcissism

Childhood Narcissism

Strategies to Raise Unselfish, Unentitled, and Empathetic Children

Mary Ann Little, PhD

ROWMAN & LITTLEFIELD
Lanham • Boulder • New York • London

Published by Rowman & Littlefield
An imprint of The Rowman & Littlefield Publishing Group, Inc.
4501 Forbes Boulevard, Suite 200, Lanham, Maryland 20706
www.rowman.com

86-90 Paul Street, London EC2A 4NE

British Library Cataloguing in Publication Information Available

Library of Congress Cataloging-in-Publication Data

Names: Little, Mary Ann, 1952- author.
Title: Childhood narcissism : strategies to raise unselfish, unentitled, and empathetic children / Mary Ann Little.
Description: Lanham : Rowman & Littlefield, [2023] | Includes bibliographical references and index.
Identifiers: LCCN 2023016176 (print) | LCCN 2023016177 (ebook) | ISBN 9781538182161 (cloth) | ISBN 9781538182178 (ebook)
Subjects: LCSH: Narcissism in children—Popular works. | Narcissism in children—Prevention—Popular works. | Child rearing—Popular works.
Classification: LCC RJ506.N37 L58 2023 (print) | LCC RJ506.N37 (ebook) | DDC 618.92/85854—dc23/eng/20230703
LC record available at https://lccn.loc.gov/2023016176
LC ebook record available at https://lccn.loc.gov/2023016177

The fate of Narcissus is to suffer
the pain of disconnection from others
and isolation from the self.

Contents

Introduction

Sharing My Toolbox for Stopping Narcissism

$\mathcal{I}$'ve been a psychologist for more than forty years and have seen just about every imaginable scenario: anxiety, eating disorders, depression, substance abuse, broken homes, self-harm, learning disabilities, grief, posttraumatic stress, Asperger's, geniuses (both talented and tormented), physical abuse, developmental delays, schizophrenia, traumatic brain injury, and physical disabilities, as well as many healthy children, adults, and families who ended up in my office due to loss, disease, or trauma or who simply wanted to be their best selves. But there is one thing I have never seen: no parent has ever told me, "I hope my child grows up to be a narcissist."

No one wants his or her child to exploit others, be selfish, demand special treatment, or lack empathy. No parent wants to see their little one grow up unable to sustain fulfilling relationships and miss finding contentment and happiness as an adult. However, despite our best intentions, narcissism in our society continues to thrive.

The study of how and why humans grow, change, and adapt across the course of their lives first captured me in college and graduate school. My interest in developmental psychology has grown over the years with broader knowledge and greater challenge and has influenced my professional training, academic specialty, and clinical placements. It has led me to focus on the relationship between parent and child and, ultimately, to search for strategies that would allow me to intervene constructively in family systems. There are countless parenting books that outline stages of child development, offer sage and well-informed advice, or present a check-the-box approach to parenting, but rehashing best practices is not the goal of this book.

The issue I discuss in this book—how narcissism starts in childhood but can be diverted—is complex. There is no simple rule of thumb that will prevent your child from being a narcissist. It's taken four decades of study, practice, and experience to develop a toolbox for stopping narcissism when it typically begins—in childhood. The purpose of this book is to share those tools with you—the parents, grandparents, aunts, uncles, teachers, and coaches who define the lives of the children around you.

MY FIVE CRITICAL OBSERVATIONS
ABOUT CHILDHOOD NARCISSISM

1. *Narcissism undermines the capacity for happiness:* The consequences of narcissism are well documented, and there is a good chance you have wondered if someone around you is a narcissist. This observation is not novel, but it is important that we consider the roots of narcissism and why we want to avoid these tendencies and traits. Fundamentally, narcissism prevents people from achieving happiness. If you are hardwired to need to believe you are better, more deserving, smarter, more attractive—whatever it might be—than others, you are destined to experience disappointment, frustration, and problematic relationships.

2. *Narcissism is often anchored in childhood:* Narcissistic tendencies and traits are, in large part, taught, adopted, and anchored in childhood and adolescence. Parents are not to blame. They do not create narcissists—but they can, often unwittingly, encourage narcissism in the child. Parenting styles that support the development of narcissism have become more dominant among *all* parents. Making this reality worse is that well-intended parents rarely recognize the systems around their children that lead toward narcissistic development. Trained therapists realize the extent to which experiences in childhood and adolescence define development, both positive and negative, reverberating over the course of a lifetime. The development of narcissistic structures is arguably the most damaging because such structures ensure that those children will struggle in ways that can be prevented.

3. *Our society increasingly promotes and instills narcissistic tendencies and traits:* Try going fifteen minutes on any day without seeing

signs of narcissistic values. Likes, shares, follows, and awards are crowd-sourced, based on perceived beauty, achievement, power, and likelihood of success. Acceptance into esteemed colleges, high schools, elementary schools, and preschools is based on relatively superficial and gameable standards. The measuring stick varies, but the structure is increasingly consistent. Children (and often their parents) vie for attention and accolades by presenting perceived superiorities to the world, whether actual or artificial.

More troubling is the fact that narcissistic messages are ubiquitous and their influence unavoidable: be beautiful, thin, or rich, no matter how you get there; get ahead regardless of who you hurt in the process; use people if it benefits you; take what you want because you need it; put others down if it elevates you—the list is long and growing. Such narcissistic values are shortsighted and ultimately problematic. They encourage narcissistic development in the child and, at the same time, undermine healthy parenting practices.

4. *Narcissistic tendencies and traits are extremely difficult to reverse in adulthood:* Frederick Douglass said, "It is easier to build strong children than to repair broken men." I could not come up with a better axiom based on my years of practice. This is not to say that "broken men" cannot be fixed. Having personally seen hundreds of patients turn around their conditions, I am more optimistic now than I have ever been. However, reversing the effects of harmful structures built in childhood is extremely difficult and increasingly unlikely, once established and fully formed in adulthood.

5. *Parents can stop and reverse narcissism:* By understanding how the roots of childhood narcissism develop and recognizing specific negative influences on the child and adolescent, informed parents can stop the development of narcissism. The keys are tied to developing an awareness of the problem, working to build healthy structures in the child, and gaining insight into your own parenting position.

The book is divided into three broad sections that address the nature of narcissism, identify strategies to avoid narcissistic development through building healthy personality structures, and explain broad parenting practices that encourage and discourage narcissism.

Part I: Narcissism Considered

In order to avoid narcissism, you have to know what it looks like and how it operates.

Before we explore the tools we have at our disposal, it is important to be able to spot narcissism and understand why it is such a damaging condition. Part I provides just that, an *overview of childhood narcissism*, its prevalence, and the various presentations of narcissists-to-be (N2B) during childhood, which include the high-achieving narcissist, the non-achieving narcissist, the bully narcissist, the daredevil narcissist, the closet narcissist, and the manipulative narcissist. This section introduces the notion of "structure," a concept that describes the processes taking place under the surface in the child that are not typically seen in exterior behavior. It identifies and discusses the emerging tendencies and traits—actual structural flaws—seen in children that are warning signs of the potential development of a full-blown narcissistic disorder in adulthood. I also describe how I came to understand N2B (narcissists-to-be) development in childhood, after struggling to treat the resulting disorder in adults for decades.

Part II: Raising a Non-narcissistic Child

The key to avoiding narcissism is to build structures that counter unhealthy tendencies.

Part II explores the four psychological structures developing over childhood that will secure emotional health and prevent narcissistic development: a healthy model of the self, a steady ability to regulate emotions, an accurate capacity to take in and process information, and a positive model of love and relationships. Each chapter is divided into three sections:

a. The development of the specific structure over time
b. Signs of the healthy or not-so-healthy structure in the child

c. Parent contributions to the development of the healthy or not-so-healthy structure in the child

The first section provides background information and is more theoretical. The second section helps parents "see" the structure under development through specific examples. The last section identifies specific parenting practices that encourage or discourage healthy development in that area.

Part III: Strategies to Defeat Childhood Narcissism

No one is perfect, so it is important for parents to be aware of narcissistic pitfalls.
Part III identifies four parent types that promote narcissism in children: hovering/directive, indulgent/permissive, critical/harsh, and inattentive/disengaged. This section also describes the likely outcomes associated with each parenting type. It explains that narcissism is, in large part, born of treatment on "both ends" of a continuum, with each extreme being formative. N2Bs either receive "too much" or "too little" of an essential something in their growing up. "Moderation parenting" is explained and shown to be the key to raising empathetic, unentitled, and caring children. For most parents, this section of the book will be particularly valuable with its focus on parenting styles that encourage or discourage narcissism. For clinicians, this section explains the underpinnings of narcissism and proposes a new theory of its development.

This book is written with different audiences in mind, and, for this reason, some direction at the outset is indicated. The reader is encouraged to *review the headings* within each chapter to decide which portions are most relevant to them and their situation. Using the book in this way will help determine which sections could be skimmed and which should be read carefully.

The website, drmaryannlittle.com, offers study guides for Part II of the book that correspond to each specific chapter:

The Non-narcissistic Model of the Self: A Guide to Development
The Non-narcissistic Ability to Regulate Emotions: A Guide to Development
The Non-narcissistic Ability to Take In and Process Information: A Guide to Development

The Non-narcissistic Model of Love and Relationships: A Guide to Development.

It also shares study guides from Part III that correspond to two of those chapters:

View and Treatment of the Child: A Guide to Assessing the Two Critical Dimensions in N2B Parenting
Identifying Parenting Positions that Build N2B Children: A Guide to Understanding and Changing for the Better.

Graphics that identify risky parenting positions—Hovering/Directive, Indulgent/Permissive, Critical/Harsh, and Inattentive/Disengaged—are also available there.

Over my years of practice, I have treated countless adults who suffered from narcissism to varying degrees or who have been involved with narcissists as spouses, parents, or children. Also, through work with parents, I have intervened to halt the narcissistic progression in children who presented with narcissistic tendencies and traits. This book is a compilation of the insights and accompanying strategies that I have developed for use in my office and in the materials created for presentation in my lectures. The tools I share here are based on those years of clinical experience and my own informal longitudinal study of witnessing the narcissistic trajectory and the varied responses to intervention in my patients' lives.

Childhood Narcissism is the culmination of my lifelong commitment to the mental health and emotional well-being of my patients and the greater community. It reflects my long-held professional bias that, whenever possible, it is better to grow strong and caring children than to repair childhood injury in adulthood.

I

NARCISSISM CONSIDERED

· 1 ·

Lessons from Narcissus

The tragedy of Narcissus is well known. A handsome youth was caused to fall in love with his own reflection in a pool. Less well known is how he earned this harsh punishment. A maiden, so angered by her failed efforts to attract Narcissus and his insensitive and cruel response to her attention, whispered a prayer that he might know what it felt like to love and not have that affection returned. An avenging goddess granted the maiden's prayer. Narcissus's agony was the result of his selfish and unempathetic response to the nymphs in the forest, and his penance was the experience of unrequited love. Sadly, his self-absorption ultimately resulted in his death.

Ovid's tale teaches an important lesson. It cautions against self-centeredness, arrogance, and lack of empathy. To be so desirable and yet so crippled internally is a tragic theme only intensified by Narcissus's youth and exceptional physical beauty.

Sadly, the fate of Narcissus is not confined to mythology. Too many youngsters are growing up with many of the unenviable traits of narcissism. They bear the same remarkable contradictions—exceptional talent, beauty, achievement, or skill that contrasts with a deprived inner self, whether malevolent, hypercompetitive, self-absorbed, mean, or simply empty. On the one hand, these children are talented and accomplished, attractive and engaging, popular and sought after socially. Yet, at the same time, they have a darker side that often goes unrecognized, most especially in childhood and adolescence. Beneath their generally appealing exterior, these children have an emerging view of themselves as better than others, a growing expectation of being accommodated by others, and a budding belief that their needs are more important than those around them.

Over time, these children, now adolescents, present more clearly to the trained eye as selfish and self-centered, lacking in empathy, interpersonally manipulative, and riddled with unseen, unconscious deficits in self-esteem, often disguised by an air of specialness or superiority. In the end, these young people bring frustration and disappointment to those who would share their emotional lives and harsh consequences to those who cross them. They suffer exceedingly when their narcissistic goals are frustrated. Going forward, being the parent, friend, spouse, or coworker of a narcissist, while initially gratifying, ultimately turns painful and unfulfilling. In the final analysis, the narcissist's injured and poorly developed self-concept leads to a lack of connection in relationships and an accompanying lack of fulfillment more generally in life, even in the face of external measures to the contrary. The numerous life trajectories that I have witnessed professionally over many years illustrate the observed patterns of development and dysfunction.

ELLIOT

Elliot was an adorable boy with a big smile, bright eyes, and a head full of strawberry blond curls. He was highly verbal and absolutely engaging. His exceptionality was evident in an instant. He seemingly had it all—brilliant, athletic, good-looking, engaging socially, and talented in almost every aspect. While many parents will not admit it, most secretly look at him, his talents, and achievements and wonder why their child cannot be more like that. He learned to read without much effort and became a recognized writing talent by third grade. He breezed through math and spent time in the after-school math enrichment program. He was identified by his teachers as "talented and gifted" when only in first grade. He started competitive soccer at four and would end up on a "select" team while still in grade school. He began playing chess in elementary school and went on to win in local and state competitions. His peers liked him and were impressed with his consistent achievements. Most boys wanted to be on his team at recess. He was invited everywhere.

In middle school, Elliot's athletic skills progressed. While both a soccer player and excellent at baseball, he gave up baseball to play in the highest-level soccer league in the city. His academics continued at a high level. His chess skills progressed too, though he gave that up to meet the demands of his athletics. He was popular and sought after by his peers given his big personality, academic achievement, and strong athletic skills.

By high school, Elliot was a clear academic standout. He excelled in all areas, proving to be stronger in math than literature but competent in all. His strategic chess skills transitioned into debate, where he performed outstandingly at the national Lincoln debate competition. Not surprisingly, he was accepted at an Ivy League college and was the pride of both parents.

In college, Elliot met many kids just like himself and he continued to do well there. But once in an environment with people more his equal, he was no longer the singular standout. He continued to achieve but was no longer a "star." He became frustrated with the lack of singular attention from his professors and peers. He joined an elite fraternity and drank heavily.

Elliot graduated college, went to an excellent graduate school, and ultimately entered the workforce. He took a job with a prestigious large corporation and made exceptional money for his age and stage in life. He was able to live in a nice apartment and travel extensively. He partied and had lots of friends who enjoyed the perks that went with being in his orbit. Somehow, though, the picture was not as rosy as it once was, as he became less satisfied with his life.

Elliot's interpersonal skills had not developed as well as his record of achievement. Now no longer the center of attention, he became more noticeably self-centered and self-absorbed. He adopted a superior attitude over the lesser people at work and tended to be intolerant of the imperfections of the people working below him. These negative traits meant that he didn't score well in terms of his "aptitude" for management. He received some negative reviews from HR, and his career was not moving as rapidly as he expected. Elliot was aggravated that he was not on the "fast track."

Handsome and charming, Elliot had numerous relationships with women. He generally broke their hearts and moved on, engaging in lengthy "flings," but never having committed relationships. The one girl who was involved with him over a longer period of time became frustrated with his self-centeredness and left him.

Elliot's parents returned to see me when he was in his early thirties, noticeably upset. They reported that Elliot was preoccupied and inattentive to them. They also worried that he was not dating women who would be "good" wives and mothers. They saw him as increasingly insensitive, self-centered, and unconcerned about the feelings of others. He had forgotten to send his mother a card for Mother's Day and didn't call his brother on his birthday. He was aggravated when his mother complained of having hurt feelings and dismissed her as "too sensitive." Somehow Elliott was not the star he once was, and neither he nor his parents were adjusting to this new reality.

ELLEN

Ellen was a cute little girl who was best described as "nice." She had an articulation disorder in preschool and saw a speech pathologist for several years. She began elementary school and learned to read with effort and determination. Early on, there was nothing to distinguish her. She learned to write and spell just like all the other children in first grade. She was a diligent student at her schoolwork and turned in her homework on time. She simply did her job and never "stood out," whether waiting in line in kindergarten or helping a classmate with their homework after school.

In middle school, Ellen was inconspicuously capable—always able to do what was required. She was likable but not the "belle of the ball." Her achievement was solid, but she was not a particularly talented student or athlete. She did not assume any leadership positions at school but was appointed to a student council committee where she did her work well and on time. She joined a youth group at her church and participated in community service projects there.

Ellen graduated from high school with a solid A average. She continued her community service work through her church. Her teachers liked her and respected her. Looking back over her career, her teachers and family members remember her as unusually helpful and noted that she could be counted on for attending to the little things. Those involved in writing her college recommendation letters realized that she had done quite a bit better than they thought and was much more involved than they knew. She did her work quietly, so her achievements went without celebration or recognition, but she often went "above and beyond" what was required.

Ellen attended a large, moderately competitive public college, and in this environment, her skills began to shine. Her independence and ability to get things done steadily advanced her into leadership positions both socially and academically. By her junior year, she was in the top 1 percent of her class as an "honorary fellow" working toward a select course of study in her chosen field. Interestingly, she was selected for her academics, ability to work with others, willingness to be a team player, and commitment to establish and work toward her goals. Ellen saw herself realistically, knowing that she was not a great intellect but rather a hard worker. She was proud of her successes and was not threatened by the talents and efforts of others. In fact, she celebrated the skills of her peers and her teachers.

Ellen went on to take a high-level government job in Washington, DC, securing a much sought-after position following an extremely competitive search. She was successful at work and was steadily promoted, consistently taking on increasing responsibility and broadening her training. She had many friends and dated regularly, patiently waiting to find the "right" relationship. In her late twenties, she met a young man who became her "best friend." She married him and has been "happily married" for years. They have three children and work well together juggling two careers and their busy lives as parents.

LESSONS LEARNED

Without question, Elliot was the child that many parents wished for as their own. He was a superstar by all standards, accomplished in so many areas and so charming. But he did not turn out to be the person that his parents wanted him to be—or a person who found satisfaction and happiness in daily life. By contrast, Ellen was a "sleeper." Her light was hidden under a bushel. While her parents delighted in her through the years, there was no consensus that she was anything more than a "nice girl" until she matured.

I have seen numerous Elliots and Ellens through my years of practice. They have come in a variety of styles and presentations, but the outcomes remain the same. As a young and inexperienced psychologist,

I was surprised at the decline in Elliot's promise into young adulthood, and at the acceleration of Ellen's competence and success over the same time period. Somehow, excellence in achievement, extraordinary talent early on, or notable accelerated development did not ensure comparable outcomes in the following decades. Nor did ordinary, unremarkable development in childhood point to unimpressive outcomes in later life. Rather, the opposite often proved true: confidence, competence, diligence, good character, and emotional intelligence usually win out over time.

When I lecture, I ask parents to choose between Elliot and Ellen as to the child they would prefer as their own as the age-related stages of their development were revealed in preschool, early elementary, later elementary, middle school, high school, college, and young adulthood. Not surprisingly, in a show of hands, the vast majority voted for Elliot as a youngster, believing he had already secured an impressive future. Ellen, for all her steadiness, did not inspire parental validation at the same points in time. But as the years passed, Elliot's early advantages and successes began to fade, and Ellen's unseen potential began to show itself. By young adulthood, the contrast was remarkable. What explains these differences? Was it possible to see Elliot's flaws earlier and change his life course? Could Elliot's parents and teachers have intervened earlier and reversed those negative tendencies and traits before becoming set in adulthood? Were Ellen's strengths recognizable early on when there was little or no acknowledgment in the real world? Can we better support the parents of the many Ellens, reinforcing their solid parenting, building their confidence in their child when outside support is lacking, and lessening the self-doubt they experience in the face of competitive failure?

HIDDEN BENEATH THE SURFACE: PERSONALITY FLAWS AND STRENGTHS IN CHILDHOOD

A careful historical look at both children's development would reveal clues along the way. Subtle hints were there all along—hidden beneath Elliot's intoxicating array of talents and impressive record of accomplishment and largely unrecognized in Ellen's understated style and relatively unremarkable achievement.

A deeper review of Elliot's history would show that the later identified problematic trends were evident early on. In elementary school, the record would reveal, he fought incessantly with his brother and was quick to anger. There were rumors that a soccer teammate changed teams because of his teasing. In middle school, he was critical of the less talented debaters on the team and overly proud of his accomplishments. In high school, he was disliked by some for being boastful and full of himself. In college, he was openly frustrated and disagreeable at no longer being the single shining star, and his academic effort diminished in the face of stiff competition. Once on the job, he was intolerant of people on his team and did not inspire a collegial atmosphere. Ever popular, his close relationships failed to have the appropriate depth. His lack of empathy meant he didn't remember Mother's Day or his brother's birthday, and he chose to spend time with his buddies drinking at the beach and miss the family reunion. His parents, for all their prior pride, suffered worry, wondering where their Elliot had gone. Tragically, what they did not know was that this was the Elliot who had been "growing up" right in front of their eyes despite all the evidence to the contrary.

Ellen's talents and competencies were also there, but neither teachers nor neighbors nor school personnel made much of them at the time. She was a good kid, without either attracting attention for misbehavior and problems or being recognized for any special talents. People liked her, but there was no one betting on her future successes. Yet solid development was evident if one looked deeper. Ellen was a hard worker from the beginning. She tolerated the frustration of not having academics come easily to her and achieved all the necessary academic competencies. Early leadership skills, while not recognized at school, were evident in smaller environments. She organized the children for a block party around Halloween. She took flowers to the old man down the street when his wife died. She played kindly with the Down syndrome boy next door. She loved her parents demonstratively, making homemade cards and creating "special surprises" for holidays. She learned to bake and took cookies to the preschool class at the church over Christmas. She was a good friend to many but had a "best friend" that remains close even now. She routinely celebrated the successes of others and was not threatened if they achieved at levels that she could not match.

Over my forty years of practice and my own informal longitudinal study, I would learn that it was the internal, invisible skills and abilities, not the external presentation, that would predict success in adulthood and later life. It is these internal skills and abilities that I refer to as personality structures. It became my mission to identify and address these signs during the developmental period—to find the underlying reasons for those accelerations and regressions and their ultimate outcomes, and to intervene while change was still possible.

A truth would become obvious. Future successes for children are the result of the development of healthy internal psychological structures and the absence of unhealthy ones as they grow and mature.

THE IMPORTANCE OF UNDERLYING PERSONALITY STRUCTURE

Personality is a set of characteristics that define a person: the thoughts, feelings, attitudes, and actions that are predictable and describe their way of being. This is their "personality." This book focuses on the development of four key personality structures that my years as a psychologist have revealed to be the essential variables that predict success or lack thereof.

Sheila smiles easily when she sees others, listens thoughtfully when they talk, touches her friend's arm gently when she greets them, attends to her dog religiously, loves nature and works steadfastly in her garden, sings while she washes dishes, always remembers her friend's birthday, laughs at good jokes, and tears up at the story of a disadvantaged child. These qualities and traits are predictable, and Sheila's family and friends expect her to behave in these ways. She is known to herself and others in these terms. This would be Sheila's personality, and it is a steady predictable way of being.

Henry has a great sense of humor and is the life of the party. He laughs easily and tells jokes, often at the expense of others. He is competitive and bright, always striving to outdo his peers. He's an engaging conversationalist and fun to be around. He rarely talks of feelings and focuses primarily on the events of the day. People like his optimism and are attracted to him. He is never moody, not a profound thinker, but generally good company.

Personalities are complicated and often evidence inconsistencies. People can be consistently steady at work and still volatile in the privacy of their homes. But the general term *personality* tends to describe the overarching presentation, the descriptor of major tendencies such as extrovert or enthusiast, or major styles such as hysterical or paranoid or overly sensitive. They also describe qualities of character such as reliability, perseverance, and honesty to name only a few. By adulthood, these tendencies and traits are considered to be largely stable and set.

One is not born with a personality. However, children are born with a biologically given *temperament* that will influence the development of that personality. Considerable research has studied and defined temperament, identifiable at birth, that can be classified as easy, difficult, or slow to warm. Longitudinal studies show temperament to be stable over time, though there is evidence that it can be modified through interactions with sensitive patient adults for the better, or through interactions with harsh, insensitive adults for the worse. Temperament will predispose children to the development of more adaptable and healthy personality traits or more difficult and unhealthy personality traits. This is a consistent finding in the research.

Personality develops over time in an orderly progression. The child, in effect, learns how to become a fully functioning person. This process unfolds as the child's brain develops in interactions with parents, friends, and the larger world.

- He develops stable ways of *defining himself.*
- He learns who he is in relation to others.
- He develops a sense of self-esteem made up of caring and concern for himself.
- He learns to count on being the same person with the same qualities, traits, and abilities from day to day.
- He develops stable ways of *defining relationships.*
- He develops an understanding of what to expect in dealings with others.
- He develops a sense of the nature of relationships, made up of care, value, and concern for them.
- He learns to count on others as being the same person with the same qualities, traits, and abilities from day to day.
- He learns the rules of social interaction initially from those he loves and later from those he knows.

In the process of these interactions with parents and significant others, the child will develop strategies to regulate emotions and process information. Personality disorders are the result of something going wrong in the orderly progression of child development toward healthy adaptation and psychological growth. If children have an unresponsive, invalidating, or insensitive parent, or experience traumatic or injurious experiences, they are susceptible to failing to develop a full mature adult personality. Various forms of poor nurture or trauma can result in the child's personality being impaired or stunted at an earlier developmental stage. The child's immature or poorly formed base—or structure—will inhibit learning the necessary skills and abilities to be a mature, fully functioning adult. The repercussions of that stunted development are far reaching. Sadly, the child's sense of self will not grow beyond childhood levels. Their ability to understand and engage in complex interpersonal relationships will not develop beyond childhood levels. Further, their ability to regulate their emotions and refine their perceptual skills will remain immature as well.

These personality deficits, if reinforced and not nurtured toward change over time, will result in a personality disorder. A personality disorder then becomes a stable, predictable pattern of personality impairment that is characterized by immature, unhealthy, maladaptive function.

Personality disorders are distinguished by the extent to which their dysfunctional behaviors cause distress to those who interact with them frequently. For this reason, most personality-disordered individuals do not seek treatment but are typically referred by spouses, family, or coworkers. It is important to emphasize that those who have personality disorders are significantly more dysfunctional than people with more mainstream neurotic issues or milder mood problems such as those seen in easily treated depression or anxiety.

There are numerous personality disorders, and they come in a variety of flavors and styles. While each presents differently, they share specific predictable and stable dysfunctional characteristics that interfere with contented, reliable function and finding and maintaining fulfilling meaningful relationships with others.

This book focuses on childhood narcissism, including its early warning signs in children and adolescents and the potential for the development of narcissistic personality disorder over childhood. Importantly, childhood narcissism represents a growing concern in American society and poses a real threat to the healthy maturation of American youth.

THE NATURE OF PERSONALITY DEVELOPMENT: BUILDING STRUCTURE OVER TIME

As I searched for explanations as to the development of narcissism in the children in my practice, the role of parents in helping or hindering mature personality development became increasingly obvious. At the same time, there was emerging research that confirmed my observations. Indulgent parenting, permissive parenting, and parental overvaluation each appears to be associated with narcissism. Parental overcontrol, both in the form of parental coldness and parental intrusiveness, also appears to be associated with narcissism. Interestingly, these general findings are consistent with clinical theories about the development of narcissism in childhood and match my clinical observations and understandings.

I conceptualize personality development as a process of structure building. In this book, I identify and explain the specifics in that orderly progression and name the important structures that mature into healthy or not-so-healthy outcomes. Some of those dysfunctions result in destructive personality tendencies or traits, while others result in full-blown personality disorders.

In later chapters, my four-point analysis of personality structure is covered in detail with case examples. Four specific structures are referenced in separate chapters and include models for: self-concept, emotional regulation, perceptual and processing accuracy, and capacity for relationships. Signs of those *healthy* structures in childhood predict who will succeed later in life. Signs of those *faulty* structures in childhood predict who will struggle later in life.

THE ROLE OF PARENTS IN PERSONALITY DEVELOPMENT

Parents can foster the development of healthy structures or contribute to faulty structures through their interactions with their child. Their child's late adolescent or early adult functioning reveals the psychological structures formed in interactions with parents throughout childhood that are necessary to insure health and well-being.

Charles, a seventeen-year-old student at a public high school, was observed playing cornhole with three friends. He and his partner were up by several points. He yelled out encouragingly to one of his opponents, "Come on, George. You can do it." Unexpectedly, the opposing team began to surge and ultimately won the match. Charles shook the hands of the winning opponents and teased playfully, "Good job, George. Next time it will be mine." This small look into Charles's life tells us something about his underlying psychological health.

A lay person can see Charles *is* a good kid. A structuralist can see *why* he is a good kid. His self-concept is securely developed such that he is strong enough to tolerate losing. His notion of friendship includes encouraging others, even competitive rivals, and appreciating their perspective. His mood is regulated, and the sudden reversal of his likely success was not upsetting to him. This small sample of behavior reveals a pattern of healthy adjustment. Such seemingly insignificant moments reveal much from a structural perspective and allow meaningful predictions concerning future adjustment.

A structural perspective allows a more meaningful understanding of various behaviors, actions, and values. The four-point analysis of personality structure reveals that much important information goes unrecognized by parents in the face of more obvious accomplishments and successes; this parental blind spot is supported by broadly accepted, but often misguided, cultural values that stress winning and individual achievement. Information that points to unrecognized but important developing abilities, on the other hand, actually predicts desirable outcomes.

Parents are encouraged to look deeper into their child's development and change their parenting accordingly. Our American culture tends to press for short-term gains. But, in terms of child development, the long game is what matters. The child's future is built on the stability and health of the identified personality structures. Kids with healthy structures will succeed and prove more resilient, while those with faulty structures will, more typically, struggle and suffer failed efforts of various kinds.

This book focuses specifically on narcissism and the associated, often unrecognized, structural flaws that compromise health and happiness. While a discussion of "structure" may be somewhat off-putting, personality development matters. It can create possibilities or problems, encourage health or deficit, ensure positive growth or thwart it. Elliott's promising early development masked underlying structural deficits that proved costly in the end. In order to change the trajectory of every budding "Elliott," parents and professionals must be able to "see" the source of the child's limitations and develop strategies to address them in childhood. Through that process, it is possible to rescue Narcissus and avoid the tragedy of self-centeredness and disconnection.

Childhood Narcissism

The Emerging Pattern—Budding Narcissism in Childhood

*A*s a young psychologist and mother, I believed that I could reliably predict how individual children would mature and could identify who would be well adjusted and successful in life. This was not an altogether unreasonable idea. At that time, my work included administering (over years) innumerable test batteries that measured children's intelligence, academic skills, psychological well-being, and emotional health. Many of these children did not have any identifiable diagnosable issues, being seen only to determine if they were gifted or would be appropriately placed in a highly competitive school. Others were assessed to screen for learning difficulties or attentional issues. Still others were referred for mild childhood distress such as problems in sleeping, separation anxiety after a parent's hospital stay, or sadness over the death of a grandparent. After each evaluation, I followed up with recommendations for school placement, specialized services such as psychotherapy or tutoring, and appropriate parent management interventions.

Over time, I began to realize that there were shortcomings in my ability to predict developmental outcomes. *Young children* who possessed remarkable skills and abilities, who did not evidence obvious difficulties in adjustment, and who had an absence of reported problems at school or home at that time ended up in my office as *older children or adolescents* referred by their parents or teachers with identified problems in peer relationships, conflict with parents or teachers, or issues in their behavior at home or school. As adults, they are referred by their spouses or bosses due to nagging issues in interpersonal relationships or struggles with emotional distress when confronted with disappointment or failure.

Many of these children had problems that went largely unrecognized by the outside world, being seen only by those in close proximity who had greater access to their lives over longer periods of time. I came to refer to these less obvious issues as "silent" problems, which included perfectionism, an absence of emotional depth, loneliness, anxiety, avoidance of emotional closeness, emotional reactivity, and depression. More obvious issues emerged as these children aged and developed; eating disorders, emotional volatility, cutting, acting out, bullying, halted achievement, and debilitating anxiety were among the issues I saw. There were holes in their self-concept, whether seen in vulnerable or grandiose self-esteem. All grew to have immature relationships with peers or parents, teachers, or coworkers. Over time, many of these interpersonal difficulties magnified, became more malignant, and resulted in unfulfilling relationships or failed marriages. While a variety of symptom patterns accompanied their underlying difficulties, interestingly, all suffered from underdeveloped or disturbed social relationships.

A pattern began to emerge from my observations: many of these children had tendencies and traits that were associated with narcissism. Because narcissism has a number of different presentations, the fact that this personality style was the overarching consideration did not become immediately obvious. Yet, once my eye was oriented toward narcissism, I developed more finely tuned powers of observation and was able to identify the narcissistic characteristics interfering with healthy development in those children at younger and younger ages. Many children with narcissistic personality *tendencies* were eventually turning into children with more stable narcissistic *traits*, and then, in the more extreme cases, emerging as pathological *narcissists*. Not surprisingly, the children with narcissistic tendencies and traits struggled in their relationships, as did children with full-blown narcissism. As would be expected, the degree of struggle matched the level of narcissism.

Pathological narcissism is not diagnosed until after the age of eighteen, but the pattern that presaged that outcome was evident much earlier. What I observed in my practice is that many narcissistic tendencies, if reinforced rather than reversed during childhood, became increasingly stable and dysfunctional over these formative years. Eventually, the interaction of temperament and experience appeared to establish lasting personality traits. In other words, those early narcissistic tendencies, if unaddressed and unmediated, often led to stable traits, which later became recognizable clinically as "problematic" or "destructive" narcissistic traits or led to a later diagnosis of "narcissistic personality disorder" (NPD).

NARCISSISTS-TO-BE (N2B)

While NPD is not accepted in the literature as a diagnosable condition in childhood, I began to identify and label those children, in my mind's eye, as narcissists-to-be (N2B). I also began to develop methods of addressing these behaviors and intervening with their parents. I came to understand that certain parenting strategies and parent messaging, if implemented, could make the development of NPD more likely, and that others could reverse a youngster's course as an N2B if addressed in childhood or early adolescence.

With these developmental progressions more clearly set in my thinking, I more readily identified narcissistic tendencies and traits in children. I began to intervene with parents earlier to shape their parenting style, informing their knowledge of the impact of their behavior on their child and building parenting strategies that did not reinforce narcissism.

Realizing that parenting styles supporting the development of narcissism were becoming more dominant among *all* parents, and that the culture was reinforcing narcissistic values generally, I began to lecture at local schools and hospitals, community centers, and clubs. I noticed it was common for attendance to double at each session over the series of three or four lectures. Clearly, there was broad concern about the subject of narcissism in children.

This book is a compilation of the strategies that I developed over forty years of clinical experience and my own informal longitudinal study of witnessing the narcissistic trajectory and the varied responses to intervention. In that period, I have intervened to halt the narcissistic progression in children who were presented with narcissistic tendencies and traits through work with their parents, and I have worked to improve the lives of numerous adults who suffered from narcissism to varying degrees or who dealt with spouses, parents, or children who were narcissistic.

NARCISSISM: AN OVERVIEW AND RECONSIDERATION

Contrary to popular lay understanding, narcissism is not a bad thing. In fact, without healthy narcissism a child cannot develop into a capable, competent, and well-adjusted adult. Sigmund Freud and Heinz Kohut, among other psychoanalysts, understood healthy narcissism as an essential quality involving an adequate sense of self-love. This necessary "self-liking" leads to an ability to love others in mature and selfless ways, devoid of manipulation, exploitation, and harm and characterized by empathy, warmth, and sincerity.[1] With adequate caregiving and nurture over time, children can develop a stronger, steadier, and more resilient self-esteem and self-confidence that actually encourages and, ultimately, enables the development of the ability to love others deeply and unselfishly.

The features of healthy narcissism are qualities every parent would want for their children. They include:

Strong self-regard, self-respect, and self-love
Empathy for others
Recognition of the needs of others
Authentic, integrated self-concept
Ability to tolerate criticism and maintain positive self-regard
Confidence to set and pursue goals
Self-efficacy and persistence
Consistent recovery from disappointment or failure
Healthy pride in the self and in accomplishments
Ability to admire and be admired
Awareness of emotions in the self and others

The child who is well loved and grows up in a secure environment develops an accurate self-concept and positive self-esteem, emerging with a sense of indestructibility, a feeling of power, and a confidence in secure support. These beliefs fortify the child against failure and disappointment and allow him to bounce back from insult or injury, all of which fuel positive growth and development toward contentment, fulfillment, and self-actualization. Self-liking encourages engagement with others, as the child believes, at his core, that he is lovable and can anticipate positive regard from others.

Since getting hurt emotionally is inevitable, from infancy through adulthood, the child with healthy narcissism recovers from injury and pain by restoring a positive sense of self and rebuilding relationships with others. Healthy narcissism contributes to building curiosity, spurring self-discovery, sustaining engagement in activities, pursuing passions, building relationships, adapting to change, and enhancing joy. There can be no doubt: healthy narcissism is both needed and necessary for a child to grow up contented, capable, concerned, and emotionally and socially well-adjusted.

It is important to emphasize that narcissism must always be considered in terms of the age and stage of development. "Age-appropriate narcissism" changes as the child grows and matures. Every item mentioned above will look different depending on the age and stage of the child. A tantrum is age-appropriate healthy narcissism for a toddler venting her demands on the world, but not for a teenager. Empathy and the ability to appreciate the perspective of another is nonexistent in early childhood but will begin to appear in the elementary school years and grow more sensitive, accurate, and strong into adolescence and adulthood.

Healthy adult narcissism includes a more mature development and reflects stable mastery of all of the less well-developed features seen in childhood:

Secure self-esteem
A capacity to establish and maintain deep and satisfying relationships
Mood regulation
An ability to delay gratification
An ability to tolerate frustration, disappointment, and failure
A capacity to express a full range of emotions
The ability to set firm and clear boundaries
The capacity to work on a team and problem solve in groups
A sense of humor, including self-deprecation
The capacity for creativity
Tolerance of risk and criticism

Healthy narcissism is a fundamental and needed resource in childhood, adolescence, and adulthood for full and healthy emotional functioning.

THE NARCISSISTIC CONTINUUM

Narcissism exists on a continuum. At one end is inadequate self-liking, self-regard, and resilience (i.e., deficient narcissism). Toward the center is the appropriate delight and confidence that goes with reaching a goal, or succeeding at a difficult task, coupled with strong resilience following disappointment or injury (i.e., healthy narcissism). At the other end, there are pathological traits that interfere with finding contentment and establishing fulfilling relationships (i.e., pathological narcissism). Healthy narcissism supplies the drive to mastery, the persistence to reach goals, and the ability to find and make social connections. In contrast, people with pathological narcissism suffer a lifetime of struggle with building and sustaining intimate, interpersonal relationships with family, friends, and coworkers and in finding personal fulfillment and contentment. (See figure 2.1.)

THE NARCISSISM CONTINUUM

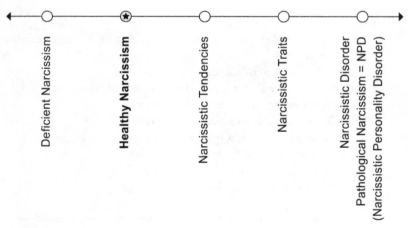

Figure 2.1.

Understanding the movement from healthy narcissism to narcissistic tendencies to traits to disorder is important as it reflects movement toward illness or pathology. Healthy narcissism is necessary to fuel emotional growth. Without it, the drive to develop is limited. However, unhealthy narcissism, by degrees, blocks positive emotional growth proportionate to the degree and pervasiveness of the narcissism.

PATHOLOGICAL NARCISSISM: NARCISSISTIC PERSONALITY DISORDER (NPD)

Narcissistic personality disorder (NPD) is a psychological disorder with a long-term pattern of behavior characterized by exaggerated feelings of self-importance, a sense of entitlement to special treatment, an excessive need for attention and admiration, a self-perception of being unique and superior to others, an exquisite sensitivity to criticism, and a lack of empathy. This constellation of qualities leads to impaired relationships, which are characterized by superficiality, manipulation, exploitation, or other emotional dysfunctions. People with NPD demonstrate punitive behavior when crossed and hold grudges when mistreated.

In a sense, the narcissist does not have the capacity for close, meaningful connections. While these individuals can be intoxicatingly charming and seductive at moments in every relationship, their deficits interfere with the development of intimacy over time. People who fall for narcissists in the beginning find themselves later in an unfulfilling relationship that becomes increasingly empty and toxic. Ironically, the same traits that initially generated attraction become a turnoff when the narcissist's lack of empathy and air of superiority begin to block out meaningful connection over time.

High achievement and functionality are associated with narcissism generally. Many highly successful individuals display personality traits that would certainly be considered narcissistic. In fact, they may be rewarded and celebrated for these successes and accomplishments. Only when these traits produce significant impairment in relationships or result in subjective distress (which is less common) is NPD considered an appropriate diagnosis.

The functioning of narcissistic traits can push individuals toward differing outcomes—relative success or relative failure. Narcissism is a strength in some situations but can be a weakness in others. Many narcissists will be successful in their careers, while others may be unwilling to compete and may refuse to take the steps necessary to be successful. Many will become CEOs or amass wealth or social status, while others will not progress in the work environment due to their inability to tolerate disagreements or criticism and inability to work cooperatively with others. Whether highly successful or relatively underachieving, their difficulties in getting along with others are always an issue. If elevated to a position of power, their deficits are typically tolerated by those around them, as their employees cannot survive pointing out flaws in their boss. If forced to share in control or work on a team, their relationship deficits will likely get them into trouble with their coworkers, clients, or bosses. A narcissistic CEO, surgeon, or litigator may not pay a price for their intolerance, self-assessed superiority, or interpersonal difficulties, while middle managers who must establish cooperation in the workplace may struggle to keep their job, much less be productive at work.

Pathological narcissists can be self-absorbed, unaware of the needs of others, controlling, intolerant of others' views, blaming, impatient, and ignorant of the effects of their behaviors on others. They often insist that others agree with them and see them as they wish to be seen. Narcissists typically become angry when others offer a different point of view or unflattering opinion. They are thin-skinned and collectors of every injustice they have suffered. Their sensitivity to perceived criticism or defeat makes them prone to feelings of worthlessness, shame, and humiliation. They may react to failure or frustration with outbursts of rage, defiance, defensiveness, or by seeking revenge.

NPD is a disorder of disturbed relationships. The dysfunctionalities of NPD are often unrecognized by those not intimately acquainted with them. Typically, only those in close relationships with narcissists can see their deficits. For others, the narcissist's underlying problems are cloaked in the outward appearance of success. Most NPDs do not recognize their traits as problematic. As they typically do not see their deficits for what they are, narcissists rarely seek therapy for their dysfunctional behavior. Most are referred to therapy by their parents, spouses, or coworkers—those who struggle with their negative traits and insist that they make some changes. If NPDs do enter therapeutic treatment on their own, it is typically prompted by life difficulties (failure at work, broken marriage, etc.) or to seek relief from another disorder, such as substance abuse, eating disorders, generalized anxiety, or bipolar disorder.

I recall being consulted by a narcissistic man who arrived in my office in an expensive suit with monograms on his cuff, handkerchief, and briefcase. His stated goal was to understand "what was wrong" with his ex-girlfriend who had recently left him. He had already concluded that she must have left based on some obviously erroneous premise. He never considered that any of his attitudes or behavior might have contributed to her departure. Despite my efforts to engage him in considering that possibility, he dismissed my words.

At this time, the effectiveness of therapeutic interventions in the treatment of NPD has not been well established. In the absence of more thorough research, most treatment recommendations are based on extrapolations from theoretical models or the experiences of clinicians who treat such individuals in clinical settings. While there is not a consensus in the literature, some believe that NPD is an incurable condition due to the narcissist's tendency to receive feedback poorly, react defensively when challenged, and quit therapy when feeling attacked or misunderstood. Skills training for controlling anger, impulsivity, and rage may be helpful but does not address the core dysfunction.

Narcissistic personality disorder usually develops in adolescence or early adulthood. It is common for children and adolescents to display some tendencies and traits similar to those of NPD, but such occurrences are usually transient, and, for this reason, do not meet criteria for a diagnosis of NPD. As a result, an NPD diagnosis cannot be made with confidence until after the age of eighteen. Some, but not all, of the characteristics must be present for a diagnosis, but the overarching criteria is that the symptoms must be sufficiently severe to significantly impair the person's abilities to develop meaningful relationships. Agonizingly for others, the narcissist's sense of superiority may cause them to monopolize conversations. They may purposefully or unknowingly devalue or disparage other people. They may overemphasize their own talents and success without realizing their social blunder. When they are made aware that their behavior is hurtful, they tend to become defensive and react with anger or contempt. They rarely take responsibility for their mistakes or missteps, often blaming the other person. When they are criticized, their anger can be disproportionate to the situation. In the broadest sense, NPD is a problem of a disordered sense of self that causes disordered interpersonal relationships.

PREVALENCE OF PATHOLOGICAL NARCISSISM

The prevalence of NPD ranges from 0.5 to 5–6, or even 10 percent of the general population. However, this is likely an underestimate since, in order to be diagnosed, the narcissist must seek treatment. Lacking insight into their struggles and believing incorrectly that the "problem" is outside of themselves, narcissists infrequently do so. My clinical practice and community experience broadly would suggest that narcissism is considerably more common than these findings would indicate. Whatever the prevalence, it is important to realize that narcissistic personality disorder has its roots in childhood.

CHILDHOOD NARCISSISM

Narcissism is nothing new. The history books are filled with vain and greedy individuals who wield power with little regard for the feelings of others. But childhood narcissists are a special breed. Still in the fragile state of development, they are not easy to spot and many of us will find ourselves confused if confronted with their seemingly ambiguous or unclear behavior. We do not expect the most accomplished student to cry over a B on an exam when it has no impact on their straight-A record. We do not expect the most popular boy, whom we saw push the handicapped child in his wheelchair at the community service site last week, to tease others unmercifully. It is these contradictions in their behavior that often befuddle us and defy early recognition especially by parents and family.

Many budding narcissists will present as downright remarkable in their achievements, being exceedingly charming, clever, powerful, talented, or accomplished. Few achieving narcissists will go unnoticed for their remarkable traits, yet their vulnerabilities or negative traits often remain invisible. Other narcissists attract attention, often identified as the most likely to succeed, the most popular, the most talented, or the most charismatic student in the school. These children outperform their peers and are often the "apple polishers" that teachers adore. Others draw attention as the class clown, the good-looking bad boy, or the seductive queen bee. All share an excessive need for admiration, whether positive or negative. What is generally not seen is their sensitivity to the slightest rebuff, their insistence on getting their own way, their need for recognition, and their primitive responses when they are frustrated or opposed.

Because these children are often unidentified, their ability to wreak havoc is intensified in the social world. Their misbehavior is so unexpected, so subtly shown, or so manipulatively managed that few peers can successfully manage a run in with them. Strategically, they are nearly impossible to outfox, and their distortion of facts makes argumentation unfruitful. Their retelling of the facts often does not match that of the group, but their insistence on the truth of their story, defensiveness, argumentation, and threat of rage often leave others feeling helpless and bewildered. Adults also fall prey to them as well. Principals, teachers, coaches, and ministers, in the face of the narcissist's compelling account, have trouble imagining the story as the whiny unathletic youngster presented it. All too often, it is easier to return to the soccer drill than take time to sort through the difficult encounter. The truth often seems elusive, and school officials have less and less time to devote to sorting through interpersonal skirmishes at school. Given the cultural demands for strong academics, high achievement, and outstanding performance, adult time is often spent elsewhere.

Identifying narcissism in childhood is problematic. Many symptoms and traits of narcissism are a normal part of child development. For this reason, narcissism cannot be diagnosed until the end of adolescence, as personality is still "under construction" until young adulthood and, therefore, is variable and may resolve before maturing. Many maladaptive tendencies are normal during childhood and are only considered abnormal if they persist long enough to become stable patterns of behavior in an adult. Even if we see the narcissistic tendency or trait in childhood, it is not always clear how pervasive the condition is or what the ultimate influence will become. However, my years of clinical experience suggest that early identification of narcissistic tendencies and traits is a worthy endeavor, as it can guide parents to intervene in ways that are most likely to reverse those trends in childhood. Early intervention is important because a full-blown narcissistic personality disorder in adulthood is extremely resistant to treatment.

One of the problems in diagnosing narcissism is the variety of presentations. Narcissists come in different sizes and shapes because the underlying functional difficulties find expression in various forms and combinations of behavior. Narcissism is also difficult to recognize, as it is now prevalent almost everywhere in the community and culture, so commonplace that it has become "normalized" and often goes unnoticed for the illness that it actually is. The publicized excesses, arrogance, and superiority of the very wealthy and famous are usually tolerated and often envied. Many aspire to be like "celebrities" at all levels and want the products and lifestyles that they model or may endorse.

TWO BROAD TYPES OF NARCISSISTS

In my clinical work, I identified two major themes in narcissistic development, which give rise to a variety of individual types. Those two themes are also noted in the research. First is the *vulnerable* narcissist who presents as more anxious and is often high achieving, typically flying under the radar. Second is the *grandiose* narcissist who tends to be more flamboyant, charismatic, controlling, and manipulative. The grandiose type is often popular and perceived to be a leader. The rather large difference between these two themes leads to problems in recognition and, ultimately, diagnosis. The chart in figure 2.2 illustrates those broad differences:

Differences in the Exterior of a Vulnerable and Grandiose Narcissist	
Vulnerable Narcissist	*Grandiose Narcissist*
More anxious	Less anxious
More understated	"Bigger" presentation*
Quieter	Louder
Softer, less obvious control	Stronger, more obvious control
More perfectionistic	Less perfectionistic
High achieving generally	Achievement level can vary
Less prone to public acting out	More prone to public acting out
Quiet aggression or drive	More obvious aggression or drive
Infantilized spoiled child	Uncivilized spoiled child
Thin-skinned	Thick-skinned
	* whether charismatic, flamboyant, or arrogant

Figure 2.2.

It is important to emphasize that the differences between the exterior of a vulnerable as opposed to a grandiose narcissist can be extreme. Many lay people find it hard to believe that the more nerdy, perfectionistic, high-achieving valedictorian has the same interior psychological structure as the popular football captain who can be manipulative, controlling, and prone to bullying others. A newer research-generated model of narcissism regards grandiose and vulnerable narcissism as two related but separate types.[2] Both share the core features of self-importance, a sense of entitlement, and disagreeableness, but they differ on the characteristics that blend with that core. This newer conceptualization better accounts for the variability in the observable traits of narcissism.

SUBTYPES OF CHILDHOOD NARCISSISTS

The vulnerable and grandiose types can be further refined, particularly in the case of children. Over time, I began to characterize budding childhood narcissists (N2Bs) into subtypes, which present with different exteriors. While most can be classified as one subtype of narcissist, there are some who evidence aspects of more than one. All shared the same underlying deficits in self-concept and self-esteem, and ultimately, as they grew older, the same disruption in developing healthy interpersonal relationships.

The High-Achieving Narcissist (Coping with Narcissistic Vulnerability through Winning)

High-achieving narcissists cope with their narcissistic vulnerability through exceptional performance. They must be the best, or practically perfect in every way. The effort they put into achievement often has a maniacal quality. They work harder because they must perform and be better than everyone else. Areas of exceptionality vary, but these are the children who make straight A's or are the teacher's pet. They write perfect essays, win the science fair, or play the lead in the school play. Schools and the current culture support and reward these children, as they are the ones that make both private and public schools look good, and teachers feel proud. High-achieving narcissists are the kids most difficult to diagnose because their perfectionistic performance masks any underlying deficiencies or distress. It is important to emphasize that the diagnosis of a high-achieving narcissist is not based on their exceptional performance but rather on what drives the need to achieve. If their self-esteem is intact and they achieve out of passion or intense interest (not a need for external validation), they are not narcissists.

I treated a high-achieving narcissist some time ago, a well-respected lawyer who had achieved an exceptional level of financial and professional success. He recounted his experience as a college student at a highly competitive university that was known for its basketball team. He told me that he particularly enjoyed studying during the university basketball games. When he was at the library studying and his peers were at the stadium, he knew that he was getting ahead of his classmates. For him, and others like him, the need to achieve had pushed out normal pleasure in service of competitive advantage.

The Non-achieving Narcissist (Coping with Narcissistic Vulnerability and Fear of Failure through Avoidance)

Non-achieving narcissists are the children who value recognition and attention but have been unable to achieve commensurate with those desires. Frustrated and hurt by their underachievement, they cope through avoidance. Some withdraw from the competition and display a kind of "don't care" attitude. Others will act out in maladaptive ways, trying to get attention through misbehavior or risk-taking. All have given up on the idea that they can succeed in a way that wins recognition and positive regard.

The Bully Narcissist (Coping with Narcissistic Vulnerability and Values through Unchecked Aggression)

Bully narcissists have an underlying "mean streak" that they exercise in controlling others. They abuse others socially, through exclusion, and physically, through ridicule and teasing, which can turn into hazing in young adulthood. Some are the queen bees and the most popular boys on campus. They often mediate inclusion and exclusion in social groups without regard for fairness or honor, with a concern only for their own power. Often charismatic and likable, their flaws are difficult to see, much less acknowledge. As their social skills are strong, their misbehavior is hard to catch. Many parents and teachers cannot sort through their active deception. It is not uncommon for a parent or principal to say, "It couldn't involve Jason. He's the most popular guy at McArthur High."

The Daredevil Narcissist (Coping with Narcissistic Vulnerability through Unchecked Grandiosity)

Daredevil narcissists are youngsters whose grandiosity has not been softened through the years. In the school-aged years, their grandiosity can be seen in eye-catching clothes or schoolyard feats like riding a bike alarmingly fast down a steep hill. Older, they can engage in dangerous behaviors that range from drug or alcohol abuse to dangerous driving and sexual promiscuity. Lack of good judgment is their fatal flaw. Their dangerousness is significantly intensified if they are in leadership positions, as their deficient judgment can encourage other children to take risks that they would otherwise not take.

The Closet Narcissist (Coping with Narcissistic Vulnerability through Association with a Narcissist)

Closet narcissists do not look like narcissists at all. Unaware of their narcissistic vulnerability, they cope by aligning with a powerful narcissistic friend or classmate, basking in the reflected glory they experience from the relationship. They seek their narcissistic supplies by association. They are content with attaching to an exhibitionistic or achieving narcissist who has high social value. They are often compliant and ingratiating, working to find a place near the throne of their popular high-status peer, and content to be near a person of talent and power. In a sense, they are a narcissist by proxy.

The Manipulative Narcissist (Coping with Narcissistic Vulnerability through the Exercise of Power—Getting One's Way)

The manipulative narcissist is intent on getting their way. They use others to achieve their goals, often without regard for their feelings. Their self-validation comes through power and the ability to control other people and the environment. Some manipulative narcissists are gifted leaders who can influence groups to reach higher, more expansive goals, and they often seek and hold political or other high-status positions. In childhood, some may earn a place on the student council or be elected captain of a team. Others have an antisocial component, which means they tend to be dishonest or live outside the rules. In childhood, that may mean they steal pencils from the school store or take desired items from a classmate's backpack. Many manipulative narcissists come from families of wealth, prestige, and power. Those youngsters are unusually hard to keep in check both at home, and, particularly, at school. What headmaster wants to risk the gift of a new football stadium to side against the narcissist and his parents over a schoolroom tussle?

It is important to emphasize that *all* budding childhood narcissists suffer from a faulty self-concept and accompanying self-esteem issues. The resulting narcissistic vulnerability forces maladaptive coping, whether through over- or underachievement, manipulation, acting out, or withdrawal. No matter the maladaptive coping mechanism used, budding narcissists build unhealthy models for relationships. The underlying psychological deficit is the same.

The shifts in the life stories of two sisters illustrate the confusing and often deceptive nature of external presentation that disguises deficiencies in internal structure. A parent told me, "If Gracie were just like Lou Ellen, our family would be just fine." In my observations, parents in narcissistic families typically see their children as "good children" and "bad children." The differences that emerge in childhood can be more pronounced in adolescence. However, snapshots of the narcissistic family over time reveal the consistency of pathology across *all* children, both those perceived as special and those seen as problematic.

In high school, Lou Ellen was beautiful and popular, a hardworking and solidly achieving student with great leadership skills. She was elected student council president in her private all-girl prep school. Given her array of talents, she was recognized as the rising star. Gracie was quite the opposite. While equally pretty and an even higher achiever than her sister, she was giving her family fits, sneaking out of the house to drink alcohol with boys, refusing to dress appropriately, and engaging in youthful promiscuous behavior. The final blow to her family happened on their exclusive holiday cruise in the Mediterranean, when they discovered that she had slept with a cabin boy. To their horrified parents, Gracie was a "bad child," and Lou Ellen was a "good child."

However, surprising as it may seem, Lou Ellen and Gracie suffered the same level of disturbance, and a snapshot of their lives twenty years later reveals the commonalities between the "star" and the "disgrace." Gracie went to rehab and got into therapy. She completed medical school and a prestigious residency, married a steady, stable med-school classmate, and had three precocious children. Her life settled down, and she established a generally contented, steady life. Lou Ellen, on the other hand, graduated from a prestigious, second-tier college but floundered in settling on a career path, not knowing herself well enough to find a place where she fit and found fulfillment. For too many years, she was unable to find a man she found suitable to marry. No one quite measured up, and no one treated her as she desired. Years later and too old to bear children, she married unsuccessfully, the relationship lasting only a couple of years. She ended up in a modestly successful but personally unfulfilling job. She lived well through extensive international travel and membership in a number of exclusive social clubs, all due to the large trust she received when her parents died. She was busy, but contentment remained beyond her reach.

Both girls grew up in a narcissistic family, one being the idealized child and the other being the devalued one, each suffering costly deficiencies in their self-concept, which played out in the repercussions of a dysfunctional model of love and relationships. Those structural limitations proved challenging for both, at different times and in different ways for each, but they were functionally the same. Gracie's relatively better outcome is a testament to the value of good therapy and the potential for redemption in a "good enough" marriage and family. Lou Ellen's relatively poorer outcome reflects the handicap of narcissistic development that remains unrecognized and uncorrected.

CAUSES OF NARCISSISM

The causes of narcissistic personality disorder are unknown. Experts typically apply a biopsychosocial model, meaning that a combination of environmental, social, genetic, and neurobiological factors (such as temperament) play a role in developing a narcissistic personality. There is some evidence that NPD, to a degree, is heritable, with a positive family history increasing the odds. However, environmental and social factors are increasingly recognized and are generally believed to have greater impacts on the development of NPD.

Influences on Childhood Narcissism

Narcissism is a tapestry woven of many threads. Clinical observation and emerging research suggest that there are numerous interpersonal and cultural influences that likely produce these maladaptive tendencies and traits, which, if unaddressed, contribute to the development and sustaining of NPD.

- Biological influences include an oversensitive temperament present at birth or some other heritable factor.
- Parental influences include overvaluation, excessive criticism, extreme expectations, neglect, overindulgence or pampering, overprotection, treatment that promotes a sense of entitlement or specialness, excessive admiration that is not balanced by realistic feedback, excessive praise for "good" behaviors, excessive criticism for "bad" behaviors, parenting based on parental needs to inflate their own self-esteem.
- Environmental influences can be divided into several different groupings.
  - Peer and broader social influences include being praised for exceptional qualities (such as good looks or wit) or abilities (such as intelligence or acting talents) by peers or adults, being harshly criticized by others for deficiencies, and learning manipulative behaviors from peers or adults.
  - Trauma includes traumatic life events such as a car wreck, physical injury, emotional hurt as the victim of bullying or rejection from a social group. Suffering severe emotional abuse, being the victim of bullying, receiving unpredictable or unreliable caregiving in early childhood, or experiencing extreme social isolation through peer rejection, adoption, or divorce would also fit in this category. The severity of injury can vary in degree, from not pitching at a baseball game after

having been promised otherwise to being robbed at gunpoint to witnessing physical abuse between parents.

o Cultural influences include the context of community mores and values and the general understanding of what it means to be successful, attractive, valuable, or worthy. Social media is a forum that easily propagates values without regard for its impact on children. Current cultural messages including over-valuing achievement, idealizing winners, underappreciating solid performance, celebrating beauty, glorifying wealth and power, and rewarding success at all costs, among many others, also encourage narcissism. All these reinforce self-centeredness and disregard for the feelings of others, which can lay the groundwork for narcissism. Not surprisingly, negative cultural values are thought to increase the prevalence of NPD. It is noteworthy that NPD has been found to be more prevalent in modern societies than traditional ones.

STOPPING NARCISSISM THROUGH EARLY INTERVENTION: ADDRESSING INFLUENCERS IN THE LIVES OF CHILDREN— PARENTS AND "SIGNIFICANT OTHERS"

The goal of the book is to decrease influences that promote narcissism and encourage change in individuals who can support positive emotional development. While people may at times feel powerless in the face of greater forces in society, the importance of singular influences cannot be overstated. Narcissism consists of two primary components: distortions in the "sense of self" and the "nature of relationships." The child's developing sense of self is influenced by input from others, primarily parents, but also important persons in the lives of children such as caregivers, teachers, grandparents, friends, and classmates. The child's developing model of relationships is influenced by early learning gathered through interactions with others, primarily parents, but also other important contacts. To stop or reverse narcissistic development, interventions must focus on the child's developing sense of self and the nature of early relationships where models of connection are both learned and played out.

Because "significant others" have such an impact on the development and maintenance of narcissism in children, and because these impacts typically occur at relatively young ages (prior to adolescence), interventions should focus primarily on the role of parents. Therapists and counselors must intercede in the family, specifically with parents, to stop and reverse the narcissistic trajectory. Intervention also includes parent education that builds understanding of the development of narcissism and the role parents and important others can play in encouraging or discouraging it. Therapists and counselors can also intervene more broadly to educate key influencers in the lives of children, from teachers to youth ministers, grandparents to neighbors, scout masters to community leaders.

My clinical work with children and families, both in my practice and through my lectures, suggests that halting and reversing childhood narcissism is possible if initiated when the child is young and the emerging dysfunctions are not yet set. This is an important finding, as the potential for change in adulthood remains more challenging and less promising. There is cause for optimism with early intervention as the key time of impact and parents as the key point of impact.

The Development of Narcissism in Childhood: A Structural Analysis

The Building Blocks of Personality: Structures under Construction

THE SCIENCE BEHIND PSYCHOLOGICAL UNDERSTANDING

$\mathscr{I}$ have a physicist friend who teases me about the nature of the "knowledge base" of psychology, as if it's some kind of pseudoscience, with psychologists being more like tarot card readers or psychics than "real" scientists. Psychology, he claims, is nothing like physics, with immutable rules, natural laws, and glorious mathematics. "Where is Schrodinger's equation?" he prods. Playful, competitive strivings aside, his understanding is anything but accurate. Psychology *is* scientific in its approach to greater understanding, even if its core principles are often generated by clinicians instead of pure scientists. Empirical evidence from persistent and intuitive experimentation has guided physics—and all science for that matter—forever. One must remember where physics was before calculus was invented or before Einstein's intellectual leap from black-body radiation to special relativity.

Like Einstein, the geniuses of psychology are cutting-edge "pattern readers" who "see" and conceptualize associations between various observable phenomena. Once patterns of evidence are identified, psychological research proves those insights by discerning operating relationships and evolving theoretical constructs to organize and elucidate the observed realities. Of course, this confirming research refines methods of intervention in clinical practice. For the field to grow thoughtfully and scientifically in its own realm, empirical validation is essential.

The purview of psychology is immense, with fifty-four divisions recognized by the American Psychological Association, ranging from the Psychology of Aging to the Psychology of Psychopharmacology and Substance Abuse, and from the Psychology of Women to the Society for the Study of Peace, Conflict, and Violence. These divisions have all the variety and depth of the numerous physical sciences. Interestingly, there is more physics in psychology today than ever before with fMRI imaging, genetic mapping, and the marvels of biochemical analyses and computational power. Obviously, there is a lot to know, explore, and discover.

What often rises to attention in the field of psychology are patterns of behavior that have significant impacts on, or present problems for, large portions of society. Childhood narcissism is one such area, with evidence that narcissism has been increasing dramatically over time and is compromising the psychological health of American youth proportionally. The growth of childhood narcissism remains not clearly understood, but patterns that describe the condition are emerging into a broader understanding that will enable increasingly successful intervention.

EMERGING PSYCHOLOGICAL RESEARCH ON CHILDHOOD NARCISSISM

Narcissism has been on the rise among American youth and contributes to a variety of social problems ranging from impaired interpersonal relationships to aggression, emotional abuse to physical violence. It represents not only an interpersonal problem but also a larger societal one. *Narcissism* has become a household word, something now experienced broadly across all social and economic strata. The world is predisposed to label celebrities and politicians as narcissists. Our contemporaries describe the behavior of children, adolescents, and adults as narcissistic. Social commentary now depicts the culture as "me focused" and generations of children as overly self-focused. Stereotypes abound. Narcissism has become front and center in our assessments of ourselves, those around us, and the world at large. The elements of narcissism have become interwoven in much of daily life.

The world of science and scientific research has mirrored the interest seen in the general population. Research databases reveal that there have been thousands of publications over many decades on narcissism, and Google searches on *narcissism* have exploded in recent years. The psychological research has followed a number of different and divergent paths. Since the turn of the century, specific empirical works on the causes of narcissism have appeared more frequently in the literature, and the more recent development of self-report measures of trait narcissism have led to a burst of empirical work in that domain. Researchers are investigating the connection between trait narcissism and narcissistic personality disorder as well as studying the correlates of narcissism. Still more is being done on treatment strategies for narcissism, and, in particular, narcissistic personality disorder.

Despite the wealth of knowledge on narcissism generally and especially in adults, relatively little is known about narcissism in children. Yet there is broad consensus that narcissism typically emerges well before adulthood.[1] Narcissism can be reliably measured in the child, for research purposes, at around the age of eight. At that age and stage, the development of the child's cognitive skills allows global evaluations of their worth and the ability to anticipate others' opinions of them. Further, researchers have already identified earlier indices that reliably predict later narcissism from preschool behavior.

The origins of narcissism are not well understood. Interest in the role of parenting in the childhood development of narcissism has also grown recently and has generated an emerging body of empirical research. A number of clinical theories and hypotheses that argue for the prominent role of parenting in causation are now being subjected to the rigors of scientific testing.

Speaking broadly, the evidence suggests causal links between particular aspects of parenting and child narcissism. That information must be taken with a grain of salt. It is difficult to describe the precise nature of these relationships for several reasons. First, researchers have used a variety of terms to characterize different types of narcissists and to describe different narcissistic traits. Those include grandiose and vulnerable, overt and covert, and maladaptive and adaptive.[2] The overlapping of traits and types in various research paradigms makes broad statements of specific causes difficult to make. Second, researchers develop new instruments as the field broadens, which means the instruments used to measure narcissism in the child can vary across research studies. Contradictory findings between studies may reflect issues around measurement instruments. Third, some studies focus more on specific aspects of parenting as it relates to outcomes, while others focus on more global measurements of parenting. When parenting behaviors are grouped into categories, the studies may be subject to the same problems in measurement and design methodologies. Finally, research that investigates narcissism as a singular construct or through the lens of specific components is a design question that makes comparison between some research studies difficult.[3] While those complexities are best left with the researchers, the tentative empirical findings offer important insights.

There appear to be several key insights regarding the links between parenting and childhood narcissism. Parental overvaluation appears to be associated with narcissism.[4] Also, parental overcontrol appears to be associated with narcissism as well as a number of negative outcomes more generally.[5] However, the latter element, parental control, may take different forms, including both parental coldness and parental intrusiveness. Finally, indulgent parenting and permissive parenting appear to be associated with narcissism.[6] Importantly, these general findings are consistent with accepted clinical theories and observations about the development of narcissism in childhood.

Longitudinal studies that look into narcissism in childhood may provide important clarification of the empirical findings and further understanding of causal factors and early antecedents. One such study investigated how narcissism develops from childhood into adolescence.[7] During preschool and elementary school, a group of children were assessed by their teachers on a standardized instrument that measured five broad categories: being the center of attention, interpersonal antagonism, inadequate impulse control, histrionic tendencies, and activity level. Those general categories included specific items evaluated by the teachers, such as lack of consideration and thoughtfulness with peers, overreaction to minor mishaps, high needs for attention, emotional volatility, and lack of cooperation, all of which make sound theoretical and clinical sense. Those children were then assessed on levels of narcissism at the ages of fourteen, eighteen, and twenty-three. All broad preschool measures predicted *later* narcissism. Importantly, this research supports the general notion that there are potential *antecedents* of later narcissism that can be *identified* in childhood.[8]

Another longitudinal study focused on the origins of narcissism in children.[9] Children between the ages of seven and eleven and their parents were assessed on four occasions in six-month intervals over two years. The researchers measured four factors through various instruments at each interval. The child was evaluated on two measures: child narcissism and child self-esteem. The parent was evaluated on two measures: parental overvaluation and parental warmth. Narcissism in the child was predicted by parental overvaluation but not by lack of parental warmth. Significantly, parental warmth was a contributor to high self-esteem and was not correlated with narcissism, suggesting that parental warmth protects against narcissism. This research lends support for the general notion that children are vulnerable to internalizing their parents' inflated views, which can result in acquired narcissism, and that parental warmth serves a protective function against the development of narcissism.

Empirical study of narcissism in childhood is important for several reasons. While there is much that further research will clarify through the years, several tentative, overarching conclusions can be made. These are particularly relevant to parents, clinicians, and parent educators— actually any adult who plays an important role in a child's life in the formative years.

- There is evidence that specific parenting practices can either help or hinder the development of narcissism in childhood.
- There is evidence that children appear to acquire narcissism, in part, by internalizing parents' inflated views of them.[10] It seems that children can come to see themselves as they believe they are seen "through the eyes" of their significant others. When children are seen by their parents as being special and are treated as such, they can internalize the view that they are superior individuals. The view of themselves as special and entitled to special treatment is a concept at the core of narcissism. Importantly, research shows that parents who overvalue their children perceive their child as more gifted than their actual intelligence scores indicate and overclaim their child's knowledge.[11] Contrary to parental belief, overvalued children are not better performing, or more intelligent, than other children.
- There is evidence that children with maladaptive personality traits tend to be at a higher risk for personality disordered vulnerability over time.[12] In other words, those demonstrating negative personality traits in childhood are at a higher risk of developing a personality disorder in adulthood. This broad finding would also apply to the development of narcissism.

- There is evidence that childhood self-esteem, as opposed to narcissism, can be predicted by parental warmth, not by parental overvaluation. The underlying perception of being accepted by parents and significant others confers benefits to children in terms of both self-esteem and emotional stability, with lowered levels of anxiety, depression, hostility, and aggression[13] and counters the development of narcissistic disorders.
- There is some suggestion that specific strategies used over the years to build self-esteem have been misguided. Society has become increasingly focused on raising children with positive self-esteem. In an attempt to enhance self-esteem, many parents appear to have relied on lavishing children with praise, telling them that they are special and unique, and giving them other exceptional treatment. Recent research suggests that efforts to raise self-esteem through a process of overvaluation and overinvestment may actually increase narcissism in children[14] and, in fact, undermine self-esteem. In contrast to lavish praise,[15] it is simply the underlying perception of being accepted by others and treated with affection and appreciation that benefits children.[16]
- Researchers and theorists continue to refine the distinction between healthy self-esteem and narcissism through attempts to more clearly differentiate between healthy feelings of worth and unhealthy feelings of superiority.[17] Researchers theorize that self-esteem can be cultivated—without building narcissism—through realistic feedback (rather than inflated praise), a focus on self-improvement (rather than outperforming others), and unconditional regard (rather than conditional regard based on achievement).[18]

The existing research to date suggests the need to more thoroughly understand the nature of narcissism in childhood personality development and the parental and cultural influences that contribute to the resulting negative personality traits. Selfish, entitled, and unempathetic youth prove problematic. Society needs a substantial portion of the population to be well adjusted, contented and secure, emotionally regulated, and concerned about the thoughts and feelings of others.

READING THE SUBTEXT:
LEVELS OF UNDERSTANDING AND ANALYSIS

Child development is complicated, and children can be confusing. Their demands are intense, their behaviors variable, and their reactions often inexplicable. That a child's development is unfolding in the face of the demands of two-parent careers, family stresses, financial worries, and the uncertainties of day-to-day living only serves to challenge an already complex and complicated process. It is not surprising that parents typically deal with their child's behavior at the most immediate and obvious level. When Bobby has lost his shin guards and the dog has just spilled his water bowl, which the toddler is now scooting through, it is more difficult, and often inconvenient, to search for deeper meanings. However, these deeper meanings tell the real story and help guide parents.

I am reminded of the story of an altercation between two brothers playing in the front yard after coming home from school. Six-year-old Eric hit his four-year-old brother with a stick. The mother began to scold Eric when suddenly she realized that this was not typical behavior. She stopped herself. "You don't normally hit your brother. What's going on?" Eric's face curled into an expression of pain, and he began to cry. "I can't read like Bobby. Everybody else can read but I can't." Eric was not a bad kid. He was struggling at school, and, with an immediacy born of immaturity, took it out on his brother. The mother comforted him, pulling him into a tight hug. Later, she reminded him that it was not OK to hit his brother. It would be best if he could "put his feelings into words." It was true that Eric was inappropriately aggressive. He did hit his brother, but the deeper meaning tells the story of *why* and would be a better point of understanding and intervention developmentally.

An adolescent in my practice explained the importance of deeper meaning with a particularly insightful observation. James was describing his handful of friends: "I really like Tom and Ed, but they're not like Clayton and JB. I don't think I'll ever be *really* close to somebody who can't read the subtext." James had an intelligence and sensitivity well beyond his years. Of course, meaning can be found at different levels, from the superficial to the profound, but there is always a deeper meaning that lies beneath a more obvious one. James recognized those differences and used insight to guide his friendship choices. The goal of "good enough" parenting[19] is to be able to "read the subtext," to search out the deeper meaning underlying their child's behavior, demands, and words, and to more fully appreciate and respond to those needs at this more fundamental level.

Understanding a condition as varied and pervasive as narcissism requires a focus on deeper meanings. Adriana and Summer are two nine-year-old girls who generally feel good about themselves. Most teachers and parents would judge them to have a positive self-view. On a standard testing measure, researchers would conclude that they both have high self-esteem. However, a more careful analysis suggests that their self-views are very different. Adriana is not particularly interested in how her competencies stack up against others her age, whereas Summer sees herself as superior to others. Adriana likes to receive compliments but can do without them, whereas Summer craves them and is upset if denied them. Adriana holds accurate, well-balanced and positive views of herself, whereas Summer holds unrealistically high, superlative views. The differences between the girls are often unrecognized in ordinary observation and most global measures. However, it is in this subtle but significant difference that narcissism lives. This explains why parents and educators—as well as therapists—must be able to "read the subtext" and search for the deeper meanings underneath a child's words and actions if they want to help them grow and heal.

PSYCHOLOGICAL STRUCTURES: BUILDING OVER CHILDHOOD AND ADOLESCENCE

Children are born with only rudimentary skills and abilities. Each skill and ability develops over time and becomes increasingly more complex and advanced. This is most obvious in physical maturation; infants cannot walk, but once grown, they can perform remarkable physical feats such as gymnastics or competitive athletics. In cognitive development, a nonverbal infant eventually ends up with capacities for high-level mathematics, linguistics, philosophy, and sophisticated reasoning, as well as almost unlimited creativity.

Less well understood are the *psychological* structures that build in the child throughout these years. These psychological structures unfold and advance over time, increasing in depth and complexity. The structures are not built in an all-or-nothing fashion; rather, they develop gradually, in a "two steps forward, one step back" fashion, but with a progressively upward trend. In a sense, these structures are continually "under construction," becoming stronger and more complex every year of a child's growth toward maturity.

As children mature emotionally, they become better able to handle complex emotions and complicated social relationships. Their "operating system" becomes more complex. But mastery is not always steadily forward, subject to backsliding under the influence of external stressors. This process is referred to as regression. For example, a child may be able to use words to deal with his frustrations, but when his sister develops brain cancer and is hospitalized, causing his mother to be unavailable, the child may revert to earlier—or more childlike—levels of managing their feelings, including grabbing, hitting, and screaming. Stressors on the child that result in regression may not always be obvious but are nonetheless powerful psychologically—an older brother going away to college, disappointment over grades, or a girl's lack of response to a boy's overture might all precipitate a backslide in emotional functioning.

Both positive and negative experiences provide opportunities for psychological structures to grow more complex and efficient in their adaptation. New social opportunities and experiences challenge psychological structures to grow in the same way that physical challenges demand increasingly complex, physical development. More time on the tennis court increases the likelihood of better ground strokes and faster, more agile movement toward the ball. Similarly, practicing calming oneself, unraveling novel problems, and resolving conflicts challenges emotional structures to adapt by forcing them to become more efficient and sturdier.

As explained, I refer to these psychological structures as operating systems. When I lecture, I explain the overarching process through the metaphor of an ever-evolving and improving computer with operating systems that expand and develop their capabilities when provided with more data and new problems to solve. Obviously, when children are born, they have limited capacities to manage psychological stress and process information. Over time, those operating systems become increasingly complex. By adulthood, well-developed operational structures can handle high levels of stress with intact integrity and efficiency and process huge amounts of complex and contradictory information. Structures that maintain equilibrium are seen as a sign of maturity and an indicator of being "well adjusted." Underdeveloped or faulty structures limit function and suffer disequilibrium and loss of control.

FOUR ESSENTIAL PERSONALITY STRUCTURES

In this book, I describe four psychological structures and delineate the nature of each as it unfolds over time. This process is remarkable in the sense that mastery of these developments is dependent on interaction with others, most particularly, with parents. Through their interactions with their child, parents can do much to promote the development of positive or negative psychological structures.

The four psychological structures addressed are integral to the development of positive emotional growth, and if their influence is mismanaged, negative narcissistic tendencies and traits can develop. Even though the four structures are interdependent, I discuss them independently in order to understand the mechanisms more fully and explain their effects. Their interdependency is more complex than the simple descriptions I provide. Nonetheless, the overall effect is better understood by the agency of each component studied in isolation.

Structure 1: Building a Model of the Self (Developing an Inventory of Strengths and Weaknesses = Self-Concept and Then Self-Esteem)

Every child must come to an understanding of their particular skills, abilities, and qualities. That formulation will eventually include an inventory of strengths and weaknesses that will become increasingly differentiated with time and experience, moving from a more global concept to a more nuanced one. "I can run" will eventually become "I am a fast (or not so fast) runner." Then, an overarching concept is built up out of an integration of a multitude of specifics ("I'm a fast runner, slow reader, good cuddler, fantastic sister, etc.) Then, the general self-concept, if viewed favorably, will turn into a stable sense of positive self-esteem. Similarly, if that self-concept is poorly differentiated or negative, it will, by degrees, result in negative self-esteem.

Structure 2: Building an Ability to Regulate Emotions (Learning to Handle Feelings = Self-Regulation and Self-Control)

Every child must develop strategies to calm themselves. This begins in infancy by crying out for support from a caring adult. Over time, children will develop more independent self-calming strategies, ranging from putting feelings into words to engaging in distraction and, eventually, into higher level strategies such as humor or intellectual understanding. By adulthood, the child should be able to tolerate frustration and upset with a sense of equanimity. The ability to regulate feelings builds a sense of self-control and confidence in the ability to tolerate frustration and disappointment.

Structure 3: Building an Ability to Take in and Process Information (Gathering Information about the World = Perceptual Accuracy, Non-distortion and Non-extreme Thinking)

Every child must develop an ability to process information that is not distorted by emotional needs, other personal bias, or externalities. She must also grow beyond thinking in terms of extremes and must build a more nuanced view of understanding any observation or interaction. The ability to gather information about the world in clear terms, supported by facts and confirmed by evidence, is a sign of both cognitive and emotional maturation. Mature thinking is nuanced and thorough, unaffected by emotional bias.

Structure 4: Building a Model of Love and Relationships (Interacting with Others and the Development of Trust = Relationship Knowledge)

Every child must develop a model for interacting with others. This model includes knowledge of the nature of love and the rules of social interaction. It is predicated upon trust, an understanding that people are predictable and can be relied upon. In the end, a healthy model reaffirms that social connections are valuable, and relationships are to be sought after and sustained.

These four psychological structures are built of a variety of individual skills and attitudes that contribute to the whole, developing incrementally and progressively over time. At specific ages, the structures should normally demonstrate a certain level of development. When working with my patients, I make assessments of the level of development of the operating structures. For example, I might guesstimate that Susie's sense of self is that of an eight-year-old, her ability to manage feelings is that of a seven-year-old, her perceptual accuracy is that of an eight-year-old, and her quality of relationships is that of a six-year-old. If Suzy is nine, her low scores likely reflect immature development. If Suzy is six, then her high scores likely reflect precocious development.

The assessment process is complicated because child development is not always linear and is stage dependent. Certain skills indicate different things at different ages. "Faster" or "earlier" is not always better. I remember sitting with a group of mothers who all had toddlers. One mother was lamenting how her child, crying uncontrollably, would not go to the daycare at the family resort they had visited last week. Another mom boasted that her child separated easily at the hotel daycare they had attended a month before. The first mother's face dropped in disappointment, while the second mother's face lit with pleasure at what *appeared* to be superiority. What the mothers did not know was that the first child's reaction was appropriate to the age and stage of this child, while the second child's reaction likely indicated some problem in attachment—not early competitive success or an indicator of "better" parenting or a more accomplished child. At the same time, it is important to note that delay is not always problematic. In some situations, the behavior might be an appropriate short-term response to a specific stressor or regression. All skills and abilities must be seen in the larger context of a complex process elaborated over time.

THE FATAL FLAWS OF NARCISSISM

The developmental progression that underlies personality structures is an orderly one but can be helped or hindered by experiences with others. As noted, temperament, trauma, parenting, peer interactions, and cultural values all can influence a developing personality.

In the case of a personality disorder, something has gone awry in that developmental progression. In narcissism, a fault has developed in some, or all, of the structures. The symptoms evidenced are a simple reflection of the flaw or weakness in the structure. Generally speaking, children with narcissistic tendencies, traits, or disorders show deficits in one or all of these structural operating systems.

A Flawed Model of the Self

Children with narcissism have developed a sense of themselves as either grandiosely valuable or, at the other end of the spectrum, as upsettingly deficient. Either form of disorder results in a faulty self-concept that is both hungry for attention and validation and/or excessively vulnerable to criticism or disappointment. Because the "sense of self" is impaired, self-esteem will also be defective in either its inflated or deflated state.

A Flawed Ability to Regulate Emotions

When life is not predictable and under control, children with narcissism have problems in self-regulation. In one presentation, these children are prone to anxiety and worry, and when things do not proceed as expected, they are easily upset. In another form, they are inclined toward emotional disruption and volatility; when frustrated or disappointed, they become overly angry. The narcissist's impoverished sense of self does not tolerate blows to the self-concept or frustration of desires, and it can set off an episode of emotional dysregulation.

A Flawed Ability to Take in and Process Information

Children with narcissism have difficulties processing or interpreting information. They may personalize the words and behaviors of others, often reaching conclusions about intention or motivation that are not accurate. They may misperceive or misinterpret various events. They may be exquisitely sensitive to the reactions of others, often misreading the specifics of an interaction. Their ability to read the facts of social realities may reflect their own perspective, which is without regard for alternative views. The narcissist's reasoning is flawed, dominated by extremes and a non-nuanced view of people and events. More generally, problems in perspective shifting may interfere with resolving differences between themselves and others.

A Flawed Model of Love and Relationships

Children with narcissism develop a defective model of relationships. In one form, they tend to expect special treatment and, more typically, seek out unequal relationships with a lesser (or caretaker) partner who is responsible for their emotional needs. In another form, they push people away and avoid emotional closeness, not expecting good things from emotional connection. If frustrated or disappointed in a relationship, the narcissist can disregard the feelings of others, often punishing or mistreating them, or can dismiss the relationship with little provocation. Solving disputes with narcissists is difficult, if not impossible, as their insistence on their point of view and disregard for the feelings of others is problematic.

WARNING SIGNS THAT CHILDREN ARE AT RISK FOR DEVELOPING NARCISSISM

As noted earlier, children are developing a variety of skills and abilities over each developmental period. A failure to develop or improve certain skills over time, as well as a failure of other skills to lessen or decline over time, can indicate that a child is at risk for developing narcissism. The following chapters will discuss in greater detail the skills and abilities that develop, or do not develop, over time.

Because of the nature of child development, certain behaviors, skills, and attitudes should improve over time, while others should decline with age. The list below covers many warning signs, all of which will be discussed in greater detail in later chapters.

- Empathy that does not develop or become more sensitive, appropriate, and accurate with age
- Cooperation (and cooperative relationships) that does not increase in frequency and complexity with age
- Misperception and misinterpretation of information that do not improve with age

- Realistic and appropriate self-esteem that does not increase with age
- Emotional volatility that does not settle and calm with age
- More mature coping strategies that do not develop with age
- Self-centeredness that does not decline with age
- Entitled attitudes that demand special treatment that do not decline with age
- Demands to "have their way" that do not decline with age
- Angry or aggressive responses to being criticized, wronged, and disappointed that do not decline with age
- Needing to win or succeed without regard for the feelings of others (i.e., who is hurt in the process) that does not decline with age
- Bullying behaviors (i.e., teasing, threatening, scapegoating) that do not decline with age
- Filtering information such that reacting on the basis of its personal impact does not decline with age
- Blaming others for bad outcomes or disappointments that does not decline with age
- Preoccupation with getting their needs met (over those of others) that does not decline with age
- Envy that does not decline with age
- A view of extraordinary self-worth that does not decline with age

Normally, certain behaviors should decline with age and others should develop. However, the identification of narcissistic behavior is further complicated by two additional factors: the frequency of the identified behavior and the intention underlying it. Many behaviors that are recognized as narcissistic are normal, at times, in the course of healthy development and in small doses. Everyone can be insensitive from time to time, but persistent insensitivity is different and can be problematic. Similarly, the motivation for the behavior is equally informative. A person can help the homeless out of general concern and empathy or to gain recognition or praise. In other words, the same behavior can have different meanings depending on the underlying motivation.

The following four chapters cover each of the personality structures that are being built over the course of child development and explain the problems that arise when there is narcissistic disruption. Each chapter is divided into three major sections: a description and explanation of the development of the specific structure over time, signs and measures of that structure in the child at different ages, and parent contributions to the healthy or not-so-healthy development of that structure. The particular ways parents, friends, and significant others may promote narcissistic outcomes is explained with examples and case studies.

II

RAISING A NON-NARCISSISTIC CHILD

Building a Non-narcissistic Model of the Self

(Developing an Inventory of Strengths and Weaknesses
= Self-Concept Leading to Self-Esteem)

The Development of the Self over Time

*E*very child must develop a thorough and comprehensive knowledge of the "self," which includes an appreciation of her strengths and weaknesses and an inventory of her assets and liabilities. If successful, the development of this solid "self-concept" contributes to a *realistic* sense of self that is neither inflated nor deflated. This healthy self-concept is built of confidence and persistence and has tolerance for frustration and disappointment. A healthy self-concept is perhaps the most important measure of psychological maturity and steady emotional function. A fully developed, mature, healthy self can hold both positive and negative self-images and can tolerate criticism, shame, and embarrassment without undue upset. Measures of the health of the self can be seen in the accuracy of the self-perceptions, being neither overly inflated nor overly self-critical, in overall contentment with the self, and in a resilient response to criticism and shame.

Self-knowledge begins in infancy and grows more comprehensive and complex as the child matures. The child must first differentiate the "me" from "not me" (i.e., this is my finger but her nipple, a rudimentary sense of me/not me). This occurs as they become increasingly aware of a world outside (i.e., someone is smiling at me and interests me). It is in this process that mothers help the child know their first "self." Some psychoanalytic writers have described the child's first meeting of the "self" in their encounter with their own reflection in their mother's eyes. Importantly, the mother's warm and accurate view of the child will encourage the fledgling sense of self. Continued feedback from important others in the child's external world (i.e., significant others, peers, teachers, etc.), along with feedback in the home will contribute to development of the emerging self.

Of course, errors are possible in this process. A "self" based on unfounded assets (a belief that the child has great talent when he does not), or inaccurate liabilities (a belief that a child has great liabilities when he does not), gives rise to an inauthentic self.

An inflated, inaccurately positive sense of self must stay pumped up artificially and requires ongoing reinforcement. A child experiences embarrassment and shame when he is found lacking. That exaggerated sense of importance relative to real accomplishments results in self-absorption, limited regard for others' needs, and a failure to appreciate the feelings of others. Most importantly, an inflated sense of self results in the expectation that the child should come first and is entitled to special treatment.

An inaccurate, negative sense of self based on unfounded deficits contributes to a feeling of worthlessness. The child becomes supersensitive to any evidence of their shortcomings and is accompanied by an overwhelming sense of shame, resulting in a need to be better than others and/or a need to put others down to avoid feeling valueless.

Superiority is a recurring theme for the narcissistic child. Competition is a way to reaffirm superiority, and the child can be either hypercompetitive or avoidant. If the former, a child often chooses areas in which she can win and prove her value. Failure cannot be tolerated, as the failure to be better than others is evidence that she is nothing at all. Such children are naturally attracted to power as a way to reaffirm superiority and/or a way to control others.

When inflated with positive attention and regard, these children can be charming, alluring, enchanting, and those around them can feel the magic. When deflated due to failure or criticism, they can be demanding, bossy, judgmental, and mean spirited.

SELF-CONCEPT: THE "UNDEVELOPED FARM" AS A METAPHOR

When I lecture and work with parents, I search for metaphors and images that allow parents to actually "see" what is going on inside the child—a way to visualize the personality structure that is forming, evolving, and building under the surface.

I understand the child's self-concept as a fertile farm that has never been planted or worked. I imagine the child's various skills and abilities as if they are agricultural operations that have recently commenced or particular crops recently laid in. Some grow easily. Some require extra care. All require nurture from the farmers—the parents—who till the soil, water and weed, and fertilize as necessary with changes in the weather and climate. Negative outside influences—such as rain, drought, storms, or pests—halt and challenge growth, but the crops persist. Different crops are planted over time, with some succeeding easily and others struggling. The farmer makes choices and mistakes. After years, the farm is working with some consistency and efficiency, its operation predictable. After many years, its assets and weaknesses are known, and the farmer puts protocols in place to encourage good habits that deal with whatever distress challenges the farm's efficiency and productivity. At some point, it is an operating farm with a stabilized history and steady operation.

Similarly, I imagine the child's self-esteem as the overarching sense of the farm's stability and predictability—its success at producing crops and its resilience under the threats of nature as it has developed over time and experience. Like a seasoned homestead, in the end, a child's self-concept and self-esteem are made up of a thorough understanding of his strengths and weaknesses and an appreciation for the overall operation and resilience of the system. The farm, like the child, is undergoing an evolution, and over time, the system runs with less attention and more ease. It is important to know that there is great variability between farms and ever-present optimism about the potential operation of each individual farm, even in the face of vulnerable crops and troubled years.

DEVELOPMENT OF THE SELF: SELF-CONCEPT LEADING TO SELF-ESTEEM

Step 1: The Development of the Self-Concept

There are two essential steps in the development of the self, and the first involves the development of a *self-concept*, an understanding of *this is who I am*. It is based on a child's recognition of her individual skills, abilities, and qualities. Since this involves *self-knowledge*, it is a complicated process. Children must learn about themselves and their capabilities through experiences in the real world. They cannot necessarily be told or taught those things. For example, a parent cannot simply say, "You are good at mathematics." Bobby must come to understand for himself that he is good at mathematics, which involves a back-and-forth process between the exercise of those skills and both his own and others' perceptions of that ability. The process can go wrong in a number of ways, ranging from a grandiose self-assessment ("I am better than everybody else at mathematics") to an overly self-critical assessment ("I'm no good at mathematics").

Self-assessments are, in part, based on actual knowledge of specific skills, abilities, and qualities. A child might actually be particularly talented in math, science, or linguistics. Genetic gifts must be mediated by real-world experiences. But it is also true that assessments are made on the basis of social comparison. Social comparison theory was first proposed in 1954 by psychologist Leon Festinger, who believed that people engage in this comparison process as a way of establishing a benchmark to accurately evaluate their own skills and abilities. Six decades of research have confirmed that individuals do determine self-worth based on how they stack up against others.

I was taught the lesson of social comparison most vividly early on in my practice when I had the opportunity to treat a number of "pageant girls." These were beautiful young women who competed in beauty contests around the country (Miss Texas, Miss America, and Miss World pageants). These women were breathtakingly beautiful, but each of them saw their physical attributes in light of the competition. They were indeed beautiful, but not exceptionally so, given the group to which they were being compared. These women taught me that, depending on the social comparison group, individuals can come up with relatively inaccurate conclusions about themselves if they do not account for the larger context.

The self-concept is made up of the many self-assessments the child will make over the years. It is the child's overarching understanding and appreciation of those skills and abilities that is key. As he grows and matures, he will further refine and integrate that knowledge.

Tom was an early reader. By the age of four, he had sounded out most picture books. By the age of six, he had moved on to chapter books. His first-grade teacher praised him constantly for his talent, and his classmates envied his effortless achievement. He became the teacher's helper and was selected to deliver notes to the principal's office. It was true that he was a more accomplished reader than all the other children in first grade, but there was a risk to this acceleration and its impact on his self-assessment. Tom's teacher attended a conference where she learned that early readers do not necessarily turn out to be particularly bright. They have a particular visual and auditory processing talent that makes reading easy, but that might not be indicative of other intellectual strengths in the future. To give Tom an inflated view of himself at this young age was to do him a disservice. The teacher learned that she should encourage his reading as an ordinary variation and search for other mastery areas that would challenge him to develop the skills of hard work and persistence. It was important that he not take *one* "superior" skill and generate a broader-ranging "superior" self-concept.

Effortless mastery is not a good teaching lesson. The right amount of challenge is good, while too little or too much is problematic. Research by the famous psychologist Jean Piaget referred to this challenge to promote growth in child cognitive development as a "pacer." The data have shown that challenging the child slightly above their current level of function is optimal. Providing material that is too easy does not encourage growth, nor does providing material that is too difficult. Tom's parents supported the teacher's recommendation to help him see himself in a less inflated way, allowing him to celebrate his special talent without taking it on as a measure of overall superiority.

Step 2: The Development of Self-Esteem

The second step involves the development of *self-esteem*, an understanding that *I am lovable and valuable as I am*. This is based *both* on a recognition and valuation of the child's individual skills, abilities, and qualities, and also on self-*acceptance*. This is a complicated process, as a child must not only learn about themselves but also make a determination concerning the value of those abilities and characteristics. Susie may be good at chess, but if chess is considered a game only for nerds, Susie must come to her own conclusions about the value of her skill and whether she wants to invest in further development of that skill. Susie may know that she is good at chess but not fully value that talent in the face of potential social ostracism. Over the course of growing up, children will try out all kinds of skills and abilities and determine if those are, or should be, valued parts of the self, based in part on their own feelings and experiences as well as on objective measures and the reactions of others.

The process of establishing self-esteem can go awry in a number of ways. One error is to mistake the absolute level of performance as the only or most meaningful measure of self-esteem. This perspective lends itself to harsh evaluations and extreme thinking: If the child is high achieving, then "He is better than you," and if the child is low achieving, then "He can't do that. He's no good." At both ends of the spectrum, extreme thinking is injurious to self-esteem. If children judge themselves to be better than others, then they are at risk of developing a superior, arrogant attitude. If children conclude that they are deficient or defective, then they are at risk of developing feelings of worthlessness. Parents who embrace a "superior/inferior" model actually undermine important concepts of the self, and thereby diminish overall self-esteem. Self-esteem is a nuanced understanding of value and competence.

Parenting practices focus generally on the goal of raising well-adjusted children who are capable and competent with high self-esteem—critical skills that are believed to translate into success. Research confirms that how children think about themselves determines how they react to the challenges they face in daily life.[1] This general understanding has fueled efforts to build a child's self-esteem for several decades. The advice of the self-esteem movement has been adopted by schools and accepted by parents based on its assumed validity. This movement has operated under the assumption that all types of efforts to boost children's self-esteem will result in emotional, interpersonal, and academic success.[2] However, there is evidence that these types of efforts aimed at building self-esteem may instead promote narcissism and undesirable consequences, such as emotional dysregulation and decreased persistence on challenging tasks.[3] Sadly, these popular and well-intentioned efforts by parents and school personnel may actually be limiting, not enhancing, a child's potential for success.

This notion that positive self-esteem is associated with success has led to an excess of poorly formulated and potentially negative parenting practices. Stories abound of children provided with trophies for almost every activity, certificates for all types of participation, ribbons and banners, accompanied by excessive applause and attention. Sadly, these types of excessive and inappropriate efforts to help children feel good about themselves backfire. It is not ribbons, trophies, or applause that results in a steady self-concept and an accompanying positive self-esteem. Rather, it is the child's engagement, demonstration, and ultimate mastery of specific skills and abilities that build self-confidence. The child must *experience* the work of achieving appropriate recognition and confirmation in order to build confidence in his ability to make progress through incremental steps of mastery. Ultimately, it is competence that builds confidence, not praise standing alone, independent of demonstrated achievement.

The inadequately understood goal of encouraging self-esteem has led parents to believe that treating the child as special will make him feel good about himself. Tragically, the "specialness" paradigm actually builds negative qualities in the child—selfishness, entitlement, inconsideration, all of which result in poor interpersonal relationships. Children do not end up feeling good about themselves guided by such parenting practices. Regrettably, they end up believing that they are *better* than everyone else. In terms of the development and maintenance of healthy interpersonal relationships, an attitude of superiority is a fatal flaw. Such children fail to develop the essential interpersonal skills of empathy and a mature understanding of emotional closeness. These deficits reflect narcissistic development, with narcissism being characterized by core beliefs of superiority and entitlement. In the simplest terms, it is a form of entitled self-importance.

Fortunately, there's an antidote to this disturbing trend in our society. Parenting practices must be reconsidered and refocused on building *healthy* self-esteem and avoiding the pitfalls of narcissistic development.

Again, self-assessments are, in part, based on actual knowledge of skills and abilities, but self-assessments also incorporate the assessments of others. There are broad social and cultural influences around what is valuable, desirable, or worthy of imitation. Others' assessments come initially from parents and family, and then secondarily, from peers, the larger social environment, and the culture.

Parents do play an important role in the development of self-esteem. Nathan was a thirteen-year-old boy who struggled with problems with his peers and the negative impact of a challenging learning disability, but he had the benefit of a loving, sensitive, and responsive mother. The evidence of her steady support was seen in a comment he made to me: "My mother loves me. *She* might be the *only* one." His face brightened with a broad smile, and then he laughed. That small observation revealed the significance of his mother's influence on his self-esteem, the steady affection that held firm in the face of adversity. He knew that love was a part of his family life, and he believed it could be a part of his future outside his family. Over time, Nathan would find a group of friends who liked him *the way he was*, kids who shared his mother's view of his worth and potential. Several months later, he found a girl who felt the same way.

Self-esteem is the integration of many self-assessments and feedback from outside sources over the years. Those valuations will be refined as self-knowledge increases and social influences change.

Elizabeth was the prettiest girl in town, naturally lean and athletic, with a big smile and wide eyes as blue as sapphires. Her curly blonde locks fell around her face in waves of golden light. It was practically impossible not to respond to her good looks. While Elizabeth's mother was proud, she understood that her looks were a threat to her self-concept. Learning to be appreciated simply because of your good looks was problematic. What if she was not always beautiful? What if she lost her good looks through accident or aging? What if her good looks brought her unearned attention that she came to expect? Her mother understood the need to build a sense of self beyond physical beauty. Every time someone would comment on Elizabeth's beauty, the mother would respond: "She's not half as beautiful on the outside as she is on the inside." Elizabeth's mother provided wonderful assistance to her daughter by allowing her the opportunity to be something more on the inside than was revealed on the outside. She gave her the opportunity to be more than beautiful, to be free of the pull of becoming overinvested in that exceptional aspect of herself, and the chance to develop a wide range of abilities and qualities beyond her physical appearance.

NARCISSISM AND THE HEALTHY OR NOT-SO-HEALTHY SELF: MEASURES OF SELF-CONCEPT AND SELF-ESTEEM

Signs of a Non-narcissistic or Healthy Self-Concept

As a psychologist, I make frequent assessments or determinations about a child's or adult's sense of self as healthy or not-so-healthy. Children with a healthy sense of self have, in the end, a sense of their particular strengths and weaknesses as well as their assets and liabilities, all of which are realistic and accurate, being neither inflated nor overly harsh. A healthy "self" is confident and flexible. It can tolerate failure, deal with disappointment, bend with change, and bounce back from insult or rejection. I judge the self-concept as one of the most important indicators of psychological maturity, if not the most important, because of the protective function it serves. A steady, accurate self-concept accompanied by positive self-esteem results in confidence, resilience, and coping. Such a sense of self is not easily influenced or injured, and it also contributes to the development and overall operation of other essential psychological structures in the personality. For example, a child with a strong sense of self does not typically become dysregulated if he does not make the traveling golf team. Similarly, a child with positive self-esteem tolerates rejection by a boyfriend or the failure to win the coveted Headmaster's Cup.

There are a number of measures that I look for in my clinical practice when assessing the sense of "self." Signs of a positive self-concept include:

An accurate and realistic self-assessment
Overall contentment with the self
Appropriate confidence around skills, abilities, and qualities
An ability to tolerate failure while working on skills and abilities
Evidence of positive self-esteem or self-liking
An ability to function without reward, reinforcement, or recognition
An ability to handle criticism or negative outcomes both academically and socially
A sense of competence
The ability to function independently
The ability to maintain loving and caring relationships
Evidence of an authentic "self" (i.e., self-perception matches actual skills, abilities, and qualities)

In general, a healthy self-concept indicates that the child believes that she is loved and is a worthy person in her family and in society.

Signs of a Narcissistic or Not-So-Healthy Self-Concept

Children with a not-so-healthy sense of self have a variety of presentations that range from low self-confidence to negative self-identification, from overconfidence to an inability to try, from an inflated sense of self to a deflated sense of self. These seemingly contradictory characteristics all stem from a disorder of the self. Signs of a negative self-concept include:

> Exaggerated sense of importance
> Inflated self-perception generally
> Extreme sensitivity to evidence of shortcomings
> Need to be better than others
> Competitive strivings that do not decline with age
> Belief in unfounded assets (i.e., greater talents than they actually have)
> Belief in inaccurate liabilities (i.e., greater liabilities than they actually have)
> Need for reward and reinforcement to function well
> Negative response to criticism or unfavorable comparison
> Demands for attention or need to be the center of attention
> A negative self-concept
> Evidence of low self-esteem
> Exaggerated sense of deficiency
> Evidence of an inauthentic self (that is, self-perception does not match actual skills, abilities, and qualities)

FLAWS IN THE SELF-CONCEPT
AND NARCISSISTIC COPING

In terms of narcissism, I have come to understand the above deficiencies in the self as a function of four different but related dynamics. One is predicated on a flaw in the self that is masked by an air of false specialness. The second is predicated on a flaw of the self that is evidenced by feelings of entitlement. The third dynamic is predicated on a flaw in the self that is related to a fear of a defective self and is seen in reactivity to criticism and failure. The final dynamic is predicated on a flaw in the self that involves demands that are put on others in order to maintain self-esteem.

Underlying Narcissistic Dynamic: Need to Be Special
(Compensatory Defense for a Deficient Self-Concept)

Many children and adults who suffer from a flawed self-concept have come to believe that they are special—actually better than other people. Their exceptional performance or special talents earn them exceptional treatment. They do not understand or acknowledge that their sense of being special is predicated on a defect. Something has gone wrong in development such that their emotional security is at risk—their self-concept does not hold worth and value when it is not recognized and supported. They have a need to be seen a certain way. Without being special, they cannot feel good about themselves.

I treated a man many years ago, a surgeon, who unapologetically explained to me that he was the "smartest person" he had ever met, and he seemed to think that I should simply accept his self-assessment. He did not see this statement as boastful or inappropriate but regarded it as a statement of fact. He had exceptional talent and was therefore exceptionally "special." He had a hard time understanding why his wife did not think she should be as responsive to him as the surgical assistants in the operating room. His ideas were simply better, his perceptions simply more accurate. His advice provided the answer and solution to whatever problem she presented. He felt that she *should* appreciate the fact that she was *with* such a talented and extraordinary person. While it is true that specific people have specific special talents, skills, and abilities that are in fact special, no person is actually better than another person in a general global sense. His perception of his own specialness was tolerated in the operating room but was problematic in his marriage. Superiority interferes with meaningful connection and contributes to problems in relationships with friends and romantic partners.

Underlying Narcissistic Dynamic: Sense of Entitlement (Compensatory Defense for a Deficient Self-Concept)

A sense of entitlement is another outgrowth of an impaired self-concept. Lacking foundational confidence and security, the child builds an artificial defense. He sees himself as exceptional, better than everyone else, and comes to expect that he should be treated as special. This translates into a sense of entitlement. The small child demands a new toy regardless of its cost. A teenager believes they are allowed to see their friends whenever they choose. An adult does not feel that they should have to pay for a parking ticket when they are only five minutes over the limit. At all ages, there is a failure to appreciate the rules and a resistance to comply with them.

From a structural point of view, the need for admiration, attention, and satisfaction of their wants and desires is absolutely necessary. It props up the deficient sense of self. Being special, doing special things, affiliating with special people, and receiving special treatment all mask the underlying impoverished sense of self. This often typically finds expression in unreasonable expectations that often prove impossible for parents, friends, or associates to fulfill. Despite parental efforts to accommodate and indulge them, the child often remains unsatisfied.

I am reminded of a patient from many years ago. At thirty-seven, he had already become a highly successful real estate mogul and enjoyed the best of everything, from a farm with exotic game to a garage full of high-performance cars. He came in to see me at the demand of his wife, who claimed that he was not adequately attentive to her needs. I would have my first opportunity to witness her concerns when I tried to schedule an appointment. He was frustrated to learn that I did not see patients on Friday. He was unwilling to bend his schedule to fit into one of the two spots I had in the following weeks. He insisted that he be seen at the end of the workday despite the fact that he was the owner of his own company and set his own schedule. This is a classic example of entitlement. He expected the doctor to accommodate his needs and was visibly frustrated when he was not accommodated on demand. Accepting the limitations of his schedule, I showed him appointments far out in my calendar. Interestingly, when he realized that he could not see me for over a month, he decided to take one of the spots available in the next week.

I also counseled a woman and her husband who co-owned a ski house with another couple on a large mountain property. There was an attached garage that was closer to the house than the pull-in parking, but she did not want the other couple to occupy their half of the garage when she and her husband were not using it. She explained: "That's my half. It does not matter whether I'm there or not." Her entitled position was upsetting to her husband, who did not share her point of view. He felt that whichever couple was using the house should have full access to the more convenient and accessible garage. Importantly, the wife was infuriated at her husband for not sharing her "accurate" notion of equality based, in her mind, on the ownership. She believed the situation should be handled based on "truth," while he thought the situation should be resolved based on "consideration" and "cooperation." In relationships, notions of entitlement do not match unentitled ones and cause friction that is difficult to resolve.

Underlying Narcissistic Dynamic: Reactivity to Criticism, Failure,
and Disappointment (Defense Revealing the Fragility and
Lack of Strength in the Self-Concept)

Many children and adults who suffer with a flawed self-concept are actually struggling with anxiety over inadequacy. They fear being insignificant, flawed, invalidated, or being unable to secure the needed rewards and reinforcements. That fear of criticism, being identified as lacking or exposed as a failure, can set off shame and embarrassment. Therefore, they require continuous recognition and constant reinforcement in order to fuel their faulty self-concept. It is as if their self-concept is a bucket with a hole in it. Accolades, rewards, and recognition fill the bucket, but when deprived of those things, the bucket cannot hold. It leaks, and the self-concept must be fueled again. A defective sense of self is costly.

I treated an impressive young woman who entered my practice after she inexplicably developed an anxiety disorder despite her great success and achievement. She well describes the dilemma of those with a vulnerable sense of self. For Irene, successful competition exceeding the performance of her peers translated into pleasure and elevated her self-concept, while competitive loss translated into devaluation, which deflated her narcissistic self. I conceptualize this process as similar to a balloon. The balloon inflates with comparative success, and exhausts with competitive loss, suffering the ever-present fragility of the fate of a pin prick. In her therapeutic work, Irene discovered that her sensitivity to underachievement or loss resulted in the development of her anxiety symptoms. Her inadequacies led her to constantly compare herself to others in terms of talent, intelligence, status, financial security, and attractiveness, all swirling around on her never-ending list. She referred to this process as "compare and despair." The comparison resulted in a negative outcome. She was always able to find someone who was more intelligent, more attractive, wealthier, more talented, or more success-ful. Her growth involved recognizing the distortions in her thinking and ultimately searching to establish her own value system based on a realistic self-assessment—not based on her relative standing in comparison to others. The process took time but afforded her a kind of security that had eluded her all her life.

Many children who are continuously reinforced and celebrated will not reveal their defective self for years. This is particularly true in the case of talented and gifted youngsters who are regularly recognized and rewarded for their gifts. I am reminded of Eleanor, a very gorgeous and talented girl whom I saw briefly in my practice for anxiety around the time for her college admission results. She did not get into Yale as an-ticipated but was put on the waiting list. This was an extraordinary blow to her self-esteem, and her anxiety resulted in anorexia, with an almost complete refusal to eat. Happily, she was removed from the waiting list after only a few weeks. Her failure to eat immediately reversed itself, and the parents no longer allowed her to continue in therapy as they felt there was "no need." Despite my efforts to encourage ongoing therapy, the parents believed that her symptom pattern was simply a reflection of a "real-world disappointment" and did not reflect any underlying structural deficit or self-concept flaw. I did not share their view. I would later learn that she performed brilliantly at Yale and continued on her path of achievement. However, I would also learn that she "fell in love" and became involved with her beau to the exclusion of all other activi-ties. When he ended the relationship without explanation, she became depressed. Several days later, she carved his initials into her arm. It was only then that the parents began to appreciate that something might be wrong with their practically perfect daughter.

What Eleanor's parents did not understand was that, despite all evi-dence to the contrary, their daughter's self-concept was not sufficiently formed and stable enough to withstand this emotional blow. It was the same weakness that emerged when she was not immediately admitted to Yale. Her high performance in almost everything else was not matched by a strong, stable, and resilient self-concept. Proof of her worthiness through attention and accolades was needed to prop up her underlying vulnerability, and without it, she fell victim to the pain and disorganiza-tion of emotional dysregulation.

Underlying Narcissistic Dynamic: Use of Others for Esteem Maintenance
(Defense Revealing the Fragility and Lack of Strength in the Self-Concept)

Many children and adults who suffer with a flawed self-concept use others for self-esteem maintenance. The defective self requires continuous recognition and reinforcement, which demands compliance from others. The child must have their needs met, their wishes granted, and their demands fulfilled. This dynamic is one of the reasons that narcissism is costly to relationships. The inability to be frustrated, coupled with the demand to be indulged, places insurmountable requirements on the relationship and does not allow for reciprocity. In other words, the relationship is one way—with the child demanding that she get her way—which will inevitably frustrate the other's needs. In a sense, the child does not have the capacity to meet the needs of others, as her self-esteem cannot withstand the insult to her self-concept. This is one of the reasons that parents all too often find themselves feeling frustrated and hopeless about how to improve or resolve the child's condition or situation.

A session with Helen, a patient who came for a consultation after having spent a "long" weekend with her eight-year-old grandson, readily illustrates this point. Edgar was a child who I quickly understood as an emerging narcissist, an N2B. Helen enumerated what she described as "unending" frustrations. Edgar complained one morning that she cooked too much bacon, the next morning that she burned the bacon, and the final morning that she had not cooked enough food. When frustrated, he refused to eat and insisted that he be given dessert-like snacks from the cupboard. He claimed it was her fault—she did not know "how to cook." He demanded that he be taken out on the boat but then blamed his grandfather when he was unable to get up on his first trial on skis. Edgar insisted that his grandfather "didn't know how to drive the boat." Back in the cabin Edgar yelled at his brother and demanded that he share his toys. He blamed his brother for losing control when Helen had observed that he initiated the conflict by insulting and then pinching him. Helen described him as "impossible to deal with." Clearly, Edgar needed to have his way. Without it, he was unable to regulate his emotions.

THE HEALTHY SELF: EXAMPLES FROM CHILDHOOD

In my practice, I make assessments of the "self" in both children and adults on a regular basis. In some cases, I am making a formal evaluation in order to make treatment recommendations. In far more cases, I am making an informal evaluation as I work with an individual in therapy. Those informal measurements have been refined over decades, and now consist of a set of questions that I have posed to hundreds, if not thousands, of patients. I routinely ask children: Tell me the three things you like most about yourself. Tell me the three things you like least about yourself. I am searching here for the child's self-concept and self-esteem. Then I typically ask: "If I could ask your friends, teachers, or parents about you, what are the three things they like most about you and the three things they like least about you. Here I am searching for how the individual's self-concept and self-esteem is shaped by others.

Below are a few samples of things I like to hear from children at different ages as they share their ideas about their strengths and weaknesses.

Six-year-old George responded:
    I'm a pretty good runner.
    My teacher says I'm a good reader, but I think it's hard.
    I like to fish, and I caught a big one with my grandpa in the pond
        behind his house.

    I'm no good at spelling—that's for sure.
    I've never made a goal at soccer. I really want to. That would be
        cool.
    My dad says I eat with my mouth open.

Nine-year-old Natalie responded:
    I love to dance. I've been working on my steps for the Christmas
        dance recital. I have a big part and I'm glad I was selected.
    I'm a good writer and I like to make up stories that I put down in
        my diary.
    I'm a good helper—I help my mom in the kitchen.

I'm not that good at making my bed. I get in trouble for that.

I wish I were better at math, but it's super hard for me. My dad says that's OK, but I should just try.

I wish I was taller—that would be helpful in basketball, and I need some help there.

Fifteen-year-old Matt responded:

I'm a good debater. I actually won the Lincoln debate tournament in Cincinnati. I mean, I wanted to win, but there are lots of good debaters.

I love to ride my trail bike. I made it down the Alpine trail in less than two hours.

I'm good at math. I think I want to be an engineer.

I stink at English.

I had a hard time learning to read and still can't spell. Thank God for spell check.

Sometimes I'm mean. My dad says I have a wicked tongue. I'm working on that.

What these show is an acknowledgment of strengths and weaknesses with greater differentiation as the child ages. There is an absence of superior-like comments and a sense of increasingly accurate self-assessments. The strengths are not treated as exceptional, but they do hint of an increasingly realistic, fair-minded assessment as the child ages. The weaknesses are not devastating. There is an equanimity in the child's overall self-portrait that leads to optimism, confidence, and positive self-esteem.

A stable, steady, positive self-concept is not closely linked to the attitudes of others. Reward, reinforcement, accolades, and wild success do not feed the self-concept, nor are they required for the individual to feel good. Criticism, shame, disappointment, and failure hurt but do not pierce the self-concept and thereby do not interfere with daily functioning. The steadiness of a self-concept and accompanying positive self-esteem is, then, like a kind of shelter in any of life's storms.

THE INJURED, NON-HEALTHY SELF:
EXAMPLES FROM CHILDHOOD

The injured self can be reflected on both ends of a continuum with either excessive bragging, unrealistic overassessment and/or superiority, or at the other end of the spectrum, in an overly critical negative stance or budding negative identification.

Below are the kinds of things I worry about when I hear children at different ages talk about their strengths and weaknesses in response to my questions.

Those at Risk for an Overly Inflated Self-Concept

Six-year-old Dan responded:
> I'm the best kid ever.
> My teacher says I'm the best reader, and I am.
> I scored six goals at soccer.

> I'm good at lots of things so I don't know what I'd say.

Nine-year-old Melody responded:
> I'm a good reader. I've read all the biographies in the school library.
> I swim on a swim team and I'm the best one in my age group.
> I like my blonde hair. Lots of my friends wish they had it.

> I'm not very good at team sports but that doesn't matter to me. It's not important. I can't think of anything else.
> Well, I wish my hair was longer, but see, it's growing out. It'll be there soon.

Sixteen-year-old Robert responded:
> I'm the baseball team captain and the pitcher.
> The best-looking girl in high school is my girlfriend.
> I have the fastest car in the school, a new BMW.

> There's not much I don't like about me.
> I'm good at a lot of stuff. I have lots of stuff. Life's good.

Those at Risk for an Overly Negative Self-Concept

Six-year-old Jonathan responded:
  I don't like reading.
  I don't like my brother.
  I can swim—that's something.

  I don't like my school. I'm no good at anything there.
  I don't eat my vegetables and I don't care.
  I can't think of anything else.

Nine-year-old Cindy responded:
  I like to read but it takes me forever—so I don't do it.
  My school papers are covered in red ink.
  I have cool clothes. Look.

  I'm the last person picked at recess.
  I only have one friend, Barbara, and she's kind of fat.
  My mom yells at me for lots of stuff.

Fifteen-year-old Dylan responded:
  I'm a bad ass.
  Most popular sophomore.
  Have a fast dirt bike.

  My parents would say my grades suck. I think they're fine.
  I'm headed to a state college. My big brother was an SAE and I'll
    be one too.
  Maybe I drive too fast on my bike, but I like speed.

  These responses diverge in two markedly different ways. In the first
cases, there is an emphasis on social comparison and superiority, whether
stated in a boastful or more understated way. Weaknesses are either not
acknowledged or dismissed as unimportant. In the other cases, there
is also an emphasis on social comparison but with a developing sense
of inferiority. Strengths, if recognized, do not carry much weight, and
weaknesses dominate the picture, or if there are strengths, they reflect
negative social values and/or a negative self-identification.

In both types of examples, there is a lack of integration of strengths and weaknesses and/or an unrealistic assessment of skills and abilities, either tending toward overinflation or unwarranted deflation. In all these situations, the self-concept is at risk. In the first types of cases, while self-esteem might seem high, it is deficient. In the latter cases, self-esteem is also impoverished but in a more obvious, recognizable way.

PARENT CONTRIBUTIONS TO THE DEVELOPMENT OF THE HEALTHY OR NOT-SO-HEALTHY SELF

Parents matter. Loved by their children and essential for support and guidance, their words have the power to support or injure, as do the behaviors and attitudes that they model. When I lecture, I try to emphasize the importance of the many things that parents do but that often go unrecognized. It is important to remember that seemingly insignificant moments and brief exchanges can influence the course of development.

Parental encouragement is essential in facilitating development. This involves applauding their child's successes and helping them cope with their defeats. With a toddler, parents clap when their child takes his first steps and help when he falls flat and bangs his head. With a school-aged child, parents encourage math mastery and help when it grows difficult. With a middle school child, parents encourage hobbies and interests from scouts to athletics and provide comfort and understanding when the child's goals are frustrated. With high school kids, parents encourage the child's own self-driven interests even if they do not delight the parents and provide support if those interests prove challenging.

I am reminded of a seventeen-year-old who decided he wanted to learn to brew beer at home. He undertook the project with high energy and with his parents' reluctant permission, studying the steps and purchasing the needed ingredients, even ordering brown bottles and finding ways to cap them. The parents struck a compromise around consumption: he could start the project with the limit that he could only drink one bottle of his home-brew on weekend days to perfect his recipe. As the father said to me with a grimace, "This was *not* the hobby I was looking for in a son." He followed with a smile, "I mean I appreciate his industry and enthusiasm, but really?" His mother worried as well but explained the couple's final reasoning to support. She knew that his undertaking would require considerable study and careful planning, with many opportunities for learning through failure. She reasoned that he would develop some skills that would likely help him in starting a business someday or in following through on an important goal.

Parents also educate in invaluable ways. Margaret and her cousin Suzie, both tweeners, were at a family reunion and the grandparents and parents were doing what is common: "Look how much Billy has grown, and Suzie, and Margaret." The grandkids were all lined up in a row and Suzie had clearly grown much taller than Margaret—even though they were just a couple of weeks apart in age. Margaret felt the competitive loss and protested, "I never wanted to be tall anyway," in an attempt to make herself feel better. An hour later, Margaret's mother called her into another room. She was not angry and warmly explained that her protest had likely hurt Suzie's feelings. Suzie was now approaching six feet, having outgrown not only all the girls in her class but almost every boy. Margaret's mom knew that this was a sensitive spot for the cousin and suspected Margaret did not. The mother took the opportunity to help her daughter without shaming or criticizing. Once Margaret realized the impact of her words, she felt terrible. She had not understood the situation and never considered the impact of her words. She learned an important lesson—that sometimes you must look beyond yourself and put your needs behind those of others. Margaret explained in her work with me that this small experience had shaped her thinking going forward. She had not meant to hurt her beloved cousin and, from then on, she tried to double-check the impact of her words before she spoke. Her mother had challenged her to see the world from a different perspective. She taught her to put herself in Suzie's shoes and understand her emotional reaction and feel *for* her. Margaret never forgot the lesson.

Structurally speaking, Margaret's self-concept at the time was not sufficient to tolerate what she experienced as a competitive loss. Her upset and self-focus forced her to make comments that minimized what she perceived as her cousin's relative success. The sting of loss interfered with her ability to appreciate the predicament of her now too-tall cousin. However, her mother's thoughtful and careful intervention allowed her to grow from the experience. It underscored the importance of seeing the world from the perspective of another and elevating the feelings and needs of her cousin over her own. It contributed to the building and consolidation of a healthy self. Parents' words—every day and in everyday exchanges—impact the structures that are developing in the personality of the child.

Parents' Comments That Either Help or Hurt the Healthy Development of Self: An Example

What parents say and do has an impact on the development of the child's emerging self. Below is a sample of *healthy* parental comments around the topic of "learning to run" and "running." The responses are sequenced over time as the child grows and continues to develop the skill of running and later competing in track. They begin with simple encouragement and reinforcement for effort above all else. They progress to establishing the child's—not the parent's—goals. Later, they help establish a realistic assessment of the child's actual abilities in light of those goals in the context of the larger community.

Positive Exchanges
- You want to run fast. Good for you.
- You are trying hard. Yay!
- You're running faster. Your hard work is paying off.
- How fast do you think you're running?
- Are you running as fast as you want?
- You're doing well. Remember that your best friend, Thomas, has helped. He always encourages you to do your best—even when you beat him. That's a friend. Running is great, but friends are even better.
- You told me you want to make the track team. How fast do you have to run to make the track team?
- How can I help you meet your goals? I will make myself available if you need an extra timer at the meet.
- You're a hard worker. Give it your best.
- How fast do you have to run to qualify for the track meet?
- How fast do you have to run to go to the state meet?
- You told me you want to run track in college. What times do you need to meet that goal?
- You are working hard. That's great. But the competition is stiff.
- You have set high goals for yourself. You're going to try and meet those goals and see if they work out. We love you no matter what.

- You've learned that you are a hard worker regardless of the outcome. We love you.
- Give it your all. We'll be with you no matter the outcome.
- There's always love for you in our hearts. Remember that.
- Friendship and love are always more important than achievement, accomplishment, and winning.
- We'll be there for you—win or lose.
- We'll be here to pick up the pieces, just like always.
- Give it your best. Go with your heart.
- Love always outshines the brightest gold star. Don't forget that.

Key Concepts in Positive Exchanges
- Parental emphasis is on effort—not the level of achievement.
- Encouragement is a primary parental goal.
- The parent is focused on the child's desires—not their own expectations for them.
- The child feels supported in his efforts.
- Gradually and over time, the parent guides the child to establish a realistic assessment of their abilities.
- The parent shows acceptance and support—regardless of the level of performance.
- The parent works to help the child understand that they love them unconditionally.
- The parent is available for emotional support—not advice or criticism—when the child's goals are frustrated or if the efforts result in failure.
- The parent provides assistance when asked but is not intrusive.
- The parent deflates their child's specialness in kind, gentle, and loving ways.

Parental *errors* that build narcissism (i.e., through building a not-so-healthy self) come in many forms, including overinvestment, overindulgence, and overinflation. All will injure the child's self-concept and interfere with building healthy self-esteem. Below is a list of parental comments that I have heard from parents, both in and out of my practice, to their children that should be avoided. They run the gamut from encouraging superiority to shaming for underachievement. Here are examples around running and then participating in track.

Negative Exchanges
- You're a fast runner. You're faster than anybody in your class. You're the winner.
- Everybody knows you're the fastest runner. You're the best one.
- You're better than Tommy, Bobby, and George.
- The track coach is going to pick you for sure.
- Quitting is for losers. You don't want to be a loser, do you?
- You'll be the best sprinter on the track team.
- You got four medals at the track meet. You're the star of the team.
- Everybody loves you because you're the best player.
- Did you see how many girls want to date the star. Wow!
- You should go to college on a track scholarship. Your mom and I won't miss a meet. That's for sure.
- A college scholarship is the best way to "get there." You know, make a name for yourself. That can lead to connections and jobs and money. There's a payoff to being the best. You'll see.
- Don't give up. That will cost you your dreams.
- Wimps quit. Only the best guys persist.
- You're great. We're great. Our family is great—all of us.
- You're amazing. Better than everybody else. You're a winner and always will be.
- You make us look good. Shows everybody that we're great parents. Who else could have raised a star like you?

Key Concepts in Negative Exchanges
- The parent treats the child's success as their own success.
- The parent overvalues their child's performance, unaware of their own needs in doing so.
- The parent treats the child as special.
- The parent reinforces the child's superiority over their peers, overvaluing competitive success.
- The parent reinforces the notion of being the "best."
- The parent takes credit for their child's success, emphasizing their own superiority.
- The parent delights and shares in their child's success.
- The parent supports unrealistic expectations in the child.

- The parent does not help the child make a realistic assessment of their skills and capabilities as they develop over time.
- The parent fuels unrealistic fantasies for success and exceptionality.
- The parental emphasis is on winning.
- The parent supports a "better than others" orientation.
- The parent underemphasizes the importance of effort, promoting outcome, not process.
- The parent reinforces the child's specialness.
- The parent resorts to harsh criticism and shaming in the face of failure.
- The parent emphasizes winning without teaching the need to mediate competitive impulses over time and due to interpersonal or social concerns.
- The parents treat relationships and friendships as a secondary concern, taking a backseat to achievement.

Over the course of healthy development, the child's self-concept is being stabilized and secured such that when the child's needs are not always met, frustration can be tolerated. As children grow and mature, their needs for accomplishment, performance, and competitive winning will be mediated by friendship, empathy, fairness, kindness, concern, and morality. They will have built the ability to take risks and the courage to fail. The ultimate developmental outcome of a healthy self-concept is one of contentment. They see themselves as likable enough, pretty enough, smart enough—good enough overall, and contentment is contagious. It translates into being a person that other people like and enjoy and contributes to their being a healthy partner, parent, and friend.

The problem with treating a child as special deserves further comment. There are many children who possess exceptional talent or skill in one or more areas—children with amazing minds, remarkable athletic prowess, or incredible creativity. Those gifts challenge the parent to find a way to recognize and appreciate those skills but without encouraging the development of a self-concept predicated on exceptionality and specialness. I recall a parent at one of my lectures who raised her hand and asked, "Aren't you anti-exceptionality, Dr. Little?" I still remember my response: "I'm not against exceptionality. I'm opposed to superiority." Specialness integrated into the self-concept as "being better than" is the problem. Appreciation, pleasure, and pride in the recognition and exercise of a true talent or skill—these reactions in the parent and the child do not result in narcissism. Instead, they are important components of positive self-esteem and a stable self-concept.

In that same lecture, I went on to explain how a healthy or not-so-healthy self-concept plays out later in life. I have known many truly exceptional children over my many years—kids with perfect SAT scores and countless awards in writing, debate, engineering, or the arts, as well as every sort of sport. As a group, these children were truly exceptional in one way or another, but individually they reacted to ending up at Yale or Harvard or Stanford in very different ways. I remember one youngster who attended Harvard who explained his delight with the academic challenge there and his descriptions of the multivariate analyses taking place in the economics department. He delighted in his fellow classmates. He explained: "My roommate's brain's just like Velcro. He reads it one time and it's stuck there forever. Wow. It's so cool what he can do with his mind." He went on to explain: "I know I'm not the smartest kid there. I'm just glad to be there." Another kind of student described being at Yale in a very different way. He noted how impressive the school was and named a number of wealthy children who were in his class, explaining how many "summered" in the Hamptons or in the south of France. He recounted a weekend trip to his roommate's family home and his travel there on a private jet. He described the academic environment in terms of his professors' credentials and their likelihood of receiving a Nobel Prize. The contrast between these two students provides an important insight. One type recognizes his exceptionality but enjoys the opportunities those skills have provided him and appreciates and celebrates the skills and talents of his classmates and professors. The other type of student is impressed with his exceptionality and delights in the opportunities it has provided him to reinforce his superiority and secure his "special" place in academia and society.

How exceptionality is integrated into the child's self-concept sets the course for adult development. In my practice, I once treated a young woman with an impressive resume. She had attended the "best" schools, secured the "best" job, and had recently captured the "best" husband. I asked her about her plans for having a family. She responded: "I want to have four kids, that way I'm sure to get *one* good one." Her overvaluation of exceptionality will undermine her capacity to be a good enough

mother at the cost of the emotional health of *all* of her children, both
those who are deemed extraordinary and those who prove to be lacking. Overinvestment in exceptionality is not healthy and costs everyone,
both parent and child.

STRATEGIES FOR PARENTS:
BUILDING A NON-NARCISSISTIC SELF-CONCEPT
AND POSITIVE SELF-ESTEEM

Parents play a profoundly important role in the development of the
child's self-concept and self-esteem. In the most basic sense, children
learn *who* they are through early interactions with their parents and
caretakers. They refine those understandings as they mature and develop
relationships farther outside the nuclear family and acquire broader experience in the world. Parents can contribute to the development of a
healthy or not-so-healthy self in a variety of ways, and this has implications for the child's narcissistic or not-so-narcissistic development. Supporting this general notion is recent research showing the central role
of the self-concept in narcissism: "Narcissism is better understood as a
compensatory adaptation to overcome and cover up *negative self-worth.*"[4]

Research has identified a number of "parental influences" on the
development of narcissism. While those investigations are still relatively
new, clinical psychologists and theoreticians have been discussing the
causes of narcissism for almost a century, from early writing by Sigmund
Freud in 1914 and following in the decades to come with numerous
psychoanalytic (i.e., Kohut,[5] Kernberg,[6] Horney,[7] Miller[8]) and social
learning theorists (i.e., Millon et al.[9]). The overarching assumption is
that parents do something that causes the child to become narcissistic,
stunting her progression out of normal narcissism and sending her into a
maladaptive, defensive love of the self as opposed to a love for others.[10]
Understanding precisely *what* that something is and *why* it has its effect
varies across theoreticians and clinicians and is the subject of ongoing
discussion, debate, and research. These findings are complicated by other
research suggesting that parental influences may differ between groups of
parents. For example, parents who produce grandiose narcissists appear
to operate differently from those who produce vulnerable narcissists.[11]
This potentially explains why parents can make errors on both ends of

a given continuum. For example, parents who are overly indulgent and those who are overly critical can both contribute to narcissistic development but in very different, often seemingly contradictory, ways. While these and other questions remain with the researchers, there are trends that can be gleaned.

Ongoing evidence suggests that, in order to avoid the development of narcissistic tendencies, traits, and disorders, parents should be invested in strategies that build a positive self-concept and strong self-esteem. The following understandings have been derived from the findings and implications of both theory and research and have been refined in my decades of experience with narcissistic children, adults, and families.

Negative Impacts

The Negative Impact of Treating the Child as Special   Parents who treat the child as special continuously reward and reinforce exceptionality. Such treatment teaches the child that they are extraordinary and, by definition, better than others. A belief in one's own extraordinariness will eventually result in disappointment when inevitable real-world experiences frustrate the child's expectations. More importantly, the child can come to believe that being extraordinary is a necessary component of being loved—a feeling that she is loved for her imaginary special qualities rather than for her true self.[12] Being treated as special also contributes to self-centeredness and self-absorption, as well as narcissism generally.

The Negative Impact of Overvaluation   Parents who are overly invested in their child, making her the center of attention in their lives to the exclusion of their marriage and other important family ties, are modeling an unhealthy relationship. Such "golden" children will expect to be attended to without exception and believe that their behaviors and actions should be treated as a priority. Similarly, parents who overinvest in their child's activities and achievement communicate to the child that he is loved for his performance and not loved for his inner being. Overvaluation tends to predict narcissism[13] and does not translate into positive healthy self-esteem; rather, it engenders and supports emotional limitations of various sorts.[14]

The Negative Impact of Overprotection   Parents who overprotect their child undermine the development of independence. Sometimes referred to as "hovering," overprotection limits the child's ability to learn from their experiences and tends to make them less self-sufficient and autonomous. The child becomes anxious when the parent is not available to them. This parenting orientation is correlated with a variety of negative outcomes including lowered self-confidence, limited coping skills, intolerance of frustration, and negative self-beliefs around competence and capability.[15]

The Negative Impact of Overindulgence and Pampering   Parents who overindulge their children through meeting their every demand and not setting limits give their children an inaccurate sense of the way the world works and the nature of human relationships. This parental style sets an unrealistic standard for the child that cannot be met in the larger world. The child who has been exposed to indulgent parenting will expect comparable treatment from others. The child may learn to employ demanding strategies that elicit favored or indulged responses in all other relationships. In addition, the overindulgent emphasis on "goods" such as toys, clothes, and gadgets reinforces the idea that external "things" are more valuable than interpersonal connection or the development of internal qualities such as honesty, kindness, and compassion. This orientation increases the desire to acquire more things and decreases the drive to invest in connection with others except as a means to secure more and better "stuff."

The Negative Impact of Overcontrol and Intrusiveness   Parents who attempt to control their child excessively and intrude into their emotional development interfere with healthy maturation. Overcontrolling strategies include manipulation of a child through withdrawal of love, the induction of guilt around misbehavior, or expressions of disappointment that shame the child. Such parental strategies have been associated with a number of negative outcomes including delinquency and depression in the child.[16]

The Negative Impact of a Lack of Limit Setting   Parents who set few limitations and boundaries for their children compromise their development. Such children are likely to feel entitled and count on special treatment, believing that they are superior, and concluding that the rules do not apply to them. Lack of limit setting may interfere with the development of self-discipline, as it is hard to learn how to discipline the self if you have not experienced limits in the world.[17] Limit-setting is needed not only to socialize the child but, more importantly, to encourage the development of essential, internal structures.

The Negative Impact of Excessive Praise.   Parents who offer excessive praise undermine the effect of actual achievement and encourage the development of an unfounded, artificial self-concept. By definition, they tend to praise accomplishment unworthy of recognition and compliment. Not only does praise lose its effectiveness, but it contributes to a sense of being special and an expectation for privileged treatment. It also carries an embedded message that love and acceptance are conditional on outstanding performance and ignores the more critical aspects of effort and self-improvement. In contrast, praise that is offered judiciously and emphasizes effort over outcome builds self-confidence. Excessive praise is problematic for children, as it impedes the development of a healthy and grounded self.[18]

The Negative Impact of Treating the Child as an Extension of the Parent. Parents who see their children as extensions of themselves tend to idealize their child. They pin their own sense of self-worth and value on their child's accomplishment, and push, as opposed to encourage, their performance. This kind of enmeshment is unhealthy and sets a problematic model for the child's current and future relationships.

The Negative Impact of Criticism and Shaming.   Parents who criticize excessively, whether overtly or covertly, damage their child's sense of self. In doing so, parents evidence their difficulties in tolerating imperfection and express dislike, and even loathing, for their child. It carries an underlying message that the child is unworthy of love and contributes to feelings of self-disregard, and potentially, self-hatred. Correction (i.e., as teaching) is a necessary and important part of parenting but is not the same as criticism. Correction addresses the problem and helps the child learn to problem solve and seek solutions while criticism pierces the child's sense of worth. A critical and shaming parental stance is associated with negative outcomes.[19]

The Negative Impact of Unrealistic Expectations.   Parents who set exceedingly high expectations interfere with the child's development of a healthy self-concept and present difficulty extending in two divergent directions. If children meet those high standards, they are at risk of developing a sense of being special and entitled. If children cannot meet those expectations, they run the risk of developing a sense of being unworthy and unlovable.

Excessive parental expectations are costly, as children tend to internalize those expectations and depend on them for self-esteem. When they fail to meet them, they can become self-critical and strive to be perfect to compensate. Recent research shows that college students' perception of both their parents' expectations and criticism have increased over the past three decades and are correlated with an increase in perfectionism.[20] Perfectionism is associated with many negative outcomes including anxiety, depression, eating disorders, and self-harm.

Positive Impacts

The Positive Impact of Unconditional Love. Parents who raise children with unconditional love contribute to a child's sense of security and belief in their own lovability. Such parents know and accept the essence of the child. They demonstrate that the child is loveable and valuable for *who* they are, not *what* they do. This allows the child to separate their sense of self from the level of their performance. In effect, it helps to build a solid positive, self-concept that is resilient in the face of frustration and disappointment.

The Positive Impact of Parental Warmth. Parents communicate warmth through acceptance, understanding, and the quality of involvement and nurture in ever-evolving ways as children grow. Children who experience parental warmth tend to have high self-esteem, are more sociable, show greater self-regulation, and evidence greater social maturity.[21] Parental warmth appears to insulate the child from narcissistic development and has not been shown to be associated with narcissism.[22]

The Positive Impact of Building High Self-Esteem. Parents who raise children with high self-esteem through the expression of unconditional love and consistent warmth teach their children that they are worthy and valuable as they are. They learn to have confidence that they are "good enough," being inherently as capable as others and not needing to prove themselves as a comparative success. Children with high self-esteem do not see themselves as more special than others but rather as kids who are satisfied with themselves and who like the kind of person they are.

The Positive Impact of Regarding Imperfection and Failure as Normal, Expected, and Valuable. Research has linked rising parental expectations to an increase in perfectionism in children,[23] and perfectionism is recognized as being unhealthy for both children and adults. Perfectionists tend to be more neurotic and are prone to dysregulation and a variety of other psychological dysfunctions. Parents can help their child by teaching them that imperfection and failure are a normal and expected part of life. Focusing on competence and skill mastery, as opposed to validation through exceptional, "practically perfect" performance, and/or social comparison, helps build a healthy self-concept and positive self-esteem.

EIGHT TAKEAWAYS FOR PARENTS TO BUILD A SECURE SELF-CONCEPT AND POSITIVE SELF-ESTEEM IN THE CHILD

Lessons from theory and research lend support for the following parenting behaviors:

- Love your child unconditionally and nurture with warmth and caring.
- Encourage the child to develop a broad range of skills and abilities, to learn about their capabilities, and to discover their passions.
- Accept the child's performance, whatever the level of accomplishment, as valued.
- Encourage the child to persist when they encounter frustration, disappointment, and failure when trying out skills and abilities.
- Help the child make realistic assessments of skills and abilities as they mature and gently deflate unrealistic self-perceptions and expectations.
- Value both effort and mastery over level of achievement or comparative striving.
- Encourage competence not excellence.
- Teach children that they should be treated with respect but should not expect special treatment.
- Encourage the child to develop an overarching sense of being lovable and valuable as an ordinary—not special—person.

THE OUTCOME: "RETURNING TO THE FARM" AS A METAPHOR

When I work with parents, I discuss parenting as an opportunity to leave a legacy. Their job is an important one. They provide foundational support in the development of their child's self-concept and, ultimately, their self-esteem. Parents have a chance to leave their child with a rich legacy of events, actions, attitudes, exchanges, interactions, and memories. These will shape the child's self, either in positive ways that provide stability and security in difficult times or in negative ways that undermine their confidence. They will leave their child with a farm that functions well or one that struggles to be productive and sustainable.

Parenting through the years requires great effort, commitment, and sacrifice. Parents have worked on the farm for many years and have contributed to the success or failure of various crops and agricultural operations. They have helped when natural disasters struck, when flooding interfered with planting, or drought-restricted growing. But the legacy of the farm as a worthy, valuable, and capable institution provides invaluable reassurance in the event of tragedy, disappointment, and failure. Similarly, a negative legacy undermines security and confidence and challenges their child's future growth. For those who have succeeded, the farm can now operate without their involvement, self-sufficient and profitable. This outcome is evidence of a job well done and proves worthy of the long-sustaining effort of parenting.

· 5 ·

Building a Non-narcissistic Ability to Regulate Emotions

(Learning to Handle Feelings = Self-Control and Self-Discipline)

The Development of Emotional Regulation over Time

*E*very child must develop the ability for self-regulation, which involves control over emotions, impulses, behaviors, and thoughts. It involves control *of* the self *by* the self, that ultimately results in the internalization of the capacity for self-control. The capability to effectively regulate emotions is essential in order for the child to develop, navigate, and complete necessary steps in emotional and intellectual growth. Self-regulation and the self-concept are personality traits that make up a considerable portion of *who* the child is at their core. As a major part of the personality, self-regulation impacts daily functioning and interactions with others.

There are different types of self-regulation. Emotional self-regulation involves influence over emotional reactions. It can take a variety of forms, ranging from resisting impulsive urges to redirecting emotions in a productive manner. Behavioral self-regulation involves controlling overt physical behavior. An angry child might not punch a classmate and opt to practice the trumpet in preparation for a recital. Cognitive self-regulation involves the control of thoughts. The child might work to stop thinking about an insult from a peer and shift thoughts to other topics.

There is a wealth of research showing that self-regulation in every-day life is positively correlated with well-being for adults.[1] Similarly, children who engage in self-regulating behavior have positive associations with higher academic achievement and lowered association with the likelihood of substance abuse and conduct disorders.[2] Adolescents who consistently engage in self-regulating behavior report enhanced life satisfaction, perceived social support, and positive affect—all measures associated with general well-being.[3] There is considerable research addressing self-regulation theory (SRT), a system of understanding that focuses on the process of guiding thoughts, behaviors, and feelings to reach goals[4] and an entire treatment protocol in Dialectical Behavior Theory (DBT) that works to strengthen emotional regulation.[5]

Self-regulation involves management of emotions, behaviors, and decisions particularly in the face of strong emotions or needs. Infants are born with limited self-regulatory capabilities. When the baby is cold or wet, he wails. When a toddler falls and bumps his head, he cries in pain and demands consoling. A school-aged child shouts angrily at the demand to eat broccoli. A middle-schooler cries over a homework paper filled with red marks. A teenager stomps out of the room when his father corrects his poor manners. An adolescent turns on his heels muttering inappropriate, hostile words under his breath when told he cannot have the car Friday night.

Over the course of development, the capacity for self-control will grow steadily. Toddlers who throw fits when they cannot have their way will eventually put those angry feelings into words. I conceptualize a continuum that begins with complete lack of control (throwing themselves on the floor and yelling), that grows into tantrums (stomping feet and banging the table), that builds into negative feelings put into words ("Mom, you're a doo-doo head"), that transforms into words that are more socially acceptable ("I don't like you, and I want to live somewhere else"), that develops further into using strong but acceptable words ("I'm really, really, really mad at you"), that finally become more reasonable and measured adult-like statements ("I am really upset when you won't allow me to go to the football game).

Children do not always maintain their highest level of achieved emotional regulation. If sufficiently distressed, a child can revert to an earlier stage. A youngster who has to sit out at recess may be mean to his brother after school. A child who receives a poor grade may tease his sister inappropriately. A school-aged child, after being called into the principal's office, may yell at his mother when he gets into the car at pickup. An adolescent, still reeling from an argument with his girlfriend, may refuse to speak to his parents or come to dinner. When noting evidence of a child's regression to an earlier level of function, the caregiver or therapist should search for and take into account the source of the underlying distress.

Emotional regulation is not an "all or nothing" process. Mastery, in an absolute sense, is never complete and always has the potential for regression. As opportunities present themselves, children and adults must work on their self-regulatory skills. Individuals never outgrow the need to self-regulate—from eating to exercising, from failing to mourning. Steady, reliable emotional management is required through the cycles of life.

When considered over a lifetime, the progressive evolution of self-regulation is remarkable. The child with growing self-regulatory capabilities will eventually refrain from throwing a tantrum when she cannot have the toy she desperately wants. A youngster will put his feelings into words instead of grabbing or hitting. A student who is unable to spend the night out because of grandma's visit will eventually redirect those feelings into playing basketball in the backyard. An athlete will refrain from telling off his peer when he missed the basket at the buzzer. A student who is tempted to join her friends after school will decide to go home and study for tomorrow's exam. An adolescent will finish her homework and stay steady emotionally after being rejected by the most popular boy in high school. A football player will not cry when he takes a rough tackle. A young adult will remain calm and polite when an angry coworker berates him for something that was not his fault. Fully developed, emotional regulation results in a state of steady emotional equilibrium.

The goal of "good enough" parenting is to raise children with a sufficient capacity for emotional regulation such that they can withstand not only inevitable life stressors and real-world injustice, but also extraordinary tragedies such as the death of a beloved family member or an event like 9/11. Resilient, capably self-regulated children can persist in the face of catastrophe.

EMOTIONAL REGULATION: THE "FEELINGS MACHINE" AS A METAPHOR

As mentioned before, when I work with parents, I try to identify metaphors that allow parents to "see" what is going on inside the child—a way to visualize the personality structure that is forming and evolving under the surface.

I conceptualize the child's emerging and evolving self-regulatory system as a "Feelings Machine." This internal apparatus takes in strong emotions, digests them, and then spits them out in a more or less "neutralized" form. By this I mean, the socially inappropriate and the developmentally inappropriate are increasingly mitigated. Over the course of development, the "Feelings Machine" will grow larger, stronger, more efficient, and better adapted to challenges. Its capacity to manage and neutralize emotions is ever improving. I imagine strong angry feelings going into a toddler's tiny machine that then exit the machine still hot. I imagine angry intense feelings going into a school-aged child's small machine that leave the device "cooler" but still warm. It will be years before the machine will be large and complex enough to more effectively neutralize incoming hot feelings into lukewarm and ultimately cooler emotion.

Life is filled with stressors and stimulation of various kinds that are realized as painful, upsetting, or threatening. In all those situations, the child experiences a strong surge of emotion. Over time, the "Feelings Machine" must find a way to de-intensify those surges by controlling, holding, containing, organizing, channeling, or harnessing them.

The "Feelings Machine" must grow in size and complexity in order to deal with the ever-increasing gratifications, threats, and overall sophistication of the child's more mature life. Small frustrations can grow into larger frustrations. Modest disappointments can grow into more injurious disappointments. Little failures might grow into embarrassing mistakes. To be a mature, healthy, well-functioning adult, the machine must grow to meet the growing responsibilities and challenges of life and the intensity of strong negative adult emotions.

THE DEVELOPMENT OF EMOTIONAL REGULATION: SELF-REGULATION INCLUDING SELF-CONTROL AND SELF-DISCIPLINE

Step 1: Self-Control

Self-control might be considered to be a more active and purposeful form of self-regulation. It involves effortful control and some degree of voluntary self-management. A child's ability to govern emotions, impulses, behavior, and cognition emerge at different developmental periods and are mastered at different ages and stages.

Self-control has two aspects. While emotions are controlled in both, the effects take different forms. One involves not responding inappropriately to negative events, stressors, disappointments, or upsets. The other involves harnessing internal reactions into proactive behavior.

The capacity for self-control, for both child and adult, tends to fluctuate over the course of a day. Research on "ego depletion" describes times when self-regulation strength is low. When a child is tired or hungry, he may struggle more to control his behavior. The urge to act is felt more intensely and the ability to restrain is lower. When an adolescent has performed poorly on a test in which she invested great effort, she may battle to not react with impatience to her sibling's teasing. Studies have shown that demanding, taxing, or upsetting experiences make it harder to regulate emotions.[6]

Longitudinal research has confirmed the significance of self-control in general adaptation and adjustment.[7] Self-control has been shown to be predictive of everyday measures of adaptive function, including positive report card grades, maintenance of a healthy weight,[8] stronger academic achievement, and better relationships with others.[9] Furthermore, measures of self-control during the first decade of life predict a number of positive adult life outcomes, including physical and mental health, financial security, income, saving behavior, occupational prestige, lack of substance abuse, and lack of criminal convictions.[10] There is some suggestion that the quality of the relationship between a parent and child serves an important function in terms of the child's ability to self-regulate. Parenting predicts adolescents' later capacity for self-control,[11] and interestingly, the adolescents' capacity for self-control also predicts later parenting success.

The process of self-control can be seen at various ages and stages of development. A healthy progression is illustrated by a patient I once saw in play therapy, a five-year-old little girl, Margaret. There had been trauma in her family with the sudden death of a beloved grandparent, and she was trying to sort through her feelings around that event. She was playing with two dolls in the playhouse. One of the dolls did something that the other doll judged to be "not nice," and that doll commented on the behavior: "Don't do that again or I'll have to talk to you about it." Still a preschooler, she was working to manage feelings through words as opposed to action, trying to bring emotions under cognitive control and resist more immature behavioral expression. This is an early indicator of the healthy progression of emerging self-control and a positive sign that Margaret was beginning to master her own upsetting feelings.

Step 2: Self-Discipline

Self-discipline is perhaps the most active and demanding form of self-regulation and self-control. It involves using several capacities to achieve a desired end including persistence on a complex long-term project, problem solving directed toward achieving a goal, and self-monitoring progress toward that target. Learning to study when you'd rather be playing, practicing the piano when you'd rather be on the computer, or taking care of your younger sibling when you'd rather be on the phone with your friends are all early examples of emerging self-discipline. Like other self-regulatory skills, self-discipline develops incrementally and in small ways with time, experience, and maturation.

Initially, children learn to achieve early goals in self-discipline as their parents help them with mastery of specific tasks. Parents support beginning efforts. For example, parents help children do their reading in early elementary school, reading with them and encouraging progress. As the child matures and becomes more proficient, they can complete their reading independently. Programs support reading with various reinforcement systems, including stars and point exchanges for valued items. External assistance and validation, which take place in different areas simultaneously, help build self-discipline in the child.

Self-discipline requires the ability to delay gratification. Short-term pleasure must be denied in the pursuit of a long-term purpose. Freud considered the delay of gratification as one of the central developmental challenges of childhood.[12] The ability to navigate conflicts between long-term goals and daily temptations reflects maturity and higher-level function and control. The capacity for self-discipline will improve with emotional maturity as the ability to regulate emotion, behavior, and attention in the presence of temptation increases over the developmental period.

"Grit" appears to be a more intense and even better developed form of self-discipline that harnesses internal drive. Defined as "passion or perseverance for long-term goals,"[13] it is particularly relevant in reaching goals of high personal value and significance.[14] Interestingly, "grit" is a better predictor of success at meeting challenging, highly valued goals than self-control standing alone.[15]

I am reminded of George, a first grader, who had planted a garden in his backyard with his mother. For several weeks, he had nurtured a giant watermelon that was growing next to the fence. He watered it diligently and visited it every day, watching and monitoring its ever-expanding size. He planned to remove it from the garden, put it in the refrigerator, and eat it over the Fourth of July holiday weekend. When George went out to harvest his watermelon, he cut the stem and lifted the fruit only to discover that ants had made their way into the melon and eaten out its center. Unable to manage the intensity of his feelings brought on by such a big disappointment, he lost emotional control and cried inconsolably. He had shown great discipline in his ability to wait for the watermelon to mature to a size sufficient to be big enough for all to share over the holiday weekend event. His emotional resources were depleted through the delay of gratification he had withstood, and he was now unable to self-regulate in the face of such pain. Self-discipline and self-control cannot always manage intense emotional reactions in a child or, for that matter, an adult. Time, effort, and experience with frustration and loss present challenges as well as opportunities for growth for the child's still immature self-regulatory abilities.

HEALTHY OR NOT-SO-HEALTHY EMOTIONAL REGULATION: MEASURES OF EMOTIONAL REGULATION

Signs of Healthy Emotional Regulation

As a psychologist, I make frequent determinations about a child's or adult's capacity for emotional regulation. Children with emerging healthy self-regulation skills demonstrate increasing adaptability to upsetting events and situations over the course of their life.

Over many years, I have identified various stages in the development of emotional regulation. These are measures that I look for in my clinical practice when assessing the capacity for emotional control.

- Phase 1: Feelings come out straight away and with gusto. Young children typically let you know about their frustrations, sadness, and excitement in direct, intense, and obvious forms. The two-year-old shrieks with delight when he sees his birthday cake from across the room. The toddler throws himself on the floor when he cannot have another cookie. The school-age child screams when her toy sword is put on a high shelf after she hits her brother with it. The adult version of such raw displays of emotion includes screaming, throwing things, cursing, and even physical violence.

- Phase 2: Feelings come out after a while and with less intensity. As children mature, they often can delay their responses for just a moment. If a child's favorite toy has been taken away, she may stand for a moment, look at you, stomp her feet, and then burst into tears. The moment of control before the emotions overflow is an improvement over the earlier phase. The adult version of this stage includes a brief pause before engaging in inappropriate words or actions.

- Phase 3: Feelings come out in unacceptable words. Young children have unique ways of communicating their frustrations and feelings once they can use words. Kids often say the strongest words they know, ranging from "You're stupid" to "I hate you." At other times, they may use phrases whose meanings they do not know but think are intense. The adult version of this stage includes cursing, name calling, and using socially inappropriate, hurtful words.

- Phase 4: Feelings come out in descriptive and more acceptable words. Children in this phase can often tell you about their feelings. They will say "I don't like it" or "It's not fair." The adult version of this stage includes mild insults, sarcasm, and teasing.

- Phase 5: Feelings come out in adult-like language. Children can share their feelings with mature language stated in a relatively calm frame of mind. They are capable of a reasonable discussion about the source of the upset. The adult version of this stage includes statements such as "I feel sad because you did not return my telephone call in a timely manner."

- Phase 6: Feelings do not interfere with the ability to focus and do work. While upset, children can still be productive. They can still finish their homework or engage in a family activity while upset. The adult version of this stage includes remaining productive on a project at work, continuing to complete household tasks, and participating in family events without evidence of emotional upset.

- Phase 7: Feelings can be harnessed or channeled in productive activities. Children can be upset but harness the energy of those feelings in productive activities. They can take a run around the neighborhood, talk to a buddy or favorite aunt about their problem, or organize their thoughts on a piece of paper. The adult version of this stage includes going to yoga class, practicing mindfulness, engaging in a hobby, calling a friend, and arranging for a consultation.

These phases demonstrate a progression from physical lack of control to ultimately high-level cognitive control. I am reminded of the joke that describes more adultlike mastery: "I may look calm, but, in my head, I've already yelled at you three times."

When working with children or adults, I determine which stage the subject most frequently relies upon and use that information in conceptualizing next steps for growth.

Parents need to recognize the gains that children make from one phase to another. Some examples: "It's upsetting that you can't go to the fair, but you didn't yell. That's great. You put your feelings into words." Or: "It's maddening what George said about you, but you didn't react immediately. You took some time to think through how to manage him and the situation." Or: "Last year, you would have thrown a fit about that. Look how much better you are at handling the same situation this year."

There are a variety of gains associated with steady, solid self-regulation. Children with this ability are more able to cope in moments of extreme stress and less vulnerable to the impacts of tragedy. Their stability makes them less likely to be negatively influenced by their peers as they have the capacity to say "no" to themselves and others. A better-developed capability for self-control leads to self-discipline, which is associated with achievement generally. Such children are more likely to establish and reach their goals despite frustration along the way and can tolerate and manage with equanimity interpersonal conflicts.

A story told to me by a father highlights the importance of self-control and self-discipline in a youngster. He and his twelve-year-old son, Pablo, were skiing one afternoon in Colorado with his son's best friend and his mother. They had taken the lift to the top of the mountain and had skied halfway down a challenging run when an ominous looking storm began moving in. Within minutes, they were caught in a "white out," able to see only a couple of feet ahead.

The father organized the group, putting them into a line and instructing them to stay close. Being on a difficult hill, the moguls were impossible to navigate, and Pablo's friend fell and struggled to get up. Soon, as visibility declined even further, it became difficult to see an outstretched hand and impossible to see any trail signs.

Pablo spoke up: "Let's ski over to the lift. We can follow it down the hill and keep it in our sites above our heads." His father recognized this as a smart solution, and they made their way across. The situation was becoming increasingly terrifying. Pablo's friend was whimpering, and his mother was crying under her breath. The group continued to make slow and steady progress when Pablo spoke up again: "We need to stop following the lift now and ski over to the left back to the other run. Then we need to ski down, and then back under the lift." His father protested, "Why?'" Pablo explained, "Don't you remember, Dad? There's a cliff underneath the lift ahead. We'll go right off it if we keep going this way." His father remembered that portion of the trail, horrified that he had not thought of it himself. Pablo's plan worked, and once down, his friend and the mother thanked him for "saving" them.

Pablo's remarkably steady problem solving illustrates the benefits of self-regulation in moments of crisis. His ability to stay self-regulated in a threatening and dangerous situation allowed his cognitive skills to function at their fullest capacity. Dysregulation is typically accompanied by impulsivity and impaired reasoning, but Pablo's capacity for self-control and careful reasoning exceeded that of his father in the face of danger and was a sign of his precocious maturity and positive development.

Later, the father made an insightful, self-deprecating comment: "I had the good sense to *follow* a twelve-year-old boy when I wasn't together enough to think our way to safety for all of us." This story illustrates the essential need for children to develop steady emotional regulation, and for their parents to support them in the process.

I am reminded of another story that a father of a college-aged young man shared with me. He explained the circumstances around his son being fatally shot in a bar. An unknown, very inebriated man in the bar made an insulting comment about his son's girlfriend. His son stood up for his girlfriend and told the man to stop. In a sense, the young man did an admirable thing—taking care of his girlfriend and her hurt feelings. Tragically, an argument ensued that ended with the unknown man pulling a gun and shooting. While no one can ever rewrite a tragic past or understand the particulars, the "what-if" around years-old situations, it is important for young people to develop the ability to restrain emotions such that they can make careful decisions as to when, and if, they should stand up for any given principle if it might expose them to danger. Emotions run high in such situations, and thoughtful assessment of the degree of risk is not always a practical possibility. However, parents should encourage the development of a child's growing capacity for emotional control and self-restraint, important life skills that can be relied upon whatever the circumstance.

It is in every parent's best interest to raise a child with solid abilities for emotional regulation to ensure the availability of clear-headed reasoning and accurate evaluation in all types of difficult, potentially dangerous, situations. Over the course of development, parents can help the child learn to effectively regulate their emotions, behaviors, and thinking, providing important practice for other situations when it may be sorely needed. The ultimate goal is for the child's self-regulation to become a competent process that is readily available when needed.

Signs of Not-So-Healthy Emotional Regulation

Children with not-so-healthy emotional regulation have a variety of presentations. In my system, they generally fall into three categories: "externalizers," "internalizers," and "transformers."

"Externalizers" are children who tend to show their upset, acting out their distress. They tantrum, rage, cry, scream, curse, and name call. They tend to have a high-voltage reaction to a high-voltage experience or event, which passes through their system without any de-intensification. The machine has short-circuited and by-passed all systems for neutralization. The child's raw display of emotion is uncomfortable for parents, who often lower their heads and sheepishly slip out of the restaurant or grocery store after their child has "acted up." This developmental pattern is an immature one and presents challenges both at home and at school.

"Internalizers" are children who tend to "bottle up" upsetting feelings. When they experience shame, fear, or frustration, they hold and contain those feelings. Such children are prone to bodily complaints (i.e., somatization), anxiety attacks, and even depression. Feelings that are managed in this way and are not de-intensified are problematic in the long term.

"Transformers" are children who harness strong emotions in negative ways. Those feelings are channeled unproductively and/or harmfully toward the self or others. Upset can be turned against the self in criticism, dislike, or even self-harm as in cutting, poor grooming, or worrisome health habits. Feelings can also be directed toward others, as in developing plans to hurt others by posting harmful words or pictures on social media, excluding children from valued events, or embarrassing others. Many types of bullying behaviors fall into this category.

The Healthy Emotional Regulator: Examples from Childhood

In my practice, I make assessments, on a regular basis, of "emotional regulation" abilities in children as well as adults. In most cases, I am making an informal evaluation to help direct my work in individual therapy. Over the years, I have devised informal measures through a series of questions that have now been posed to hundreds of children. I routinely ask: "Tell me the three things that you do when you are mad or three things that you do when you're sad." Here I am searching for the child's routine ways of dealing with emotional upset.

Below are a few samples of things I like to hear from children as they share their ideas about managing their feelings at different ages:

Six-Year-Old Christopher

I yell. Even at my mom—but not my teacher.
I hit my brother. I try not to.
Sometimes I throw things. I get in trouble for that.

Nine-Year-Old Norma

I used to cry a lot. Now I try not to cry.
Sometimes I go to my room and slam the door.
Sometimes I say stuff under my breath. If my dad hears me, he talks to me about it.

Fifteen-Year-Old Marvin
When I'm super mad, I yell. I know that I shouldn't, but sometimes
    I can't help it.
Sometimes I'm pretty mean to my dad. I mean I'm mad, but I'm
    not sure he always deserves it.
I don't really cry anymore. I mean guys don't cry—well, I mean,
    not that much. My mom says it's OK to cry. She doesn't know.
    She's not a guy.

What these responses show is an acknowledgment and acceptance
of a range of emotions and a sense of the need to manage them. Children
come to accept feelings as part of the human experience. All responses
involve the appropriate labeling of feelings and an expanding or growing
"feeling vocabulary" as they age. They increasingly recognize gradations
of feelings (i.e., a little mad, a lot mad, or simply furious). As children
age, problem solving tends to rely more on words than actions and
deliberation over reactivity. There is growing understanding of the difference between appropriate and inappropriate expression of emotions,
an ever-increasing reliance on self-restraint, and developing acceptance
of the child's responsibility for self-control.

The Injured, Not-So-Healthy Emotional Regulator:
Examples from Childhood

Not-so-healthy emotional regulation can take several forms. Children
can become enraged, throwing a tantrum with yelling, screaming, hitting, and kicking, or crying inconsolably. Children can act out their
upset by hurting others, lashing out by hitting or taking revenge. As
children mature, the forms of revenge become increasingly injurious.
A lack of remorse for their bad behavior and a lack of concern for the
feelings of those injured are negative signs.
    Below are the kinds of things I worry about when I hear children
discuss their ability to manage their feelings at different ages:

Seven-Year-Old Jennifer
Yesterday, I yelled at my mother. She deserves it. She should have
    let me go visit my friend.
I cried when I had to sit out during recess. I don't think it's fair.
I'm mad when I can't do stuff.

Nine-Year-Old Neal

My dad makes me make my bed. Sometimes I don't do it because I don't want to.

Sometimes Ray is a jerk, I'm mad enough to fight him. And I tell him so.

I yell when I want something I can't have. Sometimes if I yell long enough, I get it.

Eleven-Year-Old Henrietta

I go to my room and stay there when I'm sad.

I don't like to talk to people when I feel bad.

My mom tries to come into my room, but I won't let her.

Sixteen-Year-Old Hernando

I don't get mad—I get even. People shouldn't mess with me.

I never cry. Crying is for sissies.

Actually, I don't get mad much.

These responses indicate a generally immature understanding of feelings. In some cases, the child is completely overwhelmed by the feelings. In others, there is a lack of interest and effort in building self-control, as well as a tendency to blame others for causing the situation that precipitated the upset. In both scenarios, there is also a lack of regard for the impact of their emotional reaction or behavior on others. In some, there is no recognition of the need to control feelings to avoid negative consequences.

A case that I saw many years ago, with a five-year-old little boy, Eddie, illustrates this point. Eddie was understandably upset over his parents' divorce and the contentious relationship between the parents. His emotional dysregulation was seen in argumentative behavior with his kindergarten classmates and in general disobedience at school and home. He was a very bright and precocious little boy with an unusually large vocabulary for his age. When he began therapy with me, he referred to me as "Doctor Yuck." In every session, he would use this name, and, in every session, I would let the label stand. However, I would gradually over time address his feelings and note how he behaved when he was upset. I would comment on his use of words and actions as tools to hurt others and keep them away.

Over the course of our work together, he ceased calling me "Doctor Yuck" and referred to me as "Doctor Little." He explained that I was "a doctor for little bitty people, not real ones." By the time he left my practice, he no longer referred to me as "Doctor Little," but rather referenced me rather affectionately as "Doc." By that point in treatment, he had begun to allow himself to get close to his classmates and teacher and was no longer prone to anger and meanness. Eddie is a reminder that emotional dysregulation interferes with closeness and the establishment of emotional ties. Parents, teachers, and other important figures in a child's life can help build regulation through patience, appropriate modeling, and careful encouragement.

PARENT CONTRIBUTIONS TO THE DEVELOPMENT OF THE HEALTHY OR NOT-SO-HEALTHY EMOTIONAL REGULATION

Parents have a key role in the child's progressive mastery of emotional regulation. It will be years before infantile and childlike behavior transforms into adult-like control. Parents will not only help in soothing their child and educate about strategies to manage feelings but also model emotional regulation themselves.

Temperament is an important factor to consider in terms of understanding emotional regulation. Defined as relatively stable individual differences in emotional reactivity and regulation, temperament has long been recognized as a core component of a child's psychological make up. Research has determined that both genetics and the environment play a role in its development.[16]

Chess and Thomaes, two theorists who conducted longitudinal studies, researched child temperament over decades beginning in 1956.[17] They identified three general types of temperaments in children: "easy," "slow to warm," and "difficult." They found several dimensions or qualities that reflect temperament, including intensity of reaction, adaptability, threshold of responsiveness, activity level, rhythmicity, distractibility, approach or withdrawal, attention span and persistence, and quality of mood. These biologically based differences in emotional reactivity and regulation, attention, and motor contribute to the child's ability to emotionally regulate. Just as children have specific behavioral styles or temperaments, parents have the same. Chess and Thomaes created the term "goodness-of-fit" to refer to how well the child's temperament matches the parents' temperament, with some matches being easier than others.

Identifying the child's temperament can help parents foster a nurturing environment and encourage the child's development of self-control and self-discipline. Understanding a child's temperament can help parents develop appropriate expectations for their child's behavior in various situations.

The research on temperament is a reminder that individual children present unique challenges, and that all children cannot be managed in precisely the same manner. Regardless of the temperament of the child, parents have the same task: to help their child learn how to self-regulate. In order to learn how to self-soothe, babies and children must first experience being soothed by others. Gradually, parental support can decrease as the child develops more independent means to self-regulate. Learning to calm and control one's emotions is an essential social emotional tool.

Parents Comments That Either Help or Hurt the Child's Emotional Regulation: An Example

Parents' words and actions have an impact on the development of the child's ability to learn to self-regulate. Below are examples of *healthy* parental comments around the topic.

Positive Exchanges
- That's right. Lacey hit you. Maybe you could tell her how you feel about that. Put your feelings into words.
- It's hard to not get another cookie. I know that oatmeal raisin is your favorite.
- Look, she's crying. She must be sad about something.
- I know that you are mad that Kevin took your shovel. What kinds of things can you do now? You could take back the shovel, but what else might you do? Could you ask the teacher for help? Could you get another shovel?
- I understand you don't want to go to bed. It's upsetting to have to go to bed on time when you want to play with your dragons.
- You can be mad, but you can't be mean to your sister.

- We agreed that I would read three books to you. Tomorrow there will be more books to read.
- I understand you're mad. Explain to me what happened, and we can talk about what to do.
- What do you do when you're sad? What can you do to feel better?
- I mean, how mad are you? Are you just unhappy, a little upset, or furious?
- I know you want to have friends over after school, but I have to clean the house for an event. Maybe we can do it another day.
- Now that you've told Margaret how you feel, what can you do to solve the problem? Can you talk to her? Can you work out a plan using words? Can you undo what went wrong between you?
- I know how much you wanted to go to the football game, but it's not possible. Maybe we can do some things at home.
- I know you're upset. You forgot your lunch money, but that is your responsibility. I can help remind you if you want. Let me know what you decide.
- I will help you with your math, but I cannot do it until I finish washing the dishes.
- I know you don't like your curfew, but your dad and I have decided that it's set for this year. We would consider a special exception for a special event, but the plan is set.
- I know you don't know if Elizabeth will say "yes" if you ask her to the prom, but there is no way to know except to ask. Either way, we're here.
- I understand how mad you are, but when you call me names, it hurts my feelings.
- I know you're upset, but when you tell me what time to expect you, I expect you to follow through on what you said. If you cannot for whatever reason, you need to call me so we can discuss what's best

Key Concepts in Positive Exchanges
- Parents understand that self-control is a complex process involving a considerable amount of self-knowledge, insight, awareness, and self-control.
- Parents accept feelings but encourage more mature containment and expression.

- Parents label feelings whenever they can.
- Parents work to expand the feeling vocabulary.
- Parents inquire about feelings.
- Parents encourage the child to use words instead of actions to express feelings.
- Parents encourage problem solving.
- Parents recognize that there are no right or wrong feelings.
- Parents remain calm in the face of raw emotion.
- Parents show empathy regardless of the circumstances.
- Parents set age-appropriate limits.

Parental *errors* that interfere with the development of self-regulation come in many forms. Below is a list of comments that I have heard parents, both in and out of my practice, make to their children that should be avoided. They range from criticizing children for their lack of control to being too quick to limit the child's frustrations, from inappropriate expectations to lack of appreciation for feelings.

Negative Exchanges

- Bobby hit you, but it wasn't that hard.
- There is no need to tantrum just because you can't get a cold drink. Quit acting like a baby.
- You're fine. Just go on and play with your toys. Forget about your brother calling you a name.
- Eleanor is just being a brat. Don't act like her.
- You're sad but it wasn't that big a deal. Quit crying. You can get another bucket. There's a whole batch of buckets over there.
- What they did to you was really, really bad. You should be upset—I mean really upset.
- You don't need to do that. It will just upset you.
- You're being mean to your sister, and she doesn't deserve it. Stop it. You're behaving like a baby. You're bigger than that.
- Your language is unacceptable. Wait till your father gets home from work.
- You need to act like a grown-up boy.
- Kids don't like other kids who cry.
- You can't say things like that to your father or me. You're disrespectful and don't appreciate what we've done for you.

- Stop calling me those names. Stop it now. There is no excuse for behaving that way.
- You're not a credit to our family. You should act right.
- Being mean is simply bad.
- You call me that again and you won't see the light of day for days.
- You can say whatever you want, but it won't change anything. You're disgusting.
- Act right and act right now if you expect to ever get to do anything you want.
- Do that again and you're grounded forever. If you do that again, you won't be going to camp this summer or ever. Get yourself under control. Get hold of yourself. How old do you think people think you are when you act like that?
- Be the kind of child your mother and I can be proud of.
- You need to do your homework. You need to do it right. You need to do it on your own. You need to be a better student.
- You need to quit making excuses for acting younger than your age. Grow up and accept responsibility.
- Kids who act like that can't live here. Think about how you'd like living on your own.
- Stop it. Stop it now. Stop it before you do something else that will get you in even more trouble.
- Get over it. Life is hard. People have to learn to accept difficult things.
- Being mad isn't an excuse for behaving like a brat.
- Get it together.
- If you can't manage your weight, how do you ever expect to manage your life?

Key Concepts in Negative Exchanges
- Parents are intolerant of the child's lack of self-control.
- Parents shame the child.
- Parents withhold acceptance and love when they disapprove of their child's behavior.
- Parents threaten the children with extreme consequences.
- Parents fail to appreciate the child's feelings.

- Parents use hurtful words as they attempt to get their child under control.
- Parents try to get their child under control by using force.
- Parents fail to understand the complex process of self-regulation.
- Parents do not empathize with the child.
- Parents expect children to behave as if they are more mature or capable than they actually are.
- Parents personalize their child's misbehavior and overreact.
- Parents are embarrassed by their child's misbehavior and respond harshly due to their own discomfort.

Over the course of healthy development, the child's ability for self-control and self-discipline is being stabilized and secured such that when the child's needs are not always met, frustration can be tolerated. As children grow and mature, their capacity for regulation improves, while their sensitivity and vulnerability to injury and upset toughens. The developmental outcome of a mature self-regulation is seen in their confidence in being able to handle frustration, failure, disappointment, and hurt without dysregulating.

Emotional regulation is an important developmental acquisition. The diagnosis of an emerging N2B child is not generally made on the child's deficits in self-control standing alone. However, reactions to specific areas of distress are likely reflective of narcissistic tendencies, traits, and dysfunction. Children who display narcissistic tendencies and traits typically show immaturity in emotional regulation in response to several specific areas of upset: blows to the self-concept, a frustrated ability to get what they want, and less-than-ideal treatment from others.

- Emotional dysregulation in those with budding narcissism of varying degrees most typically responds to blows to the self-concept. The relative fragility of a narcissistic sense of self is vulnerable to threat through criticism, failure, and rejection, and it is in those situations that emotional dysregulation is seen. A child who performs poorly on a test or is criticized by a parent, teacher, or friend may lose emotional control, whether in frustration, anger, or sadness. Often, their response to that insult does not diminish as rapidly as that seen in better-adjusted children. They may carry a grudge and not get over whatever offended them for what seems to be an inappropriately long time.

- Lack of self-control for those with budding narcissism is often seen in an exaggerated response to not getting what they want. While no child reacts with equanimity to frustration of specific wants and needs, the budding narcissist can show extreme and prolonged reactions in such situations. More importantly, the better adjusted child's reactions will improve with maturity, while the narcissistic adjusted child most typically will not. Such children can tantrum or complain excessively when the dinner is not to their liking, the experience involves lengthy waiting, or the quality of a product is not what they had in mind. Parents are often frustrated with this kind of behavior because it undermines many successful family events or holidays.

- Extreme reactions to less than ideal treatment from others that do not diminish with age are also evidence of narcissistic-like adjustment. N2Bs expect special treatment and are aggravated when they feel they are not provided with what they deserve. Such children make excessive demands on their friends and their parents and feel entitled. Interestingly when their desires are accommodated, they can be charming and delightful. However, the same child, when frustrated, can be difficult and prone to disrupt interactions and social engagements.

A story shared by a middle-school-aged boy named Hakeem shows how quickly that charm can change into hurtful behavior. Hakeem had transferred to a competitive preparatory school and was slow in adjusting to the more demanding and complicated social and academic environment there. After several weeks, he had befriended a boy named Edward who sat next to him in math class. Edward asked him to go to a movie over the weekend. Hakeem was delighted at the prospect. He waited all weekend to hear from Edward, but the phone never rang. On Monday, he spoke to Edward at school, "I thought we were going to go to a movie over the weekend?" Edward responded with some frustration, "Let's get one thing straight. I don't call you. You call me." Children with narcissistic tendencies and traits expect to be treated a certain way and are aggravated when they are not. Dysregulation, whether in the form of irritation, angry words, or acting out, is common in situations where the expected treatment is not forthcoming.

It is important to emphasize that difficulties in emotional dysregulation can be hard to spot in N2B children. Such children can evidence solid self-control in any number of situations, specifically in areas in which they are not sensitive or that do not challenge their deficits. For example, the high-achieving N2B child may be able to study for hours, stay on a healthy diet, and engage in extracurricular passions—all indications of excellent self-control and self-discipline. However, N2B children who evidence excellent regulation in some areas often display significant dysregulation in others. That same child may become inconsolably distraught over their not being admitted to the Honor Society in the first round or over a single poor grade on a paper. The underlying impairment may only be evident in a small slice of their life. Often it is the types of stimulation that trigger dysregulation that identify the child with narcissistic tendencies and traits. Blows to self-esteem are the most common trigger, and their outsized response to the threat is diagnostic.

A SPECIAL KIND OF PROTECTION AGAINST EMOTIONAL DYSREGULATION IN N2B CHILDREN: IMMATURE COPING STRATEGIES

Children are required to make great strides in mastering emotional control over the developmental period. This chapter has focused primarily on the complexity of that process. At the same time, the nature of that control becomes increasingly differentiated over time and takes a variety of forms in terms of coping strategies and defensive structures. Children, as well as adults, develop habitual or characteristic coping patterns that protect the self from injury, pain, and emotional disruption.

Every child must develop more mature coping strategies as they grow. All children begin life with almost automatic reliance on a set of primitive defenses that help the child deal with overwhelming emotion. These early strategies—including crying, tantrumming, withdrawal, and avoidance—are global, undifferentiated responses. Over time, the child will develop more mature and particularized ways of coping, including distraction, verbalizing feelings, intellectualization, and even humor; all these methods of coping require more sophisticated verbal and thinking skills, higher-level organization, and greater emotional control. Importantly, it is the absence of mature defenses, not the presence of immature or primitive ones, that characterizes unhealthy development.

The subset of emotional management involving the coping strategies that develop as the child matures is noteworthy. Coping strategies, considered as a more consistent way of managing feelings and emotional upset, develop progressively throughout childhood. Lower-level strategies predominate in infancy and early childhood, being supplanted by more sophisticated, higher-level ones during the school aged years, adolescence, and young adulthood. As noted, primitive defenses operate in an undifferentiated way with the fusing of emotions, thoughts, and behavioral dimensions in a kind of global response, whereas more advanced strategies make transformations of those thoughts, feelings, and behaviors into a background of emotional steadiness or find expression in more nuanced and productive behaviors. For example, an upset adolescent may inhibit yelling at a peer or parent, and instead, decide to take a run around the block.

All children begin with lower-level coping strategies, but over the course of normal development, acquire higher level ones. Importantly, it is the absence of higher-level strategies that distinguishes narcissistic development as well as other personality disorders. Children tending toward narcissism typically rely on more immature ways of handling stress. Typical narcissistic defenses include:

- grandiosity (a need to be the best, extreme competitiveness, and inflated self-esteem),
- entitlement (the need to be treated special and indulged, a demand to have things their way),
- idealization and devaluation (criticism and devaluation of others, idealization of people perceived as being above them),
- perfectionism (unrealistically high expectations for performance in all things),
- externalizing blame (holding others, not themselves, responsible for failures or poor outcomes),
- demands on others to maintain their self-esteem (excessive need for admiration and approval, insensitivity to the needs of others),

- all-or-none thinking (experiences are segregated into all-good and all-bad categories), and
- excessive control (all sources of stress are removed through extreme management).

Defenses serve an important function, existing to protect the self from emotional injury and disruption. However, healthier structures provide greater emotional flexibility and better real-world adaptation, whereas not-so-healthy structures compromise adjustment and interpersonal connection. Narcissistic development is distinguished by both reliance on these types of lower-level coping strategies, and, more importantly, the absence of more mature ones involving sophisticated problem solving, organization, and integration of thoughts, feelings, and behavior, which result in greater emotional stability.

Lower-level emotional coping strategies are not always obvious. I treated a narcissistic man who managed his propensity for emotional dysregulation through a combination of excessive control and grandiosity. Kip revealed essential elements of narcissism in terms of his perceived superiority and use of power. He laughed one day, and told me, "You know how it works, Dr. Little: he who has the gold rules." He claimed to be teasing, but there was a kernel of truth in his quip. I would come to learn that he regarded his wealth as proof of his superiority and its influence an appropriate use of well-deserved control. Kip was indeed worth hundreds of millions of dollars and possessed the accouterments that accompany such excess—from second homes to plush furnishings and trappings—a lifestyle befitting the "rich and famous." However, the power of his wealth and his surroundings produced a detached and superior attitude that proved to be costly in his interpersonal relationships. Money insulated him from intimacy and the demands of interpersonal connection, as well as the opportunity for growth through personal change that stems from being in a close relationship. He explained that if he had a conflict with his wife about the use of space in the bathroom, he would simply build a bigger bathroom. He made it clear that he would eliminate the conflict, *not* change his attitude or behavior. Exercising this kind of control prevented him from being exposed to emotional threats and allowed him to remain emotionally regulated, while his capacity for self-control remained immature. Wealth can limit both practical and interpersonal frustrations, which inhibits the development of emotional steadiness in the face of conflict. Grandiosity and insufficient frustration maintained through excessive control buy temporary satisfaction or relief but do not encourage valuable emotional growth.

STRATEGIES FOR PARENTS: BUILDING NON-NARCISSISTIC EMOTIONAL REGULATION IN THE CHILD

In order to avoid the further development of narcissistic tendencies and traits, parents should invest in strategies that build emotional regulation in terms of both self-control and self-discipline. The following understandings have been derived from my clinical practice and the implications of both theory and research.

Negative Impacts

The Negative Impact of Being Intolerant of the Child's Dysregulation. Parents who are intolerant of raw displays of emotion undermine their child's developing emotional regulation skills. In order for children to come to understand and ultimately accept their own feelings, both positive and negative, they must see and experience that same acceptance from their parents. Parents who are uncomfortable with feelings complicate the process.

The Negative Impact of Treating the Child's Loss of Control Harshly. Parents who are impatient with their child's loss of control and intervene harshly undermine the development of self-regulation skills. Strong negative parental reactions can contribute to anxiety and upset. In infancy and early childhood, children must experience soothing by others before they can actually learn to soothe themselves. As they grow and mature, understanding, patience, and support around loss of control is indicated. Importantly, children come biologically armed with greater or lesser abilities to self-regulate beginning at birth. Understanding the complexity of the developmental progression and the contribution of temperament requires calm and thoughtful intervention. Patience and understanding do not involve a lack of appropriate limit setting based on the age and stage of the child, but rather constitute a style of interaction that supports and does not shame.

Physical discipline is one form of harsh treatment that parents exercise around behavioral loss of control. Importantly, the research shows that physical discipline does not reduce the occurrence of the child's undesirable behaviors, nor does it increase the frequency of desirable behaviors.[18] Rather, use of physical discipline has been shown to increase—not decrease—the child's behavioral problems over time.[19]

I am reminded of an interaction I observed in a toddler-focused amusement park. Three fathers were there with their kindergarten-aged sons. Each was trying to put their child on a pony that would then walk around a small track, designed such that the parent would walk alongside. One child made the transition easily with big smiles and delight. The second child was hesitant but eventually agreed to get on the "big horse." The last child began to cry. The father became enraged. "This is just a pony. It can't hurt you. It's fun. Quit crying." The child began to cry even more strongly. The father repeated: "Quit crying." Then the father pulled the boy off the horse, spanked him, and then forced him onto the horse. The child was now sobbing inconsolably. The child cried all the way around the track, at which point the father pulled the wailing child off the pony and handed him off to the mother. Different children have different appetites for novel stimulation and different capabilities for adaptation, which calls for sympathetic treatment. Harsh words and harsh interventions will not overcome childhood distress, and will only, in fact, increase the upset.

The Negative Impact of Inappropriately High Expectations for Self-Control.   Parents who set inappropriately high expectations in terms of their child's ability to self-regulate run the risk of undermining their child's progressive mastery of self-control and self-discipline. Children learn self-control incrementally and over long periods of time. Temperamental factors must be taken into consideration as appropriate age and stage expectations are set.

The Negative Impact of Too Many Limits.   Parents who set too many limits run the risk of providing too much potential for frustration and setting the child up for failure. In order to develop mastery, children are best served by being challenged slightly above their current level of skill. Too little frustration does not challenge. Too much frustration undermines success. In order for children to progress, they must regularly be provided with opportunities to succeed.

The Negative Impact of Being Overly Accommodated and Indulged. Parents who overaccommodate and indulge their children interfere with the child's ability to learn to self-regulate. Children must experience a certain amount of frustration and disappointment in order to challenge growth and require the development of more mature coping strategies.

The Negative Impact of a Lack of Limit Setting. Parents who do not set limits undermine the development of emotional regulation. Limits, by definition, introduce frustration and require the child to both regulate and control emotions as well as solve problems. The amount and degree of frustration must be age appropriate and should take into consideration the temperamental characteristics of the child.

The Negative Impact of Overcontrol and Hovering. Parents who overprotect and hover interfere with the development of self-control. Some parents constantly guide the child by telling them what to do and how to do it. Children react variously through defiance, apathy, or frustration. Other parents too quickly limit their child's frustrations and disappointments and prevent the child from becoming emotionally upset. Still other parents are ever-present and assume tasks for the child. Both postures limit the child's ability to learn on their own.

I am reminded of parents who check their children's homework religiously or, in more extreme cases, actually do the science project. On the one hand, parental involvement is positive and can ensure mastery of the material. On the other hand, the parents' hovering can undermine the child's growing self-confidence and independence. They will miss experiencing the positive feelings associated with mastery and will not know the associated negative feelings when the outcome is lacking, a necessary experience that would have contributed to future learning. Either way, the child's growth is at risk. Overinvolved parents typically raise underdeveloped children.

The research supports the notion that overcontrolling parents can interfere with a child's ability to manage her emotions and behavior.[20] An eight-year longitudinal study showed that so-called helicopter parents tend to rear children with difficulties in self-regulation and self-control, which makes them less able to deal with the challenges of growing up. Poor impulse control often translates into poor behavior in the classroom or friendship drama. Conversely, children with better impulse control are less likely to experience social and emotional problems and more likely to do well in school.

Positive Impacts

The Positive Impact of Talking about Feelings.   Parents who are comfortable with feelings set the stage for development in emotional regulation. Such parents more typically label feelings, inquire about feelings, use words that express gradations of feelings, take opportunities to talk to children about feelings, and discuss appropriate and inappropriate ways to deal with feelings. Such parenting explains what behaviors result from certain emotions, as well as the consequences of different responses.

The Positive Impact of Modeling Appropriate Management of Feelings. Parents who model management of feelings in productive and matter-of-fact ways are teaching. Such parents exhibit behavior that, at some point in the future, can be imitated by the child. Learning through observation is a valuable form of nonverbal instruction. Parents can set good examples of using positive coping strategies to manage emotions and behaviors when upset.

The Positive Impact of the Understanding That There Are No Right or Wrong Feelings.   Parents who understand that there are no right or wrong feelings can more easily encourage the child's mastery of emotional self-regulation skills and promote self-acceptance. If children are to develop a positive self-concept, they must come to terms with both liked and disliked feelings and the expression of those feelings. Over time, emotional reactions will mature, but along the way, acceptance is key to developing appropriate affect.

The Positive Impact of Encouraging Mature Coping Strategies.   Parents can encourage higher-level forms of coping as the child matures. These include encouraging distraction ("Maybe you can take a break from worrying about that test and go visit Suzy next door for a while."), intellectualization ("Maybe you can make a list of the pros and cons of taking that high school course."), alternate form of expression, ("You might want to paint a picture of the way you feel."), and humor ("There may be some funny aspects in that ridiculous situation that you might want to consider."). Specific strategies to deal with acute episodes of dysregulation include deep breathing, meditation, and guided visual imagery.

EIGHT TAKEAWAYS FOR PARENTS TO BUILD EMOTIONAL REGULATION IN THE CHILD

Lessons from clinical experience, theory, and research lend support for recommending the following parenting behaviors:

- Understand that dysregulation is a normal part of growing up.
- Love the child whether in, or out, of control.
- Help the child learn to self-regulate over time through patience and understanding and age-appropriate limit setting.
- Teach strategies for self-calming and self-control including mindfulness, distraction, exercise, and reduced stimulation.
- Help the child learn to self-regulate by modeling self-control and self-discipline.
- Teach self-discipline through encouraging mastery of progressively more complex goals.
- Realize self-control is subject to backsliding under stress.
- Do not punish the child for dysregulation or react to the child's immature responses but rather, provide support.

THE OUTCOME: "FUNCTION WITH A FULLY DEVELOPED FEELING MACHINE" AS A METAPHOR

Parents who are aware of the complex process of maturation in emotional regulation can more fully appreciate the strides their child has made over time and their own efforts to encourage that development. The child has made monumental progress in taking a tiny, brittle "Feelings Machine" and transforming it into a large, complex, flexible one that can neutralize all manner of intense emotions. This skill renders the child less vulnerable to frustration and disappointment. It provides the child with confidence in his ability to deal with complicated situations filled with strong emotion. Solid self-control and self-discipline make the child more likely to be able to set goals, make progress toward them, persist when difficulties present along the way, and, ultimately, achieve the set objectives. Finally, mature self-regulation is an essential skill in interpersonal relationships. Being able to remain steady in the face of conflict and to harness solid problem-solving skills around interpersonal difficulties are signs of emotional maturity and essential capabilities for all kinds of close and loving relationships from friendship to marriage. The "Feelings Machine" has been transformed in the same way that the child's behavior has been changed over the course of development.

Building a Non-narcissistic Ability to Take In and Process Information

(Gathering Information about the World = Perceptual Accuracy, Non-distortion, and Non-extreme Thinking)

The Development of Information Gathering over Time

*E*very child must develop the ability to gather information about the world. This involves the capacity to perceive events, actions, statements, feelings, and people such as to form an accurate understanding of them. This is no small accomplishment. The ability to correctly perceive and interpret information is a necessary step that promotes both intellectual and emotional growth. Perceptual skills impact daily functioning and interactions with others and are necessary to become a competently functional individual and a capable partner in all types of relationships.

Throughout history, theoretical conceptions of cognition in childhood have undergone continuous evolution. At one point in time, children were perceived simply as "small" adults, little people with the same abilities as adults but only in more immature form. This early notion has been disproven empirically and discarded. An entire scientific field has emerged over decades that identifies and explains the developmental acquisition of knowledge.

Jean Piaget (1896–1980) was one of the most influential figures in developmental psychology. He generated both theory and research focused on understanding how children acquire knowledge and gradually come to be able to think logically. Piaget described how a child adapts to his environment. He conceptualized mental organizers within the child that he labeled as "schemas," essentially cognitive structures that are modified over time. As children interact with the world, they continually add new knowledge into the existing organizing schemas and also construct new schemas to accommodate ever more complex information. These processes allow cognitive development to proceed and mature over the developmental period. Piaget developed four stages of cognitive development.

- Sensorimotor Stage (zero to two years): The infant learns about the world through information drawn from their senses and actions. They move about and explore the environment, and continually touch, manipulate, look, and listen. In early infancy, any object that is out of sight remains out of mind. At about eight months, the infant will search for an object when it disappears. This newfound skill requires the ability to form a mental representation, or schema, of the object and is a major achievement of this period. Children will also come to realize that they are beings separate from other people and things and that their actions can cause things to happen.

- Preoperational Stage (two to seven years): Toddlers and children acquire the ability to internally represent the world through language and mental imagery. Children learn to think with symbols, of which language is one. A name can stand for a thing. "Dada" is that tall person with a beard. Gran is the old lady with white hair who brings cookies. The capacity for logical problem solving is not yet developed. It is for this reason that children believe that nonliving objects such as toys have feelings, or why children believe that something seen on TV actually happened. Logical explanations will not persuade or affect their thinking since the ability for rational thought is lacking. Children process information primarily by the way the world *looks*, not how the world actually *is*, which is an indication of concrete thinking. For example, a researcher may take a lump of clay and divide it into two equal pieces, then roll one into a compact ball and the other into a flat pancake. The preoperational child believes the flat shape is *larger* because it looks larger, even though both shapes are exactly the same quantity. Similarly, ten pennies spaced out in a long row are thought to be *more pennies* than the same number placed tightly together in a row. The effect of perceptual persuasion (i.e., the pull of how things appear) does not allow logical thought and accounts for the inaccuracies seen in preoperational thought. Thinking is nonreversible, and the child remains egocentric, with their perspective being the *only* perspective.

- Concrete Operational Stage (seven to eleven years): Early school-aged children begin to think logically about concrete events. Piaget considered this stage a major turning point in cognitive development, as it marks the beginning of preoperational, or logical, thought. The child can now work things out internally in their head rather than having to try them out physically in the real world. The child can mentally reverse events in their mind: a melted cube of ice can be reimagined as a piece of ice and the same amount of a liquid poured into a short wide cup is now seen as equal to the *same* amount poured into a tall skinny glass. The cognitive understanding that something can stay the same in quantity even though its appearance changes, was referred to as "conservation" by Piaget and his researchers. The ability for "conservation" develops over time, with children conserving "number" at age six, "mass" at age seven, "weight" at age nine, and "volume" at age eleven. Children in this stage become less egocentric, as they are beginning to be able to appreciate a different perspective and think about how other people think and feel. Similarly, they come to appreciate that not everyone necessarily shares the same thoughts, feelings, and opinions.
- Formal Operational Stage (eleven years and above): This stage is characterized by the emergence of logical thinking and reasoning as dominant. Children in this stage can think abstractly, use deductive logic, and reason from a general principle to specifics. They can address problems hypothetically, follow the form of an argument without having to be tied to specifics, and can logically test hypotheses. This is systematic problem solving based on the rules of logic.

Piaget's formulation of cognitive developmental stages (and the steps within each) have been subjected to research over many years and validated by empirical findings. Children are not born with the ability to think logically, and thereby accurately; those skills develop in a systematic and predictable manner over the course of childhood. There is no evidence that the developmental progression can be accelerated, but it can be encouraged by providing stimulation at—or slightly above—the child's current level of function. I am reminded of a story about Piaget. He asked a preoperational child how Lake Geneva was formed, and the child explained that a big giant threw a rock and made a hole. Piaget corrected him and explained that a glacier had slid down the mountain and carved out the lake. The next day, he again asked the child how the lake was formed, and the child explained that a big giant threw a rock and made a hole. This story is a reminder that children cannot be talked out of how they understand the world when their thinking is set while in a specific stage.

Studies have shown that brain development parallels the stages of development identified by Piaget.[1] Numerous researchers have tracked key changes in the brain including the length of dendritic connections and the specific volumes of gray and white matter that parallel Piagetian stages.[2] Children cannot be taught to conserve number, mass, or volume until their ability to process information has matured sufficiently such that the next step in learning can occur. Similarly, a child cannot be convinced that a monster does not live in their closet or that a bad man will not steal their adored "Lovie." Children can be reassured through interventions that take into account their developmental level. This is why children can, at best, be calmed in the preoperational stage, not completely reassured, when you show them that there is no monster in the closet or that their adored stuffed animal is living inside a house with a locked door and offer an embrace. I have lectured for many years to help parents understand those cognitive limitations, intervene in ways that match the age and stage of the child, and learn strategies that avoid making logical arguments when children are still thinking prelogically.

Cognitive development is organized structurally and follows an established pattern over the course of maturation. Piaget's groundbreaking work demonstrated that children think and reason differently at distinct periods in their development. Since his early work, research concerning anatomical and physiological development of the brain has proliferated over the years. Various studies indicate that Piaget's stages and developmental theory are closely aligned with changes in physical development of the brain, specifically in the prefrontal cortex and also in associated brain connections.[3] The maturation of each child's brain increases in complexity during childhood and adolescence and aligns with the stages of cognitive development identified by Piaget. Children do not think like an adult until the child's brain has matured to the extent that it functions like the brain of an adult.

Children will misperceive and misinterpret "real" information based on their age and stage of development. The Piagetian-based limitations in cognition, most dramatically prior to the age of seven or eight and then prior to eleven, are set until physiological maturation allows the next step to advance.

Limitations in thinking are not only the result of cognitive factors. Emotional development also has an impact on reasoning. In other words, once a child has sufficient cognitive capacity to process information at a more logical stage of development, the child can still make errors based on immature emotional functioning. The ability to regulate emotions and to manage emotional needs becomes formative of perception and contributes to misperception and misinterpretation above and beyond whatever limitation is set by the developmental stage.

Children, and adults, can misperceive and misinterpret various events or exchanges, leading to a variety of cognitive distortions based on emotional factors. They may personalize the words and behaviors of others, often coming to conclusions about intention or motivation that are not accurate. Their ability to read the realities of social interaction may be influenced by their own perspective without regard for the perspective of others or the accuracy of their interpretations. They may be so sensitive to the reactions of others that they misread the specifics of an exchange. As is apparent, emotional distortions can be the result of a number of different types of perceptual errors.

General flaws in thinking can take different forms. Children, as well as adults, may reason in extremes, evidencing a kind of black-and-white thinking. They may jump to conclusions, overgeneralize, attend to certain types of evidence while failing to attend to others, or discount various aspects of an exchange. They may fail to develop a nuanced view of people and events. Whatever the mechanism, the net result is perceptual distortion; their view of a situation, exchange, behavior, or interaction is inaccurate. Faulty perceptions and interpretations result in impaired judgment and interfere with emotional regulation and resolving disputes with others.

Accuracy of perception and interpretation is an essential developing skill in children, but it is also vital for healthy adult function. Adults who misperceive and misinterpret information experience difficulties in interpersonal relationships. I am reminded of Marguerite who misinterpreted many of her husband's comments. He asks: "You've got a new dress?"

She *heard* his words as implying that he didn't think she should have gotten a new dress. He inquires: "Have you seen my phone?" She responded with "I didn't take it." When he asked her to turn off the light, she responded with "I didn't leave it on." Marguerite is similar to many like her who were raised in families in which they were overly criticized as a child. If you spilled your milk, it meant you were a bad person. If you made a poor grade, you were treated harshly for not meeting the family standard. If you were mean to your brother, it meant you were lacking in moral integrity. The problem with misperception is that people like Marguerite actually *believe* that what they *hear* is the truth.

Marital therapists typically encourage partners to check out their perception. I urge my patients to clarify: "I told myself that you were saying I shouldn't have gotten a new dress. Is that what you meant?" In its extreme form, misperceiving can take the form of gaslighting. At that point, misperception and misinterpretation have become the steady operational state, and interpersonal interaction becomes all the more problematic for relationships—even malignant. The person's perceptions are considered to be reality, and all other perceptions are seen as lies. Emotional reactions to differences in what is perceived to be "reality" between partners are intense, and the ensuing conflict risks destroying relationships of all sorts.

INFORMATION GATHERING: THE "LENS AND CAMERA" AS A METAPHOR

As mentioned before, when I work with parents, I try to identify metaphors that will allow parents to visualize what is going on inside the child—a way to "see" the developing mental apparatus. I conceptualize the child's emerging and evolving cognitive skills as a "Lens and Camera." The "lens" is taking in all the information that the child sees, touches, manipulates, and hears. All the senses are at work, gathering and processing information. Metaphorically, I understand the "camera" as the machine that takes the input from the lens and makes a "picture" out of it. This picture is an understanding of the information as seen through the lens. To my mind's eye, the infant and young child's lens is poorly developed. It does not provide well-defined, clear, or fully formed images. As the child matures, the lens becomes more refined and capable of discerning more detail and more complex and complete information. The camera must make what it can of the information provided from stage to stage as it evolves.

These metaphorical images reveal the limitations of each stage. The infant's and toddler's tiny camera has a rather misshapen lens. A school-aged child's camera is larger and a lens more appropriately shaped but cloudy. The adolescent's camera is larger still, with a more refined and complex lens. Over time, the lens power grows clearer and the camera handles information with greater accuracy. Importantly, all these forms of "camera and lens" are not like the "camera and lens" of an adult. Until young adulthood, children do not think as adults think or with the same level of cognitive complexity and accuracy.

There is a further complication in childhood, with emotional factors overlaying cognitive development. Beyond the limiting immaturities common to each stage of cognition, the working of all lenses and cameras are subject to distortion based on emotion. States of dysregulation, bias, and emotional need can interfere with accurate perception and interpretation. Generally, the propensity to emotional dysregulation and the intensity of emotional need can interfere with accurate perception.

THE DEVELOPMENT OF INFORMATION GATHERING: PERCEPTION AND INTERPRETATION

Step 1: Perception

Perception refers to the way sensory information is organized and experienced. Our senses are constantly collecting information from the environment, and our perceptions are built from that sensory input. Perception can be accurate or inaccurate. A child can hear a loud noise and believe that a book fell off the bookshelf. That might be true, or the same noise could have been the result of his mother dropping groceries in the kitchen. A child can see a blue hat hanging on a hook and believe it is his because it looks similar to his own when actually it belongs to someone else. A child can see an uncooked chicken on the kitchen counter and believe it will be his dinner, when actually his mother placed it in the freezer and has it on the menu for later in the week. A child can approach a stray dog that looks like his puppy at home believing it is friendly, then be surprised when it growls and bares its teeth.

Step 2: Interpretation

Interpretation is the way sensory information is understood cognitively. Interpretation, then, is the act of forming an understanding of something that is seen, said, or done. Similarly, a misinterpretation is the act of forming an erroneous understanding of what was seen, said, or done. Interpretation is typically influenced by a number of factors, including our available knowledge, our history of experiences, our thoughts, and a variety of unique psychological processes. For example, a child can hear a dog bark and believe that it means someone is at the front door. In this case, the child's perception is accurate: the dog did bark. However, the interpretation could be inaccurate if the dog barked because it saw a squirrel racing across the front lawn. Similarly, a teacher can send a child to "time out" for losing his temper when, in fact, the child did yell at a classmate. However, the child believes that the teacher gave him the consequence because she did not like him. This child's inaccurate interpretation and conclusion will make the child less inclined to work on improving his behavior, and likely harden his negative feelings about his teacher and school.

The integration of sensation, perception, and interpretation is a deeply psychological process. There is an entire field within psychology, beyond the Piagetian perspective, which involves both theory and research focusing on the workings of sensation and perception. Numerous empirical studies have proven that people perceive and interpret information in terms of context. For example, a boxy shape (i.e., two not firmly drawn, rather sketchy boxes on top of each other), when placed between the letters A and C is read as a B. The same boxy shape, when placed between the numbers 12 and 14 is perceived as 13. Clearly, context can influence perception to greater and lesser degrees in terms of emotional, social, and physical aspects.

A SPECIAL CASE OF INFORMATION GATHERING: PERSPECTIVE-TAKING

A cornerstone of Jean Piaget's theory of cognitive development was that human infants and very young children have just one perspective—their own. They are fundamentally egocentric, actually being unable to comprehend that someone else has a different perspective. They assume incorrectly that everyone sees the world as they do. As young children develop, they not only learn that another perspective exists, but also how to take that perspective and use it to understand the world and others. Once children recognize that other people have their own minds and thus, their own perspective, they are said to have developed a "theory of the mind."

Piaget, and his collaborator Barbel Inhelder (1956),[4] devised an experiment, labeled the Three Mountains Task, which attempted to determine whether (a) young children were egocentric (i.e., unable to see any point of view other than their own), and (b) at what age they were able see another perspective. In it, the child was seated at a table and presented with a model of three mountains. The mountains were different, with snow on top of one, a hut on another, and a Red Cross on top of the third. The child was instructed to walk around the model and then to sit down on one side of the table. A doll was placed at various positions around the table, and the child was shown a group of ten photographs of the model, each taken from a different position. The researcher then asked the child which photo showed the doll's point of view.

Piaget reasoned that if the child correctly picked out the card showing the doll's viewpoint, she was not egocentric. While Piaget's experiments have been replicated numerous times and outcomes have varied slightly based on changed paradigms and shifts in task complexity, the general outcomes are the same.[5] Four-year-olds do not show an awareness that the doll's view is different from their own. Six-year-olds typically select a picture different from their own but rarely the correct picture from the doll's vantage point. Seven- and eight-year-olds consistently identify the doll's perspective. Piaget concluded that thinking is no longer egocentric around the age of seven. This finding aligns with the transition from the preoperational stage to the concrete operational stage of cognitive development and marks the shift to logical thinking around concrete events, both of which are supported by now-accepted neurological changes in the brain. It is at this point that the child can "see" more than their own point of view.

Cognitive Perspective-Taking

Perspective-taking has been defined and researched along two separate dimensions: cognitive and affective (the latter of which I refer to as emotional perspective-taking).[6] Cognitive perspective-taking focuses primarily on the process of visual processing—specifically the ability to understand the way another person sees things in physical space. This is seen in Piaget's "Three Mountain Task." Studies have shown that visual perspective-taking improves from childhood to adulthood. As both children and adults age, visual perspective-taking tasks can be done with greater accuracy and speed.

Emotional Perspective-Taking

Affective or emotional perspective-taking is the ability to comprehend and take on the viewpoint of another person's thoughts, feelings, and attitudes. Perspective-taking in this area has a variety of social implications. For both children and adults, it is associated with greater empathy and prosocial behavior.[7] Research has consistently shown that instructing people to take the perspective of a person in need leads to increased compassion and empathy for them.[8] Interestingly, recent research in cognitive neuroscience has identified distinct areas of brain function associated with both cognitive and affective perspective-taking.[9]

I use Piaget's research in my everyday practice, not using a model of mountains but improvising with use of the coffee table that sits in front of the sofa in my office. On it sits a Kleenex box, a jar of candy, a container full of pens, and a small box filled with my professional cards. I ask my patients, both children and adults, to consider how these items would look if they were instructed to draw a picture from each of the four sides of the table (i.e., from one side the Kleenex is to the left of the candy jar, from another side it is to the right of the candy jar, etc.). I explain Piaget's findings and the years of ensuing research noting that perspective-shifting is a key component in empathy and an essential skill in problem solving and negotiation. It is also a model that I often use in my work with couples who are in conflict as I work to help each partner understand how any given situation looks to the other partner. Perspective-taking increases understanding and builds compassion. In all cases, I am making an assessment of how accurately they can weigh and shift perspective, and how easily they can identify and empathize with the other person's point of view.

Importantly, all children go through the transition from prelogical, to somewhat logical, and then fully logical thinking. A certain immaturity in thinking is born of this developmental progression, with visual perspective-taking skills not being adequately developed until seven or eight (and more thoroughly honed and developed by age eleven). After those ages and stages, the child has the cognitive capacity to perceive situations accurately but does not always do so based on emotional factors.

The perceptual difficulties that are common to children with narcissistic tendencies, traits, and dysfunction are not the result of the expected developmental stages and the associated limitations. Rather, their difficulties are due to a variety of emotional deficits that impact accurate perception and interpretation. These children often understand the world through the lens affected by their personality (including an impaired self-concept, unmet emotional needs, and an immature model of relationships) and/or through a state of emotional dysregulation. Unfortunately, their misperception and misinterpretation only perpetuate the tendencies and traits of narcissism.

Basic aspects of personality affect perception and interpretation. Understanding those processes is critical since misperception and misinterpretation can stunt or misdirect healthy maturation and in doing so, interfere in the establishment of meaningful relationships.

HEALTHY OR NOT-SO-HEALTHY INFORMATION GATHERING: MEASURES OF INFORMATION PROCESSING

Signs of Healthy Information Processing

As a psychologist, I make frequent assessments of a patient's capacity for information gathering. Children with emerging healthy information-processing skills make good use of real-world experiences that provide information that both challenge and build their ever-improving cognitive and processing abilities.

Children with healthy information-gathering skills tend to evidence relatively stable emotional regulation. Their upset does not lead them to misinterpret events or actions. Their cognitive skills remain steady in the face of distress. Moreover, these children's emotional needs do not interrupt or influence their perceptions. They have sufficient emotional stamina to withstand injury or insult and do not need to "see" things a certain way in order to prop up their self-esteem or support a given interpretation. Their thinking tends to be nuanced and is not prone to premature conclusion, bias, or blaming. The child is open to different points of view and is willing to concede that their view might not be right. Nuanced thinking is seen in thoughtful comments such as this is the way it "seems to me" or is how "I saw it."

The importance of this kind of stable emotional regulation and healthy information gathering is well illustrated by a patient I once counseled, an adolescent who played on a competitive basketball team and wanted to be a great player. Susie's father played college ball, and she wanted to do the same. She trained hard and gave the game her all, but the coach did not reward her efforts; she remained solidly on the second string. When she did get in the game, she played well but not exceptionally so. At the end of her junior year, she scheduled a meeting with her coach and asked for an honest assessment of her potential. The coach discussed her skills carefully and in great depth, explaining in the end that she might be able to play D2 ball. Susie was disappointed but took that information home and discussed it with her parents. She heard the coach's evaluation accurately in spite of the pain it caused her. She decided to rethink her college career plans for athletics. Over the next weeks, she asked her parents if she could schedule a consultation with a therapist to talk through the situation. Susie's ability to hear a disappointing evaluation, work through her feelings around that information, and then change her plans accordingly, are all signs of healthy emotional function.

Susie's story contrasts with that of Jackson. I met him when he was fourteen years old. He was small for his age and was considered by others to be a competent but not excellent basketball player (information that was provided by the parents). Despite what appeared to be rather obvious athletic limitations (that were unacknowledged by Jackson), he wanted to be a point guard at the highest level and fully intended to play pro ball. He engaged me in endless discussions about the Chicago Bulls, the L.A. Lakers, and the Phoenix Suns. It was obvious: Jackson "needed" to be a great player, and he could neither see nor hear any information to the contrary. After several years in therapy in which we carefully followed his athletic progress through his games and various outcomes, and after responding thoughtfully to my careful questions and ongoing support, Jackson began to identify some limitations in his skill development. It was a painful process, but he ultimately gave up his dream of playing professionally. Interestingly, he shifted his aspirations. He concluded that basketball was not his sport but that athletics was still his love. He channeled that interest into sports management, becoming a manager for the high school team and pursuing a college degree in that field. Jackson's need to be a superstar was so compelling that his perception of his skill levels remained inaccurate for a time. Gradually, he came to accept his talents for what they were, developed a broader self-esteem comprised of his many true talents, and ultimately pursued a career path that made good use of them.

The contrast between Susie's story and Jackson's story is informative. Both children had high expectations, were highly motivated, and wanted to be successful athletes. But Susie was more readily able to use her experience and the feedback of others to consider and refine her goals based on the data she collected. Jackson's needs led him to resist and misinterpret information that might interfere with his goals. He hung steadfastly to his inaccurate perceptions in the face of contradictory information for a long time. Both children eventually secured a more realistic self-assessment based on an accurate perception and interpretation of the facts. However, Jackson's situation required the assistance of therapy. A solid self-concept and positive self-esteem hung in the balance.

Emotional needs can impact perception and interpretation. Perhaps more importantly, misperception and misinterpretation can prove costly in terms of development overall and emotional adjustment, in particular. Being able to see and hear the truth when it runs contrary to one's desires is a sign of emotional health and is both a needed and necessary skill.

Signs of Not-So-Healthy Information Processing

Children with not-so-healthy information gathering skills have a variety of presentations. Typically, some basic aspect of their personality results in frequent misperception and misinterpretation. The world they perceive is often rendered inaccurately and is consistent with their emotional dynamics. The following is a list of variables that contribute to various types of misperception and misinterpretation.

- Emotional dysregulation: The child is emotionally upset and cannot perceive or interpret a given event or action clearly or is not open to alternative explanations. For example, Rachel is in a state over not being invited to the after-school party Georgia is giving. She concludes that Georgia is jealous of her and does not want her to be at the party and look pretty. I know from my work with Rachel that she believes other people's jealousy of her explains her many failed relationships. She would later learn that Georgia was only allowed to invite three children to the event— a rule imposed by her mother. While Rachel considered herself to be Georgia's friend, she did not consider herself to be in her closest friendship group. Rachel's understanding of why she was not included was inaccurate.
- Emotional neediness: The child needs to see the world in a certain way that clouds perception. For example, Henry is pleased that his classmate John complimented him on his new shirt. He sees himself as handsome and cool. What he fails to understand is that John was making fun of him. I know from Henry's mother that he often misinterprets his classmate's comments.

Another example of not-so-healthy information processing can be seen in Larry, a big-time developer in my practice who was struggling with market reversals. He refused to contact one of his primary investors to determine if he would be investing in the next fund. Larry would learn later in therapy that he needed the investor so much that he simply could not allow himself to make the phone call and suffer the upset of his disinterest and the accompanying risk to his business. His emotional needs were driving his decision-making, and his refusal to proceed in the information-gathering process allowed him to hold a faulty assumption and not suffer emotional dysregulation. He would learn later that the investor was no longer interested in investing in the fund, a fact that would have been better addressed earlier than later.

Still another example is seen in Candace's report of her family history. Raised by a demanding, critical, narcissistic mother, Candace found a way to accommodate her mother's every demand. Talented and very bright, she proved herself to be an excellent student, hard worker, and sensitive confidant to her mother. When she entered therapy, she insisted that her mother was "not that bad," as she was always well-intentioned. Over a period of time, she came to realize that she had underestimated her mother's emotional difficulties and the magnitude of the deprivation she experienced through years of inadequate nurture. She, quite literally, could not see the size of the problem because she needed her childhood to be "better" than it was.

• Bias or prejudice: The child sees the world through a clouded or impaired lens. For example, Elizabeth believed that she would win the spelling bee and that there were no children close to her level of accomplishment. Her prejudice that others were less talented, less capable, and less competent led her to a faulty assessment of the competitive field. When she placed second in the event, she was heartbroken. Her perceptual inaccuracy did not allow her to make a realistic assessment and prepare herself in advance.

• All-or-nothing thinking: The child interprets information in terms of extremes. The situation is either black or white, good or bad, right or wrong. For example, Steve believes that if he does not get a perfect score on the SAT, he will not get into Stanford. Monica believes that if she is not perfect in math, she cannot be the professor she wants to be. Margaret believes that all people who smoke marijuana are bad people, and therefore, she will not develop a relationship with anyone with that orientation.

• Jumping to conclusions: The child takes one or more pieces of information and decides the outcome. For example, Annie did poorly on two tests in economics and has decided never to follow a course of study in business. Clayton did not make the tennis team the first time he tried and decided to give up the game completely.

• Blaming as an explanation: The child searches for an explanation of a bad outcome but always places the responsibility outside of the self. For example, Margo did not get a part in the school play. She decided it was Mrs. Smith's fault who had "never liked me." She did not consider whether it was an accurate reflection of her theatrical skills. Daniel was not invited on a ski trip over Christmas and concluded that the other guys had ganged up on him because he did so well in school. He did not consider that his constant teasing of them might be an irritant to his peers, which resulted in their dislike and resistance to including him.

The preceding variables contribute to misperceptions and misinterpretations in children. There are a number of common examples of problematic information processing in N2B children. These include:

- Perceptions of the self that are inflated or grandiose
- A persistent focus on comparisons and perceiving others as competitors
- Viewing those who frustrate or challenge them as malevolent and/or inferior
- Blaming and denigrating others for their own mistakes or when things go wrong
- Perceiving others or the world as being unfair if they do not get what they want
- Devaluing those who threaten their superiority
- Incorrectly viewing others as jealous or envious of them
- Being unable to see their own contributions to problematic interactions with others

Dysfunctional information processing in N2B children can complicate understanding and the potential for change and growth.

Healthy Information Gathering: Examples from Childhood

In my practice, I make assessments, on a regular basis, of information-gathering abilities in children as well as adults. In the vast majority of cases, that evaluation is informal and serves only to direct my work. Most typically I make the determination out of information provided by my patient. In those cases, I devise questions around the situation they present. When this is not possible, I have developed sample situations that I present and ask the patient to respond to. A common sample I use involves a birthday party: "Imagine you have a birthday party and all your friends come to your house to celebrate. They bring gifts, which are placed in a big pile at the front door, but you did not see your best friend bring in a present. What do you think about that? What will you do about it?"

Here are a few samples of things I like to hear from children as they share their ideas about their perception and interpretation of that upsetting birthday party event.

Six-Year-Old Nancy
I wouldn't like that.
I'd go look to see if it's in the pile of gifts. I mean to be sure.
Maybe the tag fell off. But if I couldn't find it, I'd tell her she hurt
my feelings.

Nine-Year-Old Jenny
I know her. Something must have happened. Maybe her mom
didn't take her to get something.
Maybe she left it at home. Maybe she ran out of time.
I'd tell her she hurt my feelings. That won't end it for us. We'd find
a way to make it better.

Sixteen-Year-Old Diane
I would check and be certain that I didn't receive a gift—be sure
that a tag didn't fall off one.
If I couldn't find a gift from her, I'd check with her. She'll tell me
what happened. I know she would.
She must have had a really good reason. She wouldn't hurt me—I
mean not on purpose.

What these responses show is a willingness to check their own
perception and their interpretation. Did their friend bring a gift, or
was it simply misplaced? Did their friend have a good reason, and if so,
what was it? Did something happen that would explain what happened
and could be understood? In all responses, there is an openness to other
possibilities, facts, and explanations. There is an understanding that the
behavior is atypical and a belief that there was some justification. Importantly, there is a recognition of the stability of the friendship and a
willingness to work out whatever went wrong.

Injured, Not-So-Healthy Information Gathering: Examples from Childhood

Not-so-healthy information gathering results in consistent misperception
and misinterpretation of various events. The child's emotional immaturity both maintains and reinforces their poorly developed perceptual
skills and serves to justify their conclusion. While the reasons vary, the
impact of their immature understanding of the situation intensifies interpersonal conflict. They tend to want others to agree with their conclusions and can punish others for disagreeing with them.

Here are the kinds of things I worry about when I hear them from children as they discuss their perceptions and interpretations of the same sample birthday party situation.

Six-Year-Old Alex

He shouldn't have done that. It's not fair. I gave him a great gift. He's not being a friend. I'm gonna tell him.
He better make it right. Or maybe, I don't need him as a friend.

Nine-Year-Old Trevor

I don't know why he did that. He's a jerk.
Good friends don't do that to their best friend. There's really no excuse.
Everybody knows you take a gift to a birthday party. Maybe, I need a different friend.

Sixteen-Year-Old Frank

Why would he do that? It's messed up—not what friends do.
It's inconsiderate. It's mean. Screw him.
Let's see how he likes it when I don't show up at his party.

These responses indicate a general immaturity in perception and interpretation that suggests that information gathering may be contaminated in other areas as well. The child does not consider that there may be a reasonable explanation for the failure to provide a gift. The child does not double-check their perception. The child is angry that their needs were not attended to. There is a lack of interest in searching for any underlying reasons to explain the other's behavior. There is no orientation toward forgiveness or reconciliation. In some responses, there is the hint that the friendship could be lost over such a small violation or that it might never recover from the offense.

PARENT CONTRIBUTIONS TO THE DEVELOPMENT OF HEALTHY OR NOT-SO-HEALTHY INFORMATION GATHERING

Parents play an important role in the child's development in information gathering and perception. They work to understand how children think and stimulate and challenge reasoning, bit by bit, as the child grows and matures. In infancy, this can mean playing with a child, for example, hiding a toy under a blanket and encouraging their search for it. For a toddler, this can mean asking age-appropriate questions, such as "which man is taller" or "which dog is bigger," and listening to and accepting, without criticism, the limitations in their reasoning. For a school-aged child, this can mean helping children with their homework by reading together, learning math facts, and assisting them in scientific investigation by helping build a toy car and measuring its speed down a ramp. For an adolescent, this can mean engaging in conversations about hypothetical situations such as "what would Utopia look like" or "if we assume X is true, what will its impact be on Y." These interactions focus primarily on stimulating cognitive development from the prelogical to the semi-logical to the fully logical stages. In many cases, parental involvement takes the form of standard school-supported homework and scientific investigation.

I am reminded of a parent who shared with me a story about his sixteen-year-old son. The adolescent was trying to build a kind of transistor but didn't have time to purchase the materials himself. He gave his father a list of the needed items, and the father went to the electronics store. He dutifully sought out the items and paid for them. With no knowledge or understanding of the area of investigation, he simply followed directions. As he told me, "I had no idea if this was lunacy or an actual area of talent for him at the time, but I did it anyway. I wanted him to know that I supported him even if it didn't work out as he anticipated." From his description, the young man struggled with his invention. The creative device didn't work readily or easily, and it required several revisions with more trips for the father to the electronics store. That story is now part of "family lore" as that unsuccessful but inquisitive adolescent ended up as a very successful mathematics student at a highly competitive university and then a productive engineer at a major research laboratory. Support for cognitive development by parents can take many forms.

Parental involvement is perhaps more important in the area of emotional development, as it impacts perception and reasoning. Emotional dysregulation, unmet emotional needs, and dysfunctional or immature personality structures of various kinds interfere with perceptual accuracy. The way parents address their child's information gathering

and perceptual and interpretational skills can either encourage or discourage the development of healthy and mature thinking.

Parent Comments That Either Help or Hurt the Child's Information Gathering: An Example

What parents say and do has an impact on the development of the child's
information-gathering skills. Below are examples of *healthy* parental
comments around situations when the child's perceptions are likely
distortions.

Positive Exchanges

Child (age 8): She's a jerk, I hate her.

Parent: Can you tell me what she did?

Child: Yeah, she didn't invite me to spend the night Friday night
after she said she would.

Parent: Do you know why?

Child: Yeah, like I said, she's a jerk.

Parent: Could there be an explanation that you don't know about?

Child: No way.

Parent: But if we were to consider any possible explanation, what
might it be?

Child: Well, maybe. Her brother had his wisdom teeth taken out.
She said he looks like a chipmunk.

Parent: So it's possible his surgery got in the way. Or maybe something else?

Child: Well, maybe. I suppose I could ask.

Parent: Might be helpful to check it out. See if there was something
going on at her house that you don't know about, that got in the
way with her earlier plan.

Child (age 11): He's not my boyfriend anymore. It's over, I mean
over.

Parent: Can you tell me what happened?

Child: Yeah, he told Marjorie that her dress was pretty.

Parent: How did that make you feel?

Child: Mad. And jealous.

Parent: And what do you think it means?

Child: It means he likes her better than me. Otherwise, he wouldn't have noticed.

Parent: Are you sure that's true? Do you have any other information about what he might be thinking?

Child: Isn't that enough? He liked her dress.

Parent: Might that be something you want to check out with him. You could ask if things have changed between you or see how he feels about Marjorie.

Child: I suppose I could do that. I suppose then I'd know.

Parent: Well, it might be helpful to find out for sure if what you *think* happened actually *is* happening.

Child (age 17): Well, it's final. I'm not going to college, well, not any college I want to go to. I can't do the work. I tried my hardest and I got a "C" on my English paper.

Parent: I know that's a disappointment. I know how hard you tried.

Child: I'm no good at English. You have to put your English grades on your transcript. Right? There is no way.

Parent: Have you talked to your counselor about how this level of performance might impact your college admission? Is there any way to let colleges know that you are working on improving in this area and that they should focus on your strengths in other areas?

Child: Well, no, I actually don't know. I've been so upset about this I didn't look into what's possible.

Parent: Maybe you can check it out with Mr. Morris, your counselor. I suspect he has some ideas about how to handle this. There might be some way to address this that you haven't thought of.

Child: Okay. I don't want to do that, but I'll do it. I suppose it makes sense.

Parent: Well, we don't want you to give up on your dream until you've asked all the hard questions. And exhausted all the possibilities. Either way, your dad and I are here for you, no matter the outcome.

Key Concepts in Positive Exchanges
- The parent understands that developing perceptual accuracy is a complex process subject to gains and losses over the course of development.
- The parent is accepting of the child's emotional upset around their perception and interpretation.
- The parent understands that the child's conclusion might be inaccurate (i.e., a distortion).
- The parent raises questions without criticizing the child.
- The parent encourages exploration of the child's thinking in a kind and gentle manner.
- The parent provides an alternate understanding of the same set of facts.
- The parent encourages the child to gather information.
- The parent remains sensitive to the underlying feelings.
- The parent does not force the child to change his perception.

In this process, parents are engaged in carefully evaluating and potentially restructuring children's thinking.

Parental *errors* that interfere with the development of information gathering and perceptual accuracy come in many forms. Below are some parent comments that I have seen in responses, both in and out of my practice, that I have placed within the sample situations. They range from shaming the child for their lack of understanding to embracing the child's probable distortion by joining in.

Negative Exchanges

Child (age 8): She's a jerk, I hate her.

Parent: What did she do?

Child: She didn't invite me to spend the night Friday night.

Parent: That's mean.

Child: Yeah, like I said, she's a jerk.

Parent: You know I never really liked her? I never really thought she was very nice to you.

Child: That's right.

Parent: Maybe she's not good for you.

Child: That's just what I was thinking. Maybe Marie is a better friend, one worth keeping.

Child (age 11): He's not my boyfriend anymore. It's over, I mean over.

Parent: What happened?

Child: Yeah, he told Marjorie that her dress was pretty.

Parent: That's ridiculous. Just commenting on Marjorie's dress doesn't mean he likes her.

Child: It does to me. It means he likes her better than me. Otherwise, he wouldn't have noticed.

Parent: Cut it out. You are jumping to a conclusion without any evidence.

Child: I know what it means. You don't get me or get kids at all. Like I said, you don't understand me.

Parent: Actually, the problem is not my understanding, it's that you don't listen to me. That's the truth here.

Child (age 17): Well, it's final. I'm not going to college, well not any college I want to go to. I can't do the work. I tried my hardest and I got a "C" on my English paper.

Parent: You need to stop it. Just because you didn't get an A on that paper doesn't mean it will translate into a poor grade, and it doesn't mean you won't get into the college you want.

Child: You don't know anything about college admission. You don't know anything about what it takes to get in.

Parent: Well, I know you're a great student and you get upset every time you're not perfect.

Child: You're not listening to me. You're not accepting the truth of my situation. I don't know why I talk to you at all.

Parent: You're getting mad at me when you should be evaluating your own thinking.

Child: I'm not talking anymore, starting now.

Key Concepts in Negative Exchanges
- The parent embraces the child's distortion and reinforces it.
- The parent jumps to the same conclusion that the child has reached.
- The parent fails to kindly and gently challenge the child's distortion.
- The parent argues with the child over the distortion.
- The parent criticizes and shames the child for their lack of accurate understanding.
- The parent challenges the facts in an unhelpful way.
- The parent tries to force the child to change their perception.
- The parent does not accept the child's feelings underlying emotional need that maintains the distortion.

Over the course of healthy development, the child's ability to gather information and perceive events, actions, interactions, events, and people in accurate ways improves. As children grow and mature, their capabilities in this area build while their vulnerability to misperception and misinterpretation declines. These gains are essential as they allow children to be challenged in ways that encourage growth. Children cannot grow if they cannot "see" themselves and the world accurately. Moreover, these abilities are essential for the development of close interpersonal relationships. Children must be able to appreciate how the world is seen and understood from another's point of view. Perspective-taking is a foundation of empathy and is a key component in emotional closeness.

STRATEGIES FOR PARENTS: BUILDING NON-NARCISSISTIC INFORMATION GATHERING IN THE CHILD

Accurate information gathering is an important developmental acquisition. The diagnosis of narcissistic-like traits in a child is not generally made on the child's limitations in either perception or interpretation standing alone. However, specific ways of handling information likely reflect narcissistic tendencies, traits, and potentially dysfunction. Children who evidence such tendencies and traits typically demonstrate immaturity in their perceptual skills, often reaching inaccurate conclusions and presenting erroneous explanations. Those who might construe this as lying often miss the origin of such behavior. In many cases, it is predicated on misperception, while in others, it may be due to willful misrepresentation.

Misperception of the Truth

In some cases, the child actually misperceives the situation. The overweight boy who does not realize how fat he is or the anorexic girl who does not see how thin she is are both examples of inaccurate perception. Another instance is seen in the child who believes he is unlovable and finds support for this belief by taking every negative peer comment as confirmation of his conclusion. Or similarly, in the opposite direction, there is the child who selectively holds on to all positive feedback without regard to any negative information, maintaining a grandiose and unrealistic sense of self. In many cases, the child cannot perceive the information accurately. It may be that it is too painful or hurtful to the self-concept for the weight of reality to be accepted, or too destabilizing to allow him to give up his negative self-concept. Either way, an accurate view may challenge their theory of the world, whether positive or negative, and thereby upset their emotional stability.

I recall an interesting conversation with a lawyer who explained to me that he liked to have people on the stand who engage in this kind of distortion. He noted that these types of individuals are "compelling witnesses" as they "present stories that are likely to be believed by a jury." He continued, "I'm not saying they're lying because they believe it *is* the truth—even though it may not actually be true." Confidence in distorted, inaccurate perception does make for convincing testimony.

A highly successful accountant whom I treated possessed this sort of "blindness," relating to me that he was shocked when his wife asked for a divorce. He reported that he "never saw it coming" while his wife insisted that they had discussed their difficulties over five years and had seen numerous therapists in the interim. Clearly, he read those discussions quite differently than she did. His misperception both interfered with his ability to intervene earlier and to prepare himself if those attempts at reconciliation were not successful. Another example is seen in an angry adolescent's reaction to the poor review he received from his job. He insisted that he had performed adequately, if not better than average, while the letter noted his tendency to "show up late" and his failure to "get along well" with other staff members.

Distortion is a misperception that presents problems, even more so when it is compelling. Gaslighting is an extreme form of distortion. The term refers to the process of trying to convince someone that their perception is inaccurate. It originated from a 1938 play and 1944 film, entitled *Gaslight*. The play and movie center around a husband who attempts to drive his wife crazy by manipulating her into believing that her thinking is impaired. Gaslighting is considered a form of psychological abuse, as it causes someone to question their perception of reality and, thereby, their sanity. Distortions argued as reality are upsetting to everyone and cause upset, worry, and even anger.

Misinterpretation of the Truth

In some situations, the child misinterprets the truth. This can be due to a number of problematic mechanisms including underestimation, focusing on a single element, jumping to conclusions, and overgeneralizing. An example is seen in the "queen bee" who doesn't see her behavior as problematic, does not believe that it is a form of bullying, and blames the other child who cried in response as being "overly sensitive." Another instance is seen in the man who entered my practice complaining that his wife was unsupportive while failing to recognize that he was harsh and rude with his children and prone to drink to excess.

Willful Disguise of the Truth

In still other situations, the child knows the truth but disguises it. For example, a student might insist he turned in his paper (when he did not) and claim that the teacher is at fault because she cannot find it, or a child might claim his watch is not working, (when it was) which is why he is not home by curfew time.

Assessing the accuracy of any given child's perspective can be challenging. I am reminded of a story shared by a young mother. She came to see me upset about her son who had been hit by another student at a competitive preparatory school. Her son was not seriously hurt but was very upset. The mother was furious, setting up meetings with school administrators and demanding attention and immediate intervention. She wanted that "aggressive" student to be removed from his classroom and punished severely.

Over several days, the incident was investigated by the school through interviews with various classmates. To her dismay, she discovered that her son's description of the event was inaccurate. He had focused on the inappropriate response of the other student and failed to either see or appreciate what he had done to provoke the situation. The mother learned that her son had poked the other student with a shock pen and the other student had reacted in anger. Hitting was not an appropriate response for that student, but it was certainly more understandable given the strong provocation. When confronted with these facts, her son was overly focused on the other student's "bad behavior" and underemphasized the role he played.

The mother worked with her son to help him see his behavior more realistically and its impact on the other student. Both he and the mother apologized to the other family, and they each worked to make amends. With the assistance of school personnel, the situation improved, and the two boys actually became friendly. Over time, the mother realized her part in the event. She had too readily taken up her son's perspective and had failed to consider alternate explanations earlier in the process. She came to realize that her emotional upset had compromised her information gathering, which resulted in her own misperception and misinterpretation that only further compounded an already difficult situation.

Negative Impacts

The Negative Impact of Shaming the Child for Misperception or Misinterpretation   Parents who shame their child for their misperception or misinterpretation run the risk of injuring the parent-child relationship. Children need to know that they have a parent who is on their side and who will love them, flaws and all. Making mistakes around perception is part of growing up, and parents who explore thinking in this area should anticipate less than perfect performance. As the data and clinical evidence show, perception improves with time, not only during childhood but also throughout adulthood.

The Negative Impact of Embracing the Child's Misperception or Misinterpretation.   Parents who embrace the child's misperceptions or misinterpretation run the risk of supporting inaccurate thinking. They may reinforce immature ways of perceiving such as "all-or-nothing" thinking, jumping to conclusions, omitting essential variables in an analysis, and responding impulsively based on feelings alone.

The Negative Impact of Forcing the Child to Change His Perception.   Parents who force the child to change his perception run the risk of undermining the child's self-confidence in his own abilities. The parental response is in effect saying, "you got it wrong," and "you must change." Helpful change comes through the child's own recognition of a need for change. Without such understanding, the child will not benefit from "owning" his knowledge of a mistaken perception or mistaken interpretation.

The Negative Impact of Arguing with the Child over the Distortion.   Parents who argue with their child over their distortion model an inappropriate problem-solving relationship. Parents who do so try to assert the superiority of their point of view and devalue the viewpoint of the child. This undermines the development of a positive self-concept and contributes to negative self-esteem.

Positive Impacts

The Positive Impact of Exploring the Child's Perceptions and Interpretations in a Calm and Gentle Manner.   Parents who explore the child's perceptions and interpretations in a calm and gentle way are modeling positive problem solving. This process challenges the child's thinking in a manner that is most likely to result in careful consideration and potential change. Parents who ask thoughtful questions that encourage exploration (What did you see? How did you gather that information? How certain are you of your view of the situation? Are there other ways to understand the situation? Is there a way to check out your perspective, your impressions?) present positive opportunities for cognitive growth.

The Positive Impact of Appreciating the Child's Feelings around Their Perceptions and Interpretations.   Parents who appreciate the child's feelings around their perceptions and interpretations communicate that they value the child's thinking and their problem-solving ability. Telling a child that their feelings are important is synonymous with telling a child

that they are important. In effect, the parent is reaffirming their unconditional love for the child. Parents who fail to appreciate and respect their
child's feelings run the risk of making the child feel negatively about
themselves.

*The Positive Impact of Encouraging Perspective-Taking from a Cognitive
Viewpoint.* Parents who encourage exploration of cognitive perspective-taking are building their child's cognitive skills by reinforcing and
strengthening the accuracy of their perceptions and interpretations. An
analysis of different points of view contributes to complex thinking,
but also builds empathy and compassion. A child who can understand
how things look from a different perspective is more likely to establish
meaningful relationships and participate in productive problem solving. Seeing the world from different points of view is a positive skill in
both friendship and negotiation. Specific thought-provoking questions
(How did the other person likely see the situation? What might he have
thought about the situation? What might he consider doing given the
situation?) build important cognitive skills in their child.

*The Positive Impact of Encouraging Perspective-Taking from an Emo-
tional Viewpoint.* Parents who encourage exploration of emotional
perspective-taking not only build their child's cognitive skills but also
develop their child's emotional skills. An analysis of different points of
view in terms of feelings specifically builds empathy, understanding, and
compassion. A child who can appreciate the feelings of others is less
likely to injure them and more likely to befriend them. Such children
make better citizens of the world as they can appreciate the emotional
needs of those in different or difficult situations. Asking specific thought-
provoking questions (How did the other person likely feel in that situation? How might a person in that situation respond? Might their feelings
be hurt? Could their hurt provoke an overreaction?) builds important
emotional skills.

Parents can help evaluate and improve the accuracy of their child's
perceptions through thoughtful discussion characterized by calm,
warmth, and gentleness. The strategies noted above help parents and
children understand the basis of the child's perception, assess the accuracy of specific views, and potentially shift their position if flaws are
discovered. This process and its ultimate resolution are essential steps in
child development and illustrate the important role that parents play in
its mastery.

EIGHT TAKEAWAYS FOR PARENTS TO BUILD INFORMATION GATHERING AND PROCESSING

Lessons from theory, research, and clinical observation lend support for the following parenting behaviors:

1. Understand that misperception and misinterpretation are a normal part of growing up.
2. Encourage the child to evaluate their perceptions and interpretations through careful discussion. Helpful questions include determining if the information came from a reliable source, if all the facts have been considered, and if different perspectives based on the same situation have been considered.
3. Interact with the child in a loving, gentle, and sensitive way as you "think out loud" about their conclusions.
4. Help the child make accurate assessments of various situations, events, interactions, and outcomes.
5. Question the child's assessments without criticism or shame. Flaws in thinking include all-or-nothing thinking, jumping to conclusions, and opinion masquerading as fact.
6. Understand that perceptual accuracy is a complex process subject to both progress and regression over time.
7. Teach perspective-taking throughout the child's daily life, beginning at an early age, most especially from six or seven and up.
8. Use perspective-taking as a strategy to build empathy, understanding for others, and problem-solving skills.

THE OUTCOME: "FUNCTION WITH A TRUE LENS AND CAMERA" AS A METAPHOR

Parents who are familiar with the complex process of maturation in perception and interpretation can more fully recognize the strides their child makes over time and see the impact of their efforts to improve it. The child has made tremendous progress in taking a tiny, misshapen lens and growing it into a clear and accurate instrument. She has grown the camera into a full-sized piece of equipment that organizes, frames, and conceptualizes pictures of the world. Solid perceptual skills both contribute to mental health and are an essential part of the functioning of all human beings. This fully functional camera can now take pictures from different angles and different distances, from above an object and below an object, from beside an object and even within an object. Those expanding and maturing developments in perspective-taking change the child from a selfish and self-centered being to an empathetic and sensitive partner in all types of relationships. The transformation from a child's way of thinking to an adult's mature way of thinking is a remarkable achievement.

• 7 •

Building a Non-narcissistic Model of Love and Relationships

(Interacting with Others and the Development of Trust = Relationship Knowledge)

The Development of a Model of Love and Relationships over Time

$\mathcal{T}$he relationship is the mechanism of psychological transformation and growth that provides the path to maturity. Every child will develop a model of love, a way of understanding human connection and a sense of predictability around social interaction. This constitutes the basis for understanding social relationships and determines the desire for and nature of interpersonal engagement.

A healthy model of love is built on trust, which creates a sense of security and safety in the child. He knows that if he is cold, he will be given warmth; if he is hungry, he will be fed; if he is upset, he will be comforted; and if he is lonely, he will be provided company. Such a model teaches the child that people are predictable and therefore trustworthy, and that they can be relied upon. In the end, the child comes to understand that connections are valuable, and they should be both pursued and maintained. Importantly, this early model will be elaborated in future relationships, from friendship to marriage, from coworker to employer, from family member to stranger. Notions of love begin in infancy and become more complex and comprehensive as the child matures. A person's model of love and relationships is the bedrock of social understanding and social engagement and has a profound impact on overall function, from contentment to depth of connection.

Psychologists are always on the lookout for signs of a healthy relationship. I recall hearing a heartwarming story from a friend whose daughter gave him the nickname "Glad Dad." When she began to use the term in late preschool, he was uncertain what she meant: "Why are you calling me that?" She responded with typical pre-operational logic: "It means I'm glad you're my dad." His daughter is now grown with

151

three teenage children of her own, and still uses that term of affection: "Happy Birthday, Glad Dad," "Good to see you, Glad Dad." Signs of meaningful connection are sometimes hard to miss.

It is important to emphasize that healthy relationships are not "picture perfect." Every relationship must make sense of disappointing aspects in the other and in its operation. Psychologists are mindful of *how* negative qualities are integrated into the relationship. Lawrence was a handsome, high-achieving, hardworking entrepreneur. Despite his emphasis on high standards that often proved challenging to his children, he was a warm, loving, and devoted father who spent hours of meaningful time with each. His youngest son clearly recognized the limitations of his father's world view and nicknamed him, "Captain Negative." Whenever his father noticed a below-standard performance in the world—whether in politics, social commentary, interpersonal injustice, or achievement—his son would tease: "Anything else you would like to add, Captain Negative?" This is an illustration of a child who has integrated his father's negative trait into a clearly loving, positive, and secure relationship, as well as a father's ability to accept the truth in his son's teasing. The story of Captain Negative is a reminder that parents do not need to be perfect to be deeply loved.

Negative qualities can be integrated into a working marriage with the same success. I am reminded of Dan and Helen, who enjoyed a good marriage. They, like all couples, had struggled and, in the process, found ways to integrate the disappointments that every spouse must come to terms with in their partner. Dan had not proved to be the same workhorse that Helen was, nor did he readily notice things that needed to be done around the house. Over the years, they developed a clever shorthand that allowed Helen to make her point without offending and discouraging him. She would tease: "That damn pool boy didn't clean out the skimmers or remove the leaves from the pool," or, "I'm going to fire that pool boy. He didn't take out the trash." Dan got the message and enjoyed playfully teasing back: "It's really hard to get good help," or "Agreed, that pool boy is a problem." The exchanges brought a laugh and a growing closeness over the years. It was a sign of the health of the marriage and the depth of connection between them. Marriages, like people, are not perfect. The resolution of imperfection in relationships of all sorts bonds people together in meaningful ways.

A not-so-healthy model of love complicates many aspects of child and adult function. Most typically they are built on a lack of trust; the child suffers insecurity, and her confidence is undermined by the lack of predictability in human interaction. If she is upset, she cannot be confident she will be provided with comfort; if she feels isolated, she cannot be certain of companionship; if she is cold or hungry, she cannot be confident her physical needs will be met. In many cases, the development of an unhealthy model of love is predicated on inconsistent parental treatment. Sometimes, the parent attends to the child's needs and can be comforting and attentive. At other times, the parent is disengaged and inattentive for any number of reasons. Research has demonstrated the negative impact of a depressed mother on the child[1] as well as that of an angry, volatile parent.[2] The development of an unhealthy model also can grow out of abusive parenting, including physical, sexual, and emotional maltreatment. In some cases, extreme trauma can shatter a healthy model of love, and the resulting PTSD symptom pattern reflects a shift toward an unhealthy model. For example, a young woman whose husband was killed by a random shooter in a mall no longer trusts in the safety and security of the world or relationships, is terrified to be in or near similar physical circumstances, and may resist similar love relationships going forward.

When children are very young, their model of love and relationships is developing in simplistic but foundational ways. I am reminded of a clever three-year-old who had recently begun preschool. His father was reading him a beautifully illustrated alphabet book that went, as expected, from "A is for alligator" to "Z is for zebra" with quite a few exotica like "Q is for quetzal" in between. The little boy's uniform reaction to the unfamiliar ones was: "Is it nice? Does it bite?" Clearly, he was trying to fill out a basic understanding of his rapidly expanding world by knowing who or what he should trust.

A mother of a precocious fifth grader shared a story with me that is an excellent illustration of a child's model of love and how it can be gleaned in everyday interactions with children. When she told the story, she seemed to delight in the humor of it, never realizing that she had told me much more than simply relating the facts of the event. Her son, Blake, had been studying Shakespeare in school. When she went in and kissed him good night, he threw up his arms and spoke with dramatic flair: "Oh kiss again, bright angel, for thou art as glorious as the night."

His mother was astonished, "What are you talking about?" "Come on, Mom. Shakespeare, remember? 'Oh, speak again, bright Angel, for thou art as glorious to this night as a winged messenger of heaven.' Something like that. Romeo and Juliet." She laughed and hugged him. Then he played with her again. "I just adapted it for a good night kiss—from you." This exchange told me that Blake believed in love, that he saw it as a glorious thing, an experience close to heaven on earth. The playful but poignant interaction between the two revealed the obvious closeness in their relationship and suggested that this is how he understands his relationship with her. This is a healthy model of love, reflecting secure attachment and an interest in seeking warm and predictable interaction.

LOVE AND RELATIONSHIPS: THE "OPERATIONAL HANDBOOK" AS A METAPHOR

When I lecture and work with parents, I search for metaphors and images that allow parents to actually "see" what is going on inside the child—a way to visualize the personality structure that is forming, evolving, and building under the surface.

I understand the child's model of love and relationships as a kind of "Operational Handbook." I have been told that major fast-food chains develop handbooks that describe in detail every operation required to manage the store, from how to mop the floor to how to run the cash register. Similarly, I conceptualize that the healthy handbook begins as a small book filled with blank pages. Over time, it will come to spell out the nature of love and the rules of human interaction, from beginning impressions and interpretations of daily events and knowledge of the people they have known through the course of life. In time, the book will be more fleshed out, with added phrases, sentences, and paragraphs illustrated with pictures and drawings. Imagine the rudimentary handbook of an infant. It might read: expect people to come when you cry; expect people to change you when you're wet; expect people to rock you when you cannot fall asleep; expect people to hold you when you're lonely; expect people to smile at you and make funny faces when you smile at them . . . and so the list would go.

Over the course of development, the operational handbook will grow larger, evidencing deeper understanding and certainty around its operating principles. It will specify the nature of love with more variety and complexity. Its chapters on human interactions would be considerably more nuanced than those of a younger child. Imagine a school-aged child's handbook. It might read: expect people to be kind; expect people to listen when you have something important to say; expect people to help when you are in distress; expect people to love you even when you make mistakes or misbehave; expect people to stay with you even when you disappoint or hurt them . . . and the list goes on. By the time a child is in high school, the handbook would have well-defined rules for friendship and beginning rules for dating relationships. Information would be highly differentiated, remarkably complicated, and carefully thought out and understood with growing certainty.

Life is filled with stressors and setbacks. Over time, the child's model of love and relationships must make sense of disappointments in love and account for negative experiences with others. A child must learn to differentiate between those who will be kind to them and those who will mistreat them. Much of this learning occurs through trial and error, and for this reason, pain and failure are part of the process that stimulates growth. One must trust in a relationship and experience heartache in order to learn both the signs that better guide the selection of friends and coworkers in the future. Recovery from such disappointment provides the opportunity to build resilience, confidence, and strength.

In the same way that a healthy, positive model is developed, a child can acquire a negative model of love and relationships. Whether based on insensitive parenting, maltreatment, abuse, or trauma, such a handbook is composed of negative notions about the nature of love, which shape the rules of interaction. Imagine just a few of those rules: people are not trustworthy; never count on others to love you unconditionally; learn to take care of yourself because you cannot count on others; don't expect people to stay with you through thick and thin; keep your distance, as closeness will only hurt you . . . and the list goes on.

THE DEVELOPMENT OF A MODEL OF LOVE AND
RELATIONSHIPS: LESSONS ABOUT TRUST AND SECURITY

Attachment in Infancy

Attachment is the emotional bond developed between an infant and a primary attachment figure. This role usually falls to the mother, although the father or other caregiver can also be the primary attachment figure. The infant shows a number of attachment behaviors, such as smiling, crying, clinging, following, and sucking, all of which serve to keep the attachment figure nearby. Attachment, in a Darwinian sense, serves to protect the immature child and increase the likelihood of survival.

John Bowlby, a British psychoanalyst and psychiatrist, developed the theory of attachment after studying the negative impact of maternal deprivation on infants and young children. His observations revealed pervasive ill effects of institutional and hospital care on young children separated from their mothers. He theorized that the social and emotional responsiveness of the primary caregiver provides the infant with knowledge about the workings of other people and the world. Through these interactions, the child gathers information regarding the availability and reliability of others, notions that underlie basic security. Bowlby (1969) referred to this information as an "internal working model," conceptualized as a mental and emotional representation of the infant's first attachment relationship.[3] Bowlby hypothesized that early attachments could significantly affect a child's emotional development and that later relationships are a continuation of that early attachment paradigm.[4]

Mary Ainsworth, an American psychologist, who worked with Bowlby early in her career, engaged in empirical research in Uganda in 1953 where she undertook her first "mother-infant observation." Her observational research continued in the United States where she identified individual differences in the quality of mother-infant interactions. In her early work, she categorized three primary attachments: secure, insecure, and not-yet-attached.[5] She found a strong relationship between secure attachment and maternal sensitivity. Sensitive mothers tended to raise securely attached babies, understood them, and were familiar with their behavioral and emotional cues. Secure babies cried less, and more freely explored in the presence of their mother. Insensitive mothers tended to raise insecurely attached babies and were less tuned in to the nuances of their child's behavior. Insecurely attached babies cried frequently and were less likely to explore in the presence of their mother.

Ainsworth devised an assessment technique called the "Strange Situation" in which researchers observed children, between the ages of twelve and eighteen months, as they responded to a situation in which they were introduced to a stranger, briefly left alone, and then reunited with their mothers. Her groundbreaking studies[6] revealed the profound effects of attachment on behavior. She identified three major attachments: secure attachment, insecure avoidant attachment, and insecure ambivalent/resistant attachment.[7] She concluded that these attachment styles were the result of early interactions with the mother. Later, researchers added a fourth category, insecure: disorganized attachment.[8]

- Secure attachment: Securely attached infants composed the majority of the sample in Ainsworth studies.[9] These children use the attachment figure as a safe base to explore the environment. They welcome their caretaker's return after a separation and, if distressed, are readily comforted.[10]
- Insecure avoidant: Insecure avoidant infants do not orient to the attachment figure when investigating the environment.[11] They avoid proximity or interaction with the caregiver on reunion, and do not seek contact with the attachment figure when distressed.[12]
- Insecure ambivalent/resistant: Anxious, resistant infants show ambivalent behavior toward caregivers, being intermittently clingy and dependent and also rejecting. They have difficulty moving away from the attachment figure to explore surroundings. When distressed, they are difficult to soothe and are not easily comforted by interaction with the attachment figure.[13]
- Insecure/disorganized: Insecure/disorganized infants demonstrate odd, ambivalent, or contradictory behavior toward the parent such as running up to them, immediately pulling away, hitting the parent, curling up in a ball, or avoiding and rushing away.

Studies suggest that attachment remains consistent over childhood.[14]

While Ainsworth's focus was on the impact of maternal sensitivity on attachment, Kagan proposed that temperament is an important factor in predicting different attachment types.[15] His theory is supported

by research[16] that evidences predictable connections between temperament and attachment style: babies with an "easy" temperament are more
likely to develop secure attachments, babies with a "slow to warm"
temperament are more likely to have insecure avoidant attachments, and
babies with "difficult" temperament are more likely to have insecure
ambivalent attachments. Innate temperament appears to be an important contributor, but the nature of that influence is not altogether clear.
Temperament might also help or hinder the mother's ability to respond
sensitively to her infant's needs. "Easy" babies are simpler to understand
and more easily soothed than "difficult" ones, which might contribute
to a mother's degree of success in reading the baby's cues, thereby improving or undermining her confidence and responsiveness over time.
Regardless of the contribution of these other variables, parental sensitivity remains an important and perhaps the primary factor in determining
a child's model of love and relationships.

Both theory and research support the fundamental importance of a
child's need to experience a warm, responsive, and continuous relationship with an adult in early life. This relationship provides security from
which the child can explore the environment. The internal model developed in early childhood predicts how the child will handle emotional
stress, including anxiety, hostility, and upset, as well as their motivation
to seek closeness and support from others. Those early experiences influence the way an individual relates to others going forward and predict
one's level of confidence in the availability of other figures to provide
security and safety especially in times of distress.

The Child's Development of Trust and Interest in Engagement
Fuels Emotional Growth

Trust involves forming a firm belief in the reliability, ability, or strength
of another person. It builds confidence in interactions with them and
involves a perception of the other's dependability, which establishes faith
in the future of the relationship. Numerous theorists address trust. In his
theory of psychosocial development, Erik Erikson identified trust as the
first and most important stage in his model, a factor that was considered
to shape the child's view of the world as well as their overall personality.[17] He believed mistrust, the alternative negative outcome, could
contaminate all aspects of life and ultimately deprive the child of love

and companionship. Attachment theory recognizes trust as a component of individual differences in attachment, whereas interdependence theory conceptualizes trust as a unique construct that develops within new relationships.[18] Regardless of any theoretical differences in this understanding, a child will acquire a sense of trust or mistrust as he matures, and that model will determine the extent of his interest in engagement and guide future relationships.

I conceptualize the development of trust as a two-step process. The child must make determinations, ranging from negative to neutral to positive, on two dimensions: how he understands an experience with a person, and how that experience shapes his view of the person. In the eyes of a child, the process would look something like this: If he has positive experiences with his mother over time, he will eventually develop a positive view of her. This will establish trust. If those experiences suddenly turn negative and persist over time, he will be forced to modify his positive view of her to a more negative one. Thus, this new experience undermines his trust, which, by degree, will be replaced by mistrust. This process is cumulative and iterative.

I once treated a four-year-old boy who had experienced trauma in his early life. Benjamin was exhibiting separation anxiety and signs of emotional distress. In a session that I have never forgotten, we were seated on the floor playing. He looked up at me with tear-filled eyes: "I called out for you, Dr. Little. I called out for you over and over again. And you didn't come." I later learned that he had become upset over the weekend and had wanted help. Sadly, with the limitations of his preoperational (i.e., prelogical) thinking at the time, he did not fully appreciate that I neither heard his words nor refused to come. Clearly, Benjamin had issues with trust and, over the course of our work together, he would come to believe in the reliability of others. Three decades later, he is married and is a wonderfully sensitive and responsive father of three little boys.

The child's drive to engage fuels emotional growth in a number of ways. The relationship with the primary caretaker invites the child to know himself better and the world of others. It is in this interaction with the caretaker that the child's sense of self, including both self-concept and self-esteem, will mature. In the same way, this relationship with the caretaker helps develop the child's knowledge of others, which will grow increasingly complex and sophisticated. The knowledge of self and knowledge of the other grow in a kind of back-and-forth manner, with each inviting next steps and both inviting and encouraging maturation.

Attachment in Adulthood

Early childhood attachment patterns and the development of trust or mistrust show themselves in predictable ways in adult life. A basic principle of attachment theory is that there is some continuity between early attachment and the quality of later adult relationships.[19] This idea is based upon the notion of a mental representation—or internal working model—which serves as a template from the infant's primary attachment experience and extends as a model for future relationships. The research on adult attachment is covered briefly in this section to emphasize that early models of love and relationships remain important over the course of development.

Mary Main and her colleagues developed the Adult Attachment Interview, which asks for descriptions of early attachment events and descriptions of how those relationships and events had affected later personality.[20] Administered to an experimental group, the investigators evaluated the ways adults recounted and interpreted their childhood attachment experiences and their relationships in general. The analysis revealed three major attachment patterns in those recollections and understandings: secure (autonomous), dismissive-avoidant, and preoccupied (anxious).

Theorists have hypothesized that the experience a child has with their caregiver leads to the expectation of a similar experience in later relationships.[21] Adult attachment styles describe a person's comfort and confidence in close relationships, their fear of rejection and desire for intimacy, and their preference for self-sufficiency or interpersonal distance.

Early attachment has an impact on later adult relationships generally. Research suggests that securely attached infants as adults tend to have happier, longer-lasting adult relationships.[22] On the other hand, insecurely attached infants tend to find adult relationships more difficult, are more likely to divorce, and believe finding and securing love is relatively rare. Similarly, research suggests that attachment style is correlated with relationship satisfaction.[23] Secure attachment is positively correlated with one's relationship satisfaction, whereas insecure attachment is negatively associated with relationship satisfaction.

Adult attachment styles consist of two primary components, those involving notions of the self ("Am I loveable?") and those involving notions of others ("Can I depend on her in times of distress?").[24] Individuals can hold either a positive or negative sense of self and a positive or negative sense of others, a theoretical paradigm that results in one of four adult attachment styles. These adult attachment styles are displayed in the following chart.[25]

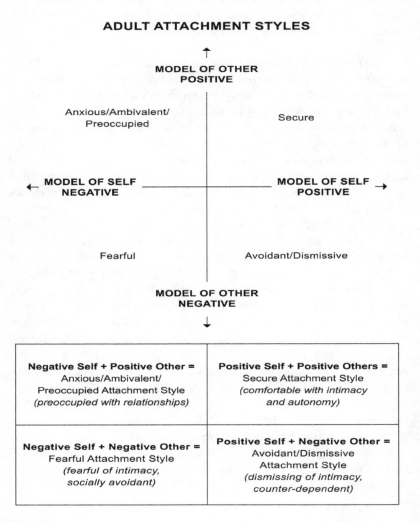

ADULT ATTACHMENT STYLES

↑

**MODEL OF OTHER
POSITIVE**

Anxious/Ambivalent/
Preoccupied

Secure

← **MODEL OF SELF
NEGATIVE** ——————————— **MODEL OF SELF
POSITIVE** →

Fearful

Avoidant/Dismissive

**MODEL OF OTHER
NEGATIVE**

↓

Negative Self + Positive Other = Anxious/Ambivalent/ Preoccupied Attachment Style *(preoccupied with relationships)*	**Positive Self + Positive Others =** Secure Attachment Style *(comfortable with intimacy and autonomy)*
Negative Self + Negative Other = Fearful Attachment Style *(fearful of intimacy, socially avoidant)*	**Positive Self + Negative Other =** Avoidant/Dismissive Attachment Style *(dismissing of intimacy, counter-dependent)*

Figure 7.1.

This information can also be understood in this way:

- Positive Self + Positive Others = Secure Attachment Style (comfortable with intimacy and autonomy)
- Positive Self + Negative Other = Avoidant/Dismissive Attachment Style (dismissing of intimacy, counter-dependent)
- Negative Self + Positive Other = Anxious/Ambivalent/ Preoccupied Attachment Style (preoccupied with relationships)
- Negative Self + Negative Other = Fearful Attachment Style (fearful of intimacy, socially avoidant)

Positive Model of Self and Positive Model of Others = Secure Attachment Style.   Securely attached adults typically display openness in expressing and sharing their thoughts and emotions with others and are both comfortable depending on others for help and comfortable when others depend on them.[26] They value relationships generally and speak openly with insight about previous relationships. They tend to describe romantic relationships as trusting and happy and are able to accept and support their partners despite their partner's faults or limitations. Their relationships tend to last longer. Research has shown that securely attached adults report warm relationships with parents during childhood.[27]

Positive Model of Self and Negative Model of Others = Avoidant/Dismissive Attachment Style.   Dismissively attached adults prefer to avoid close relationships and intimacy with others in order to maintain a sense of independence and invulnerability. Their internal working model appears to be based on an avoidant attachment established in infancy. These adults deny experiencing distress associated with relationships and downplay the importance of attachment in general. Their love relationships are characterized by fear of intimacy. They are often unsure of their feelings toward their romantic partner, believing that romantic love is not likely to last.[28] Dismissive adults suppress their emotions at the behavioral level, but still experience emotional arousal internally.[29]

Negative Model of Self and Positive Model of Others = Anxious/ Ambivalent/Preoccupied Attachment Style.   Anxiously or ambivalently attached adults strive for self-acceptance by attempting to gain approval and validation from others. They typically require higher levels of contact and typically crave intimacy. However, they remain anxious as to whether their romantic partner will meet their emotional needs.

Autonomy and independence can contribute to anxiety. Their relationships tend to be characterized by obsession, extreme sexual attraction, emotional highs and lows, jealousy, and a desire for reciprocation and union. Research has shown that anxiously attached adults had colder relationships with parents during childhood.[30]

Negative Model of Self and Negative Model of Others = Fearful Attachment Style. Fearfully attached adults display behaviors typical of avoidant children, being untrusting of others and socially withdrawn. They cope by distancing themselves from relationship partners. Such individuals prefer casual relationships and may date for prolonged periods of time. Research has shown that these individuals are likely to have more sexual partners.[31] This pattern may provide a way to get physically close without having to be emotionally vulnerable. Such individuals may be reluctant to share too much information about themselves, and if threatened with too much exposure, may rapidly shut down. They tend to expect problems in relationships but may also contribute to those difficulties by blaming partners or expressing jealousy. Research suggests that these individuals have grown up in a household that is chaotic and disruptive.[32]

While there is an indication that there is continuity in early attachment, there is also evidence that some adults evidence distinct attachment patterns in different types of relationships (friendship, romantic relationship, etc.). This suggests that attachment style may be, in part, context specific. There is also some indication that attachment style may shift over time. In a twenty-year longitudinal study,[33] researchers reevaluated young adults who had participated as infants in an earlier experiment on attachment. They found that 72 percent of the participants received the same attachment classification (i.e., secure or insecure) as they did during infancy. The majority of participants who changed attachment patterns had experienced major negative life events. This suggests a continuity of attachment patterns generally but demonstrates that a secure attachment can be undermined by negative emotional events through tragedy or trauma. The importance of setting a secure attachment in childhood cannot be overstated, and parents and caregivers should make every effort to develop that foundation for future relationships.

DEVELOPMENTAL ACHIEVEMENTS MAKE POSSIBLE
A MATURE MODEL OF LOVE AND RELATIONSHIPS:
GROWING COMPETENCE AND DECLINING
DEPENDENCE FORGE STRUCTURAL CHANGE

As a child's competence grows, he becomes increasingly self-reliant and, in the process, less dependent. Those accomplishments are accompanied by a stronger, sturdier, more capable sense of self. His changes in capability necessitate changes in the relationship, allowing the child to create a new model of love and relationships, one that is more adult-like and is increasingly *other* focused. This is the paradigm that the child will take into mature adult relationships later in life. The potential for reciprocity, balance, empathy, and caretaking are now apparent (see figure 7.2).

Matrix of Development from Dependence to Independence in the Self and Relationship

- Dependent Self + Dependent Relationship = Unequal relationship (Caretaking relationship between child and parent characterized by service by one and care provided to the other)
- Dependent Self + Independent Relationship = Undernourished relationship/lack of nurture (Child requires more support than the relationship provides)
- Independent Self + Dependent Relationship = Overnourished relationship/overindulged (Child is given more support than is needed)
- Independent Self + Independent Relationship = Equal Relationship (More mature relationship develops between child and parent characterized by empathy, reciprocity, and fairness)

Developmental Change in the Structure of the Model of Love and Relationship: A Concern for Fairness = *A Relationship of Inequality Transforms to a Relationship of Equality*

The infant begins life in a state of total helplessness, and the parental responsibility is one of complete care. Time and maturation change that paradigm. The shift from other-reliance to self-reliance is accompanied by a decrease in dependence and increase in independence, allowing the parent and other significant others to have newfound value and importance in the eyes of the child. Appreciated for more than their caretaking

MATURATION AND THE CHILD'S CHANGING MODEL OF LOVE AND RELATIONSHIPS

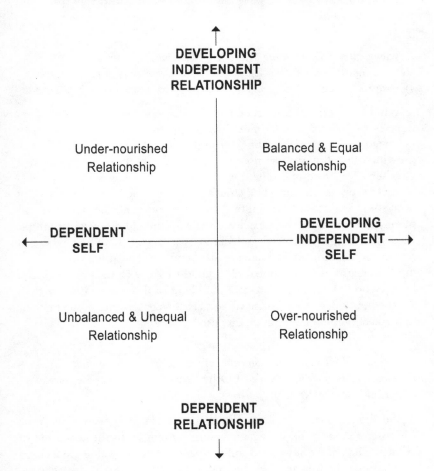

Figure 7.2.

ability, relationships broaden to include a kind of regard that involves the notion of reciprocity. The age-old adage of what is good for the goose is good for the gander is apt here, evidencing underlying notions of equality and fairness. Children will begin to share in responsibilities (i.e., "I'll take out the trash today since you did my laundry," "I'll bring the snack on Tuesday since Ellen brought it last Friday.") This is a major developmental shift. The young child's paradigm of "I need a lot, and someone must provide all of it" has shifted to "I can do my part, and you can do yours."

Developmental Change in the Structure of the Model of Love and Relationship: The Growth of Empathy = *An Egocentric Perspective Gives Way to Consideration and Valuing of the Perspective and Feelings of Others*

It is in the transition from dependence to independence and from other-reliance to self-reliance that the child begins to develop empathy. With her needs now less demanding through maturation and in the face of growing capability, she can now both see and appreciate the perspective of others. This accomplishment marks the transition away from egocentrism and self-absorption. The child's ability to "see" the perspective of others will expand to the ability to feel for another. The development of empathy increases the capacity for friendship and close relationships. Understanding is enhanced and kindness increases. Children who can feel for others tend to be kinder, more sensitive, and more understanding.[34] Empathy is foundational for a child to grow to be a good citizen in the world. They can appreciate the plight of those less fortunate than themselves and express concern for well-being beyond those in their immediate family or friendship circles.

Developmental Change in the Structure of the Model of Love and Relationship: Putting the Needs of Others First = *Selfishness Declines in Appreciation for the Needs of Others*

As the child matures, selfishness diminishes. The preoccupation with the self lessens as the child grows increasingly attentive to those outside of himself. The child's newfound ability to appreciate and value the feelings of others as much as he does his own is a major developmental milestone. With this new knowledge and competence, he is able to put the needs of others before his own, something he was incapable of doing as an infant and small child. Children will first feel for others, then exercise the ability to care for them. Concern and care for others at this higher level of engagement is a significant sign of maturation and is indicative of transformative growth, which spurs change in a multitude of directions.

I remember reading about Leonard Bernstein, the late legendary conductor of the New York Philharmonic. When asked to name the most difficult instrument to play in an orchestra, he responded with "second fiddle," the second-chair violinist who sits just behind the first chair and is second to the concertmaster. He continued: "I can get plenty of first violinists, but to find one who plays second violin with as much enthusiasm . . . now that's a problem. And yet if no one plays second, we have no harmony."[35] The maestro's clever insight is a reminder that the ability to "be second" requires great strength of character and is an essential life skill. It is a hallmark of psychological maturity and health.

Developmental Change in the Structure of the Model of Love and Relationship: Learning to Care for Others = Neediness Diminishes as the Capacity to Care for Others Grows

The transition from "self-care" to "other-care" comes with maturation and developing competence. Learning to recognize the feelings of others eventually leads to recognizing the needs of others, then to acting on those insights. Daniel Goleman describes this phenomenon aptly: "True compassion means not only feeling another's pain but also being moved to help relieve it." For the first time, a child may understand that a peer or parent needs comfort. They may have a headache or stomachache and not want to play. They may need a glass of water or want to take a rest from a game of basketball. This developmental acquisition sometimes develops unknowingly.

I am reminded of Maggie, a sixteen-year-old girl I knew, whose mother fell on the tennis court and broke her wrist. The way the circumstances unfolded, Maggie was thrust into a caretaking role. She secured ice and a firm method to support her mother's arm, then drove her to the hospital and waited during the medical procedure. Maggie spoke thoughtfully about how odd it seemed to provide the care and concern that her mother and father had provided for her over the years. A babysitter, camp counselor, and good friend, she had grown into becoming a caretaker in her own right at this young age. Development and maturation had taken its course, and the traditional parent-child roles had reversed. Maggie has the skills and abilities that any parent would wish for. Whenever time and health dictate, she will be well suited to care for aging, potentially incapacitated, parents. She has literally grown from "being taken care of" to "being a caretaker" for those she loves. She can, as a maturing adolescent, give to others what was given to her.

NARCISSISM AND THE HEALTHY OR NOT-SO-HEALTHY MODEL OF LOVE AND RELATIONSHIPS: MEASURES OF THE CHILD'S MODEL OF LOVE AND RELATIONSHIPS

Signs of a Non-narcissistic or Healthy Model of Love and Relationships

As a psychologist, I make frequent assessments or determinations about a child, or adult's, notions regarding love and relationships. Children with a healthy model of love and relationships see people as predictable and trustworthy and relationships as valuable. They take active steps to secure and maintain connection.

There are a number of measures that I look for in my clinical practice when assessing the model of love and relationships. Signs of a positive model around love and relationships include:

- A positive perception of others generally
- Belief in the predictability and reliability of others (i.e., trust)
- An interest in engaging others
- Confidence in the potential success of relationships
- Lack of fear, avoidance, or hesitation when engaging others
- Willingness to work on relationships when they encounter difficulty
- An ability to tolerate frustration in relationships
- Appreciation and understanding for the feelings of the other (i.e., empathy)
- Demonstrated capacity to put the needs of others before their own
- Evidence of caring for others without any overt request
- Interest in fair, equal, and reciprocal relationships
- Respect for the values and limits of others
- Tolerance for difference and disagreement in relationships

Signs of a Narcissistic or Not-So-Healthy Model of Love and Relationships

Children with a not-so-healthy model of love and relationships have a variety of presentations, which range from clinging behavior and over-investment to avoidance and difficulties in engagement. These seemingly contradictory characteristics all stem from an underlying negative model of love and relationships. Signs of a negative model around love and relationships include:

- Doubts about the reliability and trustworthiness of others
- Excessive focus on the other and a need for constant companionship
- High demands for interpersonal attention and engagement
- A disengaged orientation toward others, keeping people at a distance
- Struggles in building or maintaining relationships of all sorts from friendship to family
- Emphasis on a "special" relationship or better-than-others relationship
- Expectation of being taken care of without a reciprocal role mentioned
- Lack of empathy for the other in a close friendship or relationship
- A pattern of idealizing and devaluing others
- Excessive frustration when needs are not met
- Excessive desire for control in relationships
- Disrespect of others through teasing, manipulation, or threat

In terms of narcissism, I have come to understand these often seemingly inconsistent deficiencies in the model of love and relationships (i.e., ranging from doubts around consistency to both overinvestment in relationships and avoidance of others) as a function of five different but related dynamics. They involve superiority, lack of empathy, demands for compliance, needs for adoration and proof of love, and the exploitation of others.

Underlying Narcissistic Dynamic: Need for Position of Superiority Produces an Unequal Relationship = Need for a Caretaker. Many children and adults who suffer from a flawed model of love and relationships believe that relationships are unequal. The need for superiority, by definition, requires an inferior partner. I reference this paradigm as "one-up/one-down."

It typically involves a more powerful, controlling, or special, individual (i.e., the "one-up" person) who is paired with a compliant or less valued partner (i.e., the "one-down" person), who is typically the caretaker of the other and the relationship. While the forms and presentations vary, this inequality is typical in narcissistic relationships of all sorts.

Importantly, differences in power and accommodation take place in healthy relationships but shift from one partner to the other around specific tasks and activities and are arrived at through negotiation and compromise. It is the frequency and permanence of the "one up/one down" paradigm and the demanding and controlling nature of it that defines it as narcissistic.

A couple I worked with illustrates this paradigm. Max was a highly successful entrepreneur, and Jane was an equally capable, beautiful homemaker and volunteer. They had recently purchased a large home, and the wife was exhausted, having spent days packing the house. The day before the mover arrived, Max announced that he was "taking to-morrow off to help with the move." Jane was angry. She said that all the work would be done before his arrival and explained that he would only be there to "watch" the movers carry boxes. Importantly, in the prior days when she had been packing, he had steadfastly refused to help. She explained what she "knew" would happen next: Max would announce to their friends and extended family that he had "helped" with the move, offered as evidence of his being a "good husband." In the course of our work together, I would learn that this was an ongoing pattern: he gave direction, and she executed the tasks or created the activities, and then he claimed himself to be an equally involved partner and full contributor. This imbalance in their relationship was a recurring source of conflict and frustration.

An elderly woman whom I visited in a rest home shared a story that illustrates the contrasting healthy paradigm. She reminisced with me, explaining that when she was in elementary school the teacher had a quotation posted on the bulletin board. It read: "A gentleman is some-one who is equally kind to everyone regardless of their station in life and regardless of whether they could be of any use to them." Beyond the politically incorrect aspects of a generationally old and now dated story, the kernels of truth are evident. Healthy relationships do not derive from status or utility but are based on equality. A healthy relationship is one that nurtures both partners; fulfills both sets of needs; and attends to the goals, interests, and desires of each through a process of give-and-take.

Underlying Narcissistic Dynamic: Lack of Empathy and a Disregard for the Feelings of Others. Empathy involves the identification of and appreciation for the feelings, thoughts, and attitudes of another person. Self-centeredness and superiority interfere with empathetic responses. A lack of empathy and disregard for the feelings of others is a common component in a narcissistic relationship. In such relationships, one person is focused on their needs being met and is typically unconcerned with the needs of the other.

I am reminded of Sean, a lawyer I treated in my practice who had contacted me over recurring marital struggles. When I interviewed Sean's wife, I learned that her chief complaint and ongoing frustration was his "self-focus." Sue identified a pattern of behavior that involved putting "his needs" above those of the family. He was a runner and a triathlete and ran several miles every Saturday morning. If the children's athletic events conflicted with his run, he chose to "get in" his miles and not attend the sporting event. Sean insisted that Sue attend those events so "someone" from the family would be there. He rationalized his lack of attendance as "necessary for his health" as he had a highly stressful, demanding job. He felt that this explanation should be sufficient for Sue and the children.

A story about a high school freshman illustrates the contrasting healthy model. Brook played Bob in a match for the final spot on the freshman tennis team. Bob was an accomplished, highly competitive player. When Brook arrived home from the match, his mother asked how it went. He explained that he won, but she did not know what to make of the distressed look on his face. "Mom, he's better than me. He plays matches all over the state. This is *his* sport. Now he won't make the team. I'm not sure what to do. I don't know if I should take the spot." His mother asked, "But you won? Fair and square? Right?" Brook responded, "But Mom, I played select soccer, and I know what it *means* to care about something and have it just out of reach." Brook set up a meeting to talk to the coach and explained the situation. He decided it would be better if he gave up his position and let Bob take the spot if that was the only way for Bob to make the team. This clearly precocious adolescent was developing into a thoughtful and sensitive young man. His well-developed empathy guided his behavior.

Underlying Narcissistic Dynamic: Demands for Compliance and Agreement from Others.   Many narcissistic relationships are characterized by unequal status, one acting as caretaker and another acting as the receiver of care. Such an arrangement is not predicated on mutuality but rather compliance. Caretaking involves not only compliance but also agreement on values, activities, attitudes, and opinions.

I am reminded of a lesbian couple that I treated. One of our sessions focused on the anger that Anne had for her partner, Georgia, who did not particularly like New York City. Anne, a woman of wealth, visited the city often, taking in the opera, ballet, and art on a regular basis. Georgia was willing to go along in those activities but explained that she preferred places that provided more outdoor activities such as Montana or Colorado. Anne was angry that Georgia did not join her in her appreciation of New York. She believed that Georgia should shift her thinking and "like New York" out of affection for her. To not appreciate the city as fully as she did was unacceptable and insulting to her.

The contrasting healthy model is noticeably different, with affection, not demands for compliance, as the primary emotional driver. One of my patients, a seventy-year-old man named Tim, underwent an orthopedic procedure and needed some assistance getting to the doctor and doing certain exercises. His thirty-year-old daughter Sarah helped out when she could. Tim told me that he thanked Sarah for helping with his care. He shared her response with me: "You cared for me a long time ago. Of course, I'll care for you—now or whenever." Over the course of my practice, I have come to differentiate between different types of attitudes in caregivers who manage their elderly parents. Those who have had secure attachments do not typically experience their care for the parent as a burden but rather as a way to express their affection and appreciation for the earlier kindnesses extended to them. Those who have had less positive attachments tend to see caretaking as a weighty responsibility that they do out of duty, not affection.

Underlying Narcissistic Dynamic: Need for Adoration and Proof of Love.   Human beings want and need to feel loved and appreciated in their primary relationship. However, in a narcissistic relationship, the demands for positive regard are excessive, which is seen in needs for adoration and support for their exceptionality. They want to be seen as the best lover, partner, or friend. A failure to reinforce their specialness and their superiority is seen as an offense, taken as a blow to both the self-concept and self-esteem. I typically describe this process in my work with patients as demands for "proof of love." It can take different forms. One involves being provided with the needed adoration and the other involves anger over perceived slights.

I once treated a couple that struggled with narcissistic issues, and each of them kept lists in their minds of the other's emotional failures—the time he forgot her birthday, the dress he bought in a color he "should have known" she hated, his failure to know the kind of tea she drank after fifteen years of marriage. His list was equally long—her failure to "want" to include his parents for Thanksgiving, her "mean words" that accused him of being "selfish," her failure to thank him for the expensive diamond bracelet without being prompted. Interestingly, none of these offenses ever came off the list over their years of marriage. They were kept there and simply relitigated each time they had an argument. Not surprisingly, they each accused the other of "not being loving." It soon became apparent that neither could hold on to the feeling of being loved in the face of a perceived insult from the other.

Interestingly, secure relationships do not require ongoing reinforcement of each partner's worth. If value and affection are regarded as givens, there is an absence of demands for compelling positive regard and an absence of injury over slights or insults. I discuss this process in therapy with patients through a story: "Imagine that it is your wife's birthday and Aunt Matilda's birthday, both on the same day. Aunt Matilda is a much-loved relative who is lonely and in need of attention. You have been busy and have planned poorly. It is *only* possible to purchase and deliver one gift. Whom do you get a gift for?"

Many couples respond that the wife should be given the gift as she is "more important." The better answer is Aunt Matilda. With couples who have a secure relationship and who have confidence in each other's affection, one partner's poor planning would be explained, integrated, and understood. Alternate strategies would be accepted—a handwritten note, the playful singing of a love sonnet, or a shower of kisses would suffice until a proper gift could be gotten. Aunt Matilda, on the other hand, is an old lady and would be mightily hurt by the oversight. In a secure relationship, both partners would understand that and mobilize their efforts toward the greater good and beyond their own needs and feelings. In other words, partners do not require ongoing proof of love and can tolerate small blows and disappointments in the light of their mutual regard.

Underlying Narcissistic Dynamic: Using Others to Meet Their Own Needs. Narcissistic relationships are typically characterized by use of the other to meet their own desires. Others are valued instrumentally as a means to achieve goals. In a sense, these relationships have an exploitative quality. The narcissist requires the other to fulfill their own expectations and, in the process, is unconcerned with the needs of the other. This often involves boundary violations: an overstepping of the bounds of an appropriate request into an inappropriate demand. I conceptualize this aspect of the narcissistic relationship in terms of antagonism, which is defined in biology as an interaction between organisms so that one organism benefits at the expense of another. Such interactions serve an evolutionary purpose in the animal kingdom, but in relationships, they create interpersonal conflict, dissatisfaction, and estrangement.

I know of a woman who made fresh cookies for her husband every day. That certainly sounded like a daunting task, but I later learned that it impacted her life in an even larger way. She was not able to go on solo trips with her girlfriends or family because her husband wanted the cookies "fresh" and was unwilling to accept them in any other form.

The contrasting healthy model involves reciprocity. Difficulties are resolved through compromise and negotiation, with each partner having an opportunity to have their needs met at various times and in various ways over the course of the relationship. I am reminded of a couple who struggled over where to live. They actually struck a compromise that involved living in his preferred location for a set number of years, then moving to her preferred location for another number of years. Such negotiations do not necessarily require such large or equivalent solutions, but the process is what matters. Each person felt heard, understood, and respected throughout the problem-solving discussions, and satisfied with the conclusion.

A HEALTHY MODEL OF LOVE AND RELATIONSHIPS: EXAMPLES FROM CHILDHOOD

In my practice, I make assessments of a patient's "model of love and relationships" on a regular basis. In most instances, I am making this determination to inform my work with the patient, whether the person is a child in play therapy, an adult in traditional therapy, or a couple in marital therapy. Learning a person's attitude toward others is invaluable in terms of "knowing" them and establishing a therapeutic alliance. As might be expected, a working relationship is more easily established with a securely attached person than an insecurely attached one. From the outset, I need to know whether the patient can trust me and how hard I must work to establish and maintain that trust.

I have developed a number of informal measurements, which consist of a set of questions that have been administered to hundreds, if not thousands, of patients. I routinely ask children: "Tell me the three things you like most about your mother." "Tell me the three things you like least about your mother." I am searching here for information about the primary attachment figure and working to understand that first attachment. Then I typically ask: "Tell me the three things you like most about your father." "Tell me the three things you like least about your father." I am searching here for information about the secondary attachment figure or to determine if he might be the primary attachment figure. Then I ask if there was any other "important person" in their early life—a nanny, grandmother, or live-in aunt. Then I ask the same questions involving their three most liked and disliked qualities. In this series of questions, I am trying to identify the child's early notion of love and how it was experienced in childhood, knowing that this understanding has likely set the stage for later relationships.

Below are a few samples of things I like to hear from children as they share their ideas about the most important people in their young lives. Both mothers and fathers are referenced individually.

Concerning Mother

Four-Year-Old Shaeffer

She reads my favorite book over and over every night.
She cuddles with me, and we listen to music in bed.
She likes my drawings of pictures or airplanes, rockets, planets, and bugs. She hangs them up on the refrigerator.

She makes me go to bed at 7:30 and I don't like it.
She sends me to timeout if I'm mean to my sister.
She makes me eat vegetables. I hate them.

Eight-Year-Old Bart
She kisses me goodnight every night and scratches my back.
She lets me build tunnels and caves out of chairs and blankets and
    pillows. One time she actually crawled inside it. That was funny.
She taught me to make my favorite chocolate cake.

She makes me do my homework and won't let me play until it's
    done.
She makes me read books in the summer when it's too hot to play
    outside.
She gets mad if I don't put my clothes in the hamper or brush my
    teeth every day.

Twelve-Year-Old Rick
She comes to my baseball games and tells me I played great even
    when I didn't strike out a single batter or walked in a run. She
    tells me she loves me anyway. She's like that.
She let me build a treehouse and then let me spend the night in it
    last Friday.
She helped me build paper chains for the Christmas tree and a big
    star with foil on the top.

She won't let me have candy every day when I'm playing golf.
She makes me sweep the driveway and do other jobs for my al-
    lowance.
She makes me write thank-you notes.

Fifteen-Year-Old Nora
She always listens to me and never makes me feel bad about my-
    self—even when I did a pretty dumb thing.
She believes that people can learn from their mistakes and that
    things will always get better—that your dreams can come true.
If I ask her to help me, she always tries. She talks to me about boys
    and what she did when she was my age.

She won't let me ride in cars with boys who already have their
    license. That's not a fair rule.
She sticks to the curfew even when I'm having a really good time.
She won't let me wear magazine makeup or super-short skirts.

Concerning Father

Four-Year-Old Emily

He tickles me at the funny part of the books he reads to me. We laugh lots.

He sings songs to me and makes up silly words.

He helped me build a castle with pillows and sheets and played with me inside it. I dressed up as a princess, and he pretended he was the king.

He raises his voice and tells me to stop when I pull the dog's tail.

He makes me clean up if I splash water in the bathtub.

He makes me put my books back on the shelf and eat all the green vegetables.

Eight-Year-Old George

He thinks I'm great and tells me he loves me.

He let me build a treehouse with scraps from the new house next door.

He taught me how to build a fire for cooking hot dogs.

I have to help him rake the yard and take out the trash.

When I build things, he makes me clean up the mess and take care of all the tools.

He won't let me leave my bicycle out in the rain or stand up in the boat when we're fishing.

Twelve-Year-Old Connie

He listens to me. If I ask him, he'll tell me how a boy thinks.

He does what I ask him to if it's really important, like driving the carpool to the dance and not saying a single word.

He loves me and helps me work to get the things I want. He believes I can do important things just as well as a boy.

He doesn't like it when I'm mean to my friends and always says I should apologize.

He won't let me stay out late at my friend's house on school nights.

He won't let me ride my bicycle after dark.

Fifteen-Year-Old Harold
He taught me to fish, hunt birds, and drive a tractor.
He talks to me about growing up—standing up for what's important. He doesn't tell me what to believe in but says I have to figure that out for myself.
He remembers what it's like to be a kid. We talk about the difference between being scared and acting stupid and when to back down from a dare.

He won't let me speak rudely to adults or tease younger kids.
He gets mad and won't let me make excuses when I don't do my work.
He tells me I should tell the truth and never lie about anything.

What these show is a fundamental belief in the strength and benevolence of love. It is both valued and sought after by the child. Interactions are characterized by trust and predictability. To the extent that growth and health are imperative, the availability of love is assumed. This is the foundation of trust. These significant others, most often parents, are present as steady sources of support and guidance. Equally important, they are seen as having both strengths and weaknesses and thereby evidencing an integrated and realistic view of the parent. Emotional closeness is ever present in all the mundane acts of engagement and intimacy.

THE INJURED, NOT-SO-HEALTHY MODEL OF LOVE AND RELATIONSHIPS: EXAMPLES FROM CHILDHOOD

The injured, not-so-healthy model of love and relationships can be reflected on both ends of a continuum with unrealistic, perfection-seeking, or better-than-other orientations at one end of the spectrum, and an untrusting, negative attitude marked by ambivalence, anxiety, avoidance, or dislike at the other. Below are the kinds of things I worry about when I hear them from children as they self-report about these most important people.

Concerning Mother

Six-Year-Old Donald
She loves me soooo much. Just ask her.
She says I'm the best kid ever.
She makes whatever I want for dinner

I get mad at her when she doesn't get me what I want. Most of
the time she does.
She sleeps late on Sunday when I want to get donuts.
She makes me visit Grandpa, and he's really old and boring.

Nine-Year-Old Melody
My mother is perfect. She is totally beautiful, and everybody likes
her.
She buys me wonderful clothes. See these shoes? She picked them
out. They're all the best.
When my friends come over, she lets us stay up really late.

I can't really think of anything bad about my mom. She's perfect.
There's nothing wrong with her. I mean it.
She's the best.

Sixteen-Year-Old Carl
She's ok—not that nice.
She loses her temper a lot and argues with Dad.
They say her mother was just like her—mean.

Well, the list of negatives is long [he laughs].
She doesn't really like me that much.
She says she'll be glad when I'm in college. She says she doesn't
mean it, that she's just teasing. She's not.

Concerning Father

Six-Year-Old Jonathan
He has a big job, and we have a big house.
He is tall and good looking. They say I look like him.
He drives a cool car. It's fast.

He works all the time. My mother says he wants to be there.
He corrects me and gets mad when I make a mistake.
He says I'm mean to my sister when I'm not.

Nine-Year Old Cindy
He's the best dad ever.
He gets me cool stuff and doesn't care how much it costs.
He takes me to play miniature golf whenever I want.

I don't have many negatives.
Well, he works a lot and he's gone a lot.
Sometimes he yells at my mom.

Fifteen-Year-Old Dylan
My dad is rich—and I mean, really rich.
We have a cool house at the beach.
We fly there private.

My dad says my grades suck and gets mad at me.
My dad expects me to be perfect like he was.
My dad yells—I wish he didn't. It doesn't help.

These responses reflect problems in a variety of ways. In some cases, the parent is seen as perfect, and there is a family orientation toward being the best or better-than-others. In other cases, the parent provides "things" that are understood by the child as a form of connection and has adopted an indulgent understanding of meaningful interaction. In still other cases, the parent is mean, distant, critical, and/or volatile.

STRATEGIES FOR PARENTS: BUILDING A NON-NARCISSISTIC MODEL OF LOVE AND RELATIONSHIPS IN THE CHILD

While education and instruction matter, the behaviors and attitudes that parents model have a greater impact on the development of a child's understanding of love and relationships. Parents may preach that the children should be kind to others, but if they are not kind to their spouse, the message will not hold. If they teach that empathy is a valuable skill but do not demonstrate it with the child, the lesson is likely lost. If they educate about the importance of fairness in friendship but do not treat the child fairly, the words are not likely to influence. In terms of the development of a healthy or not-so-healthy understanding of love, what the parents do, demonstrate, and show remains the primary vehicle of influence.

In order to avoid the development of narcissistic tendencies, traits, and disorders, there is ongoing evidence that suggests parents should be invested in strategies that build a positive model of love and relationships. The following understandings are derived from the findings and implications of both theory and research as well as my long experience working with narcissistic children, adults, and families.

Negative Impacts

The Negative Impact of Both Overnurture and Undernurture.   The process of nurturing, caring, and providing for the child over the years is complicated, as the child's growing skills and abilities demand changing accommodation. Nurturance is best understood on a continuum with errors that can be made on either extreme. A child who is inadequately nurtured suffers in terms of security and self-concept. However, too much attention can also compromise development, with expectations arising out of overindulgence. In a healthy relationship, love must remain constant, and the quality and degree of support must match the child's evolving developmental needs.

The Negative Impact of Treating a Child as Special as Well as Judging a Child Too Harshly.   Parents are presented with an often-challenging balancing act: they must communicate their love to the child without treating them as special but also without limiting or judging them too harshly. This balance must be struck between providing love and limits such that the child's treatment does not build notions of exceptionality and superiority or inferiority. Setting a standard for loving relationships that demands consistently extraordinary treatment is certain to fail in the larger world. Similarly, setting a model that is void of minimally sufficient nurture is also hurtful. The child must believe that she is loved just the way she is and that her successes will be celebrated and her failures accepted and understood. Getting this balance right is critical as the quality of that early parent-child relationship will set the stage for other relationships.

The Negative Impact of Parenting That Does Not Match the Child's Competence, Capability, and Need for Support.   The nature of child development makes parenting an ever-changing task. Children must be supported until they can master various skills and abilities and then learn to exercise those behaviors independently. Parents push their child on the swing set until a child learns how to "pump" on their own. Parents prepare food for their children when they are preschoolers but must later teach them how to make their own sandwich and pack their own lunch. Parents organize weekend activities but then teach their children how to organize their own calendars as they mature. This back-and-forth, iterative process of mastery means that parenting must be ever flexible to allow independence to flourish. Even more complicating is the fact that, temperamentally, some children push harder for independence and personal mastery while others tend to give in to parental care. Styles of "fit" between parent and children are almost endlessly varied.

The Negative Impact of Modeling Unhealthy Relationships. As human beings work to carve out a connection that works for both parties, there is always struggle and disappointment. Parents sometimes lose their cool, say things they wish they had not, behave childishly, and fail to display their "best" selves. These negative behaviors are part of living and are easily integrated into a child's secure and stable model of love. However, if they become habitual, they will be integrated into the child's life and set the stage for dysfunctional relationships.

Positive Impacts

The Positive Impact of Developing a Trusting Relationship Based on Warmth and Reliability. The foundation for trust is established in early relationships with the parents. If parents are sensitive and responsive to their child's needs, the child develops a sense of security, a core belief that the world is a safe place where others can be relied on. In the process, they come to feel that they are worthy of being cared for and loved. There is evidence that parents shape their children's beliefs about trust.[36] Parental behaviors that build trust include overall warmth and sensitivity, as well as predictable and reliable caretaking.

No relationship is perfect. Both parent and child must find ways to steady conflict and repair around injury. Research suggests that the frequency of parental conflict is not necessarily the problematic variable, but rather is evidence that the conflict is not resolved. I like to imagine an argument in a highly verbal, expressive, stereotypically warm and loving Italian family with a mother and a father raising their voices and waving their arms in heated debate. A compromise is struck, and the couple ends up in a huge hug filled with kisses and words of reconnection. This kind of conflict does not injure children but rather teaches not only that conflict is part of living, but that it is manageable and survivable. Security and steadiness remain unshaken when connections are threatened. Love can thus be sustained through conflict and disappointment. This example is clearly not an ideal situation or the best form of conflict resolution, but it is a reminder that even less-than-perfect management can be neutralized.

The Positive Impact of Modeling and Teaching Empathy. Empathy is a critical component in all human relationships. It has been shown to improve the quality of family relationships, enhance satisfaction in intimate relationships, decrease family problems, and build cohesion in groups. Parental empathy has been shown to build close family ties as well as reduce children's aggressive and "acting out" behaviors.[37] Teaching empathy to the child develops compassion, encourages prosocial behavior (i.e., helping others in need, feeling for those in distress, etc.), and improves the child's capacity for establishing and maintaining meaningful connections with others.

The Positive Impact of Modeling Healthy Relationship Behaviors in Marriage and Friendships. Parents can model healthy relationships through friendship and marriage. Healthy partners rely on each other and give each other the benefit of the doubt. They acknowledge different points of view and engage in meaningful give-and-take. They "fight fair" and resolve arguments by solving problems and identifying solutions. They demonstrate confidence in themselves and each other. They value each other and establish appropriate boundaries. They balance self-care with other-care. They rely on each other for support and affection. They are satisfied with and content in the relationship.

Observation of such a healthy partnership communicates a larger message to the child—people are good, and relationships are valuable. It is important to emphasize that children can also learn about healthy relationships through learning from observation of others outside the immediate family. If children have been exposed to parental conflict through divorce or other difficult circumstances, the child can still develop a positive model of love and understanding of relationships through interactions with, and observation of, other significant people.

EIGHT TAKEAWAYS FOR PARENTS TO BUILD A POSITIVE MODEL OF LOVE AND RELATIONSHIPS IN THE CHILD

1. Model healthy relationship behaviors in friendship, work, and marriage.
2. Treat your child with warmth and sensitivity.
3. Provide reliable and predictable caretaking.
4. Do not set or model unrealistic expectations for love relationships through adoration or specialness.
5. Value fairness in relationships through mutual respect and appropriate boundaries.
6. Teach empathy through identification and appreciation for the feelings of others.
7. Model acceptance and appreciation for different points of view in a relationship.
8. Treat all relationships as valuable and work to maintain them.

THE OUTCOME: "AN OPERATIONAL HANDBOOK BUILT ON TRUST" AS A METAPHOR

Over the years, the child has fleshed out his "Operational Handbook" with pictures, paradigms, and observations. Built on trust, it has spelled out the rules of love and the operating principles for relationships. A positive handbook has concluded that people are trustworthy and reliable, that love is a worthy and wonderful endeavor, and that relationships should be sought after and valued. But even more importantly, it has differentiated and reinforced more mature forms of connection. It understands healthy relationships are characterized by equality, mutual respect for each other's needs, a concern for fairness, the development of empathy, the ability to put the needs of others before their own, and a willingness and ability to care for others. Each of these accomplishments is noteworthy and essential for emotional health and continued growth.

The "Operational Handbook" is relied upon by the adolescent and young adult exploring important love relationships beyond the immediate family. The process of dating and developing deeper connections with others allows the handbook to become more sophisticated and better differentiated. It will direct marriage and friendship choices, enabling the young adult to make more practiced assessments of individuals that guide decisions as to those who should be sought after and those who should be distanced from.

When I lecture, I challenge parents to imagine what their son's or daughter's handbook might say. It has proven to be an excellent tool for helping parents evaluate their own parenting behaviors, as well as set their goals for future education and modeling. One mother told me, "I hope Brian understands that issues can be talked through and solved. I'm afraid he'll think that arguing, like I do with his dad, is how relationships work." Another father told me, "I hope Ellen knows I love her. I mean I only correct her and criticize her because I want her to be the best she can be." Still another said, "I tell him I love him. I hope that's enough." The metaphor of the "Operational Handbook" is an excellent way to consider and concretize the love lessons we hope to be both modeling and teaching.

III

STRATEGIES TO DEFEAT CHILDHOOD NARCISSISM

· 8 ·

General Parenting Styles Associated with Positive and Negative Outcomes

Styles of Parenting

*Y*ears ago, I treated a patient who suffered from incapacitating anxiety around parenting. Every session, she tore herself apart, wondering if yesterday's scolding or last week's mismanagement would injure her child forever. Although my patient's distorted thinking often brought her to extreme, inaccurate conclusions—"there are literally a thousand ways I can mess up my kid"—her confusion and angst bring up a valid point. How many types of parenting practices are out there? How do professionals categorize them? Are some parenting styles better for children than others?

The four structures addressed in this book involving the development of the self, feelings, perception, and relationships are all influenced by parents. Parenting practices assume the goals of ensuring the child's health and safety, preparing the child for life as a productive adult, and transmitting cultural values. Parents adopt broad-based child-rearing strategies, which can be understood as their standard, or characteristic, ways of dealing with children and childhood issues.

Within the large body of research that has investigated parenting strategies, the work of Baumrind is most relevant to our discussion of narcissism. Through research regarding parenting styles, she identified and investigated specific parenting practices and child outcomes.[1] Parenting "styles" describe the ways parents interact with their child and consider a number of dimensions. She identified three parenting styles—authoritative, authoritarian, and permissive. Later studies identified a fourth parenting style—neglectful.

189

FOUR TYPES OF PARENTS

The Authoritative Parenting Style

Authoritative parents are accepting and warm, but clearly set limits and expectations. Support—rather than control, punishment, or criticism—is used to encourage children. These parents place a high value on social responsibility, self-regulation, and cooperation. They tend to promote autonomy by encouraging independent problem solving.

The Authoritarian Parenting Style

Authoritarian parents typically rely on inflexible, strict rules in the household and regard discipline as the most important and effective parenting practice. They avoid negotiation with the child and focus on obedience. They typically are disinterested in the child's point of view and/or in exploring differences between them.

The Permissive Parenting Style

Permissive parents tend to be responsive to the demands of their children but are reluctant to exercise control over them. They fail to set firm limits or monitor children's activities closely. They do not insist on appropriate behavior and tend to avoid confrontation. While encouraging creativity and individuality, these parents do not set standards in the form of discipline.

The Neglectful Parenting Style

Neglectful parents take on a limited parenting role. They spend little time in conversation, play, or other activities with the child, being largely uninvolved in the child's life. There tend to be few rules in such households. Children do not receive much guidance, nurture, or attention.

A number of specific parenting behaviors (such as overprotection, support, restrictiveness, responsiveness, and enforcement of rules) describe various parenting styles. Over the years, researchers have identified "warmth" and "control" (generally understood as the setting of limits) as important factors in each parenting style. I have presented the four parenting styles in terms of the essential elements of warmth and limit setting in the following list:

> *Warmth and Limits as Critical Elements in Parenting Styles*
> Warmth + Limits = Authoritative
> Lack of Warmth + Limits = Authoritarian
> Warmth + Lack of Limits = Permissive
> Lack of Warmth + Lack of Limits = Neglectful

FOUR TYPES OF PARENTS: A LOOK AT OUTCOMES

Baumrind's research has consistently shown that children of authoritative parents have the most favorable developmental outcomes. Authoritarian and permissive parenting are both associated with negative developmental outcomes. Children of neglectful parents have the poorest developmental outcomes. These findings have been replicated by other researchers.

The Authoritative Parenting Style

The authoritative parenting style has consistently been associated with positive outcomes in children, including emotional and social competence (involving resilience, optimism, self-esteem, and self-reliance) and academic achievement.[2] Children from authoritative homes have better social skills, higher grades, balanced attitudes about achievement, less depression, and lower rates of substance abuse than children from either permissive or authoritarian households.[3]

The Authoritarian Parenting Style

The authoritarian parenting style has been correlated with negative outcomes such as aggression, delinquent behaviors, anxiety, and somatic complaints.[4] While children from authoritarian homes tend to be conforming and obedient, they also evidence high rates of depression, poor social skills, and low self-esteem.[5]

The Permissive Parenting Style

The permissive parenting style has shown association with internalizing psychological problems (including anxiety, depression, somatic complaints, and withdrawal) and externalizing behavior problems (including delinquency and school misconduct).[6] However, it has also shown a positive association with problem solving and social skills.[7] While children from permissive homes can be likable and social, they tend to be impulsive, immature, and less able to understand and accept the consequences of their actions.

The Neglectful Parenting Style

Children of neglectful parents have shown the least favorable outcomes in many areas, including limited self-regulation and social responsibility, social incompetence and poor self-reliance, antisocial behavior and delinquency, and anxiety and depression.[8] Children from neglectful homes tend to have low self-esteem and limited self-confidence, and often seek inappropriate role models in what may be an effort to substitute for the neglectful parent.

BEYOND PARENTING STYLES: CRITICAL DIMENSIONS OF PARENTING

Additional research involving factor analytic techniques has identified two specific parenting dimensions—parental support and parental control—derived from the various parenting styles. These global measures have then been sorted into more specific subsets of parental behavior.

Parental *support* describes the emotional nature of the parent-child relationship as indicated by warmth, involvement, emotional availability, acceptance, and responsiveness.[9] Support has been related to positive developmental outcomes in terms of the prevention of alcohol abuse and deviance, depression and delinquency, and acting-out behaviors.[10]

Parental *control* has been divided into two subcategories: behavioral control and psychological control. *Behavioral control* generally consists of attempts to guide or regulate child behavior through enforcing rules, disciplinary strategies, rewards and punishments, or supervision.[11] Those results are nuanced and necessitate careful examination, as the type and extent of control can contribute both negatively and positively. An appropriate amount of behavioral control has a positive effect on child development, while both insufficient control (i.e., poor parental monitoring) or excessive behavioral control (i.e., parental physical punishment) have been correlated with deviant behavior, misconduct, depression, and anxiety.[12]

Psychological control pertains to an intrusive type of control in which parents attempt to manipulate children's thoughts, feelings, and emotions.[13] It includes guilt induction, love withdrawal, and intrusiveness. Such parental control, likely due to its manipulative and intrusive nature, has been associated with depression, antisocial behavior, and relationship problems.[14]

TWO "TAKEAWAYS" FROM THE RESEARCH ON PARENTING STYLES

Decades of research on parenting styles generates a variety of important insights for parents. The data consistently recognizes the importance of parental support as seen in the development of a warm, loving, and trusting relationship with the child and the importance of parental control as seen in age-appropriate limit setting and age-appropriate supervision.

Takeaway 1: The Importance of a Healthy Emotional Connection (Getting the Relationship Right through Warmth, Understanding, Acceptance, and Love)

Due to the variety of terms used throughout the literature, it is often difficult to describe the essential aspects of a healthy parent-child relationship. Baumrind, the original theorist and researcher on parenting styles, uses the term *warmth* as a defining aspect of parenting. Later research on parental practices refers to *support* as a most important factor in the relationship. Still other terms are favored by developmental theorists. Erikson, in his theory of psychosocial development, uses the term *trust* to characterize the essential aspect of the relationship typically developed with the mother in infancy. Maslow, in his theory of human motivation, references the term *love and belonging* as an essential life task. Bowlby and Ainsworth use the term *secure attachment* to describe the early bonding between parent and child. Finally, numerous authors use the term *unconditional love* to describe a related relationship quality. The number of terms used by both theoreticians and researchers often makes summarizing difficult and drawing conclusions even more complicated.

Components of a Healthy Parent–Child Relationship
Warmth refers to a relationship involving caring and fondness.
Emotional support refers to the process of aiding, protecting, sustaining, or helping another.
Love and belonging refers to a relationship involving feelings of deep affection.
Predictability refers to an individual in a relationship who behaves in expectable, consistent, reliable ways.
Affection refers to feelings toward another involving liking and tenderness.
Security refers to a state of being free from danger or threat in a relationship.
Trust refers to confidence in a person and the relationship process.
Attachment refers to the establishment of a deep and enduring emotional bond.

As the list indicates, the secure parent–child relationship consists of interrelated themes around the quality of involvement, understanding, acceptance, and the ongoing sense of being loved. It is important to recognize that these themes and connections are communicated on different levels and in different ways as the child grows and matures. Maternal or paternal sensitivity is essential in the relationship-building process. It includes the synchronous timing of a parent's responsiveness to the child—her emotional tone, her flexibility in behavior, and her ability to read the child's cues both verbally and nonverbally. Regardless of how the components are labeled or described, the mechanisms of connection are both subtle and powerful.

Groundbreaking researchers Beatrice Beebe and her colleagues videotaped mother–infant interactions, and then conducted a frame-by-frame analysis of their exchanges.[15] The data showed that infants at only four months of age are already extraordinarily communicative and responsive to the emotions and movements of the parent. Importantly, those early infant interaction patterns reliably predicted the child's later attachment styles. Through careful research, Beebe translated the infant's nonverbal language, as well as that of the mother, into words. Describing the communication as a kind of dance between mother and baby, she tracked the mother's and baby's signals to each other and labeled the reading of each other's cues—to advance and withdraw, to share delight and recognize frustration, to engage and avoid. The exchange between parent and child involves subtle details of interaction that are too rapid to grasp in real time with the naked eye, but this research documents the nascent connection, occurring long before verbal communication takes precedence. The complex process of moment-to-moment exchanges that will eventually be called a "relationship" sets the stage for the child's learning about herself and the nature of human interaction.

Over time, the mechanics of how a relationship is established and maintained have been addressed by theoreticians, both shaping research and encouraging the development of strategies to intervene in families for both parent educators and therapists. That work exceeds the scope of this book, but several key notions are noteworthy.

The steadiness and reliability of a healthy parent–child relationship must be secured before healthy learning can take place based on an established channel of parental influence. Children must come to *trust* in their experience of parental love. As an illustration, I remember having missed a school program in which one of my children received an award. I had been at work and had not been notified. Later that afternoon, I apologized profusely, explaining that I would have been there had I known. He looked up at me with bright eyes: *I know that, Mom. I know you love me, but you were helping your patients. It's OK.* He was only in third grade at the time, and I did not know that he already understood the steadiness of our relationship. I was prouder of him for his understanding than for the award. Such an innate awareness is more predictive of a child's future as a competent, secure, loving human being than any performance metric along the way.

A healthy relationship also allows a child the sense of *being known*. It involves an accurate knowledge of the child: *Billy is difficult when he's hungry. He loves me to scratch his back. He wants to hear the same story fifteen times. He is a great storyteller. He can be mean to his sister when she takes his toys. He puts things off and then does them at the last minute. I must say, he likes girls, I mean a lot.* The tuned-in parent knows these things about the child, and, as a result, their child feels "seen" and "heard."

The same connection of understanding and being understood exists between adults. A patient once explained to me that his wife *knew* that something was wrong when he had not called her after work. In fact, he'd had a heart attack and was in the emergency room. She had reportedly grown worried, knowing that something was amiss in their communication, a violation of an established pattern that meant something. This small comment revealed the quality of the relationship and the degree of understanding between the partners, a kind of understanding that is comforting and reassuring. Often unconscious, it is an indication of a deep connection and confidence in the predictability of each partner.

For adults, and, even more importantly for children, being known is not enough; the *permanency* of the relationship must also be realized. The child must also know that despite an incidence of bad behavior, disagreements, disobedience, angry words, and unmet expectations, the connection remains unbroken and the relationship is secure. Billy needs to know that he will be loved even if he gets a poor grade. Susie needs to know that her parents will value her even if she's not a ballerina. Tom needs to know that life will not come to an end because he called his sister a bad name. The child must experience the enduring quality of unconditional love as it plays out in her young life, building confidence in her own likeability and lovability.

Children must know that they are *loved*, but this is not always straightforward. Critically, children must know that they are loved for *who* they are, not what they *do*. This applies to both positives and negatives. Children must know that they are not loved *because* they are the valedictorian, made it to Stanford, or are a prima ballerina. They also need to know that they are loved if they did not make the select soccer team, did not get into MIT, or acted rudely to their mother. Children must know that they are valuable and important in their parents' eyes for their internal qualities, not their external accomplishments.

The relationship, with all its component parts, is the instrument of communication. It creates a forum that allows the parent to impart knowledge beyond instruction in which the child experiences, observes, learns, and grows. It is here that the lessons of belonging, trust, and affection take root. It is here that the child's foundation for basic security is set. It is here that the child's model of love and all its operational rules are both experienced and internalized.

Takeaway 2: The Importance of Limit-Setting in a Relationship (the Need for Limits and Introducing Age-Appropriate Frustration)

Another major aspect in the parent–child relationship involves limit setting or control. The term *control*, a consensus term used by many researchers investigating parent practices, can be confusing, as it has both positive and negative connotations. Moreover, there are a number of different dimensions of control depending on the quality and extent of the parental practice. In other words, exercising too much or too little of each control dimension can be problematic.

Below I have summarized the specifics of limit setting in terms of several factors.

Aspects of Parental Control/Limit Setting

Providing appropriate limits = clarifying what is expected and acceptable and establishing the consequences of not behaving appropriately.

Providing discipline = setting age-appropriate rules and expectations to create order, regulation, routines, and habits.

Providing supervision/monitoring = providing direction, oversight, and guidance.

The research consistently supports the importance of parental control as seen in age-appropriate limit setting (which is neither insufficient or excessively strict and punishing) and age-appropriate supervision.

Unlike moments of connection, discipline and limit setting are not typically met with smiles or hugs. On the contrary, children express anger, frustration, withdrawal, even contempt when they do not get their way. It is generally easier to understand the protective function of unconditional love and harder to appreciate the equally important protective function of discipline and limit setting in child development.

Throughout their lives, children must encounter hurdles that challenge adaptation and promote learning. Limits come in a variety of sizes and shapes, but they are essential for children to grow into mature, contented, and successful adults. I once worked with a young mother who came to my practice with a feisty toddler. The child's reactivity and ensuing tantrums were large, loud, and difficult to manage. The mother had simply given up disciplining the child, allowing her to break many rules and was pleased that, as a result, she had settled down. Yet somehow, she worried. Providing her child with the breakfast she demanded every day, allowing her to go to bed when she felt tired, and letting her get a snack every time they were at the grocery did stop the tantrums. The mother asked me: "Can't I just let her have her way—I mean only until she's old enough to understand the reasons why she can't do this or that? Once she understands, she won't be upset."

Over weeks, I worked with this mother to help her understand that it was the setting of limits that set the stage for emotional and structural growth—that her child needed to learn to manage her feelings, to tolerate frustration, and to count on her mother to help her through her upsetting episodes. The challenge was a difficult one, as her daughter did indeed throw herself on the grocery store floor when not allowed to get candy. We developed a progressive program, starting with small frustrations and gradually instituting more appropriate rules. It was a long and arduous experience for both mother and daughter. Today, her daughter is a young adult who tolerates rules and frustration well. In fact, she tends to be more of a rule follower than her sibs and parents—often remarking to them: "You know you shouldn't do that. It's not good for your health."

This story is a reminder that parenting is a process aimed at structure building and that short-term pain for long-term structural gain is well worth the effort. However, it is often hard to keep sight of long-term goals when the immediate frustration and level of psychic pain are very high. A child's upset, frustration, or emotional loss of control can weigh heavily on a parent exhausted from a hard day at work, one struggling with money worries, or one who is simply sleep deprived.

Limit setting, in various forms, provides frustration that is essential for the growing child to mature, providing fuel for the personality to grow as it must learn to handle a world that does not always accommodate. The first form of limit setting involves *physical* limits, which consist of prohibitions (You cannot eat food in your bedroom) and demands (You must make your bed, take out the trash, lock the front door when you get in). There are also *psychological* limits, where parents must weigh in on whether the child is the best grandchild or the most talented rider at the stable. Other limits are *environmental*, provided by the external environment to the child—when they do not get into the school they wanted to attend, when they are not tall enough to ride the roller coaster at the amusement park, when they are forced to leave the school dance when the principal announces its ending. Reactions to limit setting depend in part on the temperament of the child and also on how invested the child is in a desired outcome. Not being allowed to go to "the coolest party of the year" is much more upsetting than being denied a trip to Target for new socks.

Parents easily understand the physical limits, such as setting bedtime hours or prohibiting various unacceptable behaviors, but the nature of psychological limits is harder to grasp. I am reminded of my children, each of whom wanted to be the *best* child. I responded playfully but clearly frustratingly by saying: "You are my favorite first son. I can imagine no better first son." And: "You are my favorite second son. I cannot imagine any better second son." The meaning of my answer is clear. I refused to weigh in as to a favorite child and insisted that they each had an important place in my heart. Later my words turned into a joke. "I know I'm your favorite first son. Right, Mom?"

The challenge of being the *best* or favorite one typically plays out when little boys want to marry their mother. All of my boys wanted to marry me when they were five or six. My first two sons asked, and I explained that I loved them very much but was already married to Dad. My third son asked me the same question and I gave the same answer. "I love you very much, but I can't marry you. I'm already married to Daddy." He responded: "That's not true. You could marry me if you wanted to. I know because Jacob's mom is divorced." I knew I needed to respond and frustrate him even further, explaining the truth of the situation. I responded, "That's true, I could marry you if I wanted to. But Daddy is the one I chose to marry." Then I said the words that were hardest to say: "I love you dearly, but I don't want to marry you. Someday, you will find someone who you love and who loves you, and you will want to marry them, and they will want to marry you." This is the kind of parenting response that takes courage.

No parent wants to hurt their precious little boy or girl, to feel like they are breaking their hearts. But, paradoxically, breaking their hearts in caring, gentle, thoughtful ways allows children important opportunities to deal with frustration and learn to accept unwanted realities, both being essential steps in growing up to be healthy adults. This was one of my son's first experiences around the limits of love—that someone can love him dearly and unconditionally, but that he cannot always secure everything he desires or wants from them. This is a fundamental understanding for finding fulfillment in a love relationship with others later in life. My son, and all children, must learn that love has limits and always will. Still, love remains the most positive element of the human experience and remains a driving force for meaningful connection.

Deflating children's unrealistic belief in their skills and competencies is also important. I am reminded of Edward who was six years old, whom I treated when I was still an intern. He was placed at a special school, and he entertained fantasies of grandeur that interfered with real human connection. He stood up and lifted a light plastic school chair with feigned effort and announced to me: "See? I'm Superman and I can raise this chair." I knew that my goal was to help him realistically assess the strength involved in such a feat. I made an intervention that my supervisor would later praise. "You know, I'm not Superwoman and I think I can do that." My words were clear and to the point. I was attempting to confront his overinflated self-image gently and with kindness. But my words did not work as anticipated. He looked straight into my eyes and shrugged his shoulders. "That's too bad. I got it first." Over weeks of our work together and with many comments aimed similarly at his grandiosity, he would eventually come to soften his air of superiority.

When I tell this story in my lectures, it brings peals of laughter, but there is a serious purpose in my telling it. It is a reminder that parents can get it right with an appropriate intervention but still not achieve their goal. Child development can be resistant to change, but it should not deter our efforts, which often require time and patience before we see substantial improvement.

Many people believe that parenting is primarily an educational or caretaking process. Most do not fully understand that the quality of the relationship between the parent and the child is, perhaps, the larger influencer. In a sense, learning is taking place *in* the relationship. I have learned over decades that the better the relationship, the more receptive the child is to education and influence of all sorts. For this reason, it is critical that parents develop a healthy emotional relationship with their child.

Within that relationship, parents provide support through a series of related and reinforcing functions that teach, demonstrate, and encourage.

The Mechanics of Parenting

Nurturing = meeting the child's physical and emotional needs.

Modeling = showing the child what is important and how relationships operate through observation.

Educating = teaching the nature of love and what can be realistically expected in relationships.

Teaching values = showing and teaching what is important in love, relationships, and life.

Disciplining = limiting and modifying a child's behavior through structure and rules.

The role of parenting requires numerous skills and abilities, as well as the effort of continuing care, attention, and patience. Establishing a stable, steady, secure parent-child relationship is never easy. It is built through struggle, and upon a unique combination of affection, connection, authenticity, and firmness requiring ongoing work and constant repair. Like most things of value, it is neither easily achieved nor always rewarding. Once set, the relationship provides a kind of comfort and security that is reassuring and constant, ever steady and resistant to failure or loss. For the good of all of us, healthy, well-established relationships hold when all other things fail.

· 9 ·

Assessing the Two Critical Dimensions in N2B Parenting

Identifying and Explaining the Primary Parenting Components: View of the Child and Treatment of the Child

*T*heoreticians and clinicians have identified a number of different but related parenting behaviors that contribute to narcissism. These include under- and over-parenting; cold, controlling, and strict parenting; intrusive parenting; and permissive parenting. The state-of-knowledge is often contradictory, suggesting that narcissism may arise either from excessive parental admiration and overindulgence or from the opposite, parental neglect or rejection. This seeming paradox has led to frustration and confusion, aptly expressed by Millon: "Will the real narcissistic child please stand up?"[1]

Research to date offers support for specific aspects of each of these theories. While there is some overlap between theoretical constructs and empirical findings, there is no compelling explanation for those differences and similarities or any overarching principle to explain the divergences. While the research continues to illuminate, its piecemeal nature limits more comprehensive understanding. In the meantime, clinicians must make thoughtful decisions as to how to best intervene with children and their families.

This book has attempted to address that problem by distilling and summarizing the research on childhood narcissism in an effort to help both parents and professionals. It is through that process that I have come to my own theory of the development of narcissism. In doing so, I have come to value "moderation" and the importance of a "sliding scale."

THE IMPORTANCE OF MODERATION AS AN
ORGANIZING PRINCIPLE

Greek philosophers valued "moderation" in all things. Aristotle found fault in reliance on "absolutes" in understanding virtues and presented his emphasis on moderation in his "doctrine of the mean." In this, he referenced moral principles on a sliding scale, with one end indicating deficiency and the other indicating excess. This principle can be illustrated by consideration of courage, a quality that is, on the face of things, inherently valuable. But if seen on a continuum, where too much courage results in rashness and too little courage results in cowardice, moderation is clearly advisable. Virtue was then defined by Aristotle as the desirable middle ground between two extremes, arguing that either deficiency or excess destroys virtue. From that perspective, nothing was inherently good or bad but, rather, was dependent on the dose. The conceptualization of the "middle ground" attempts to avoid problems inherent in formulations predicated on absolutes.

Statistics also address the concept of the "middle ground" with a group of mathematical operations being classified as "measures of central tendency," each of which is considered to be a valuable and meaningful way to understand large quantities of data. The mean, median, and mode attempt to describe the conceptual middle, functional measurements intended to discern the characteristics that govern everyday information in innumerable charts and graphs.

Conceptualizations of moderation and the middle ground range from scholarship to common sense. The British pediatrician and psychoanalyst D. W. Winnicott posited the idea of the *good enough mother,* a term that reminds that the parenting goal is somewhere between perfect and deficient and places more emphasis on adequacy of the essential elements needed for a child to mature. It is seen in folklore as well, captured in the story of Goldilocks, who sought the right-sized bed, being neither too big nor too small, and the right temperature for her porridge, being neither too hot nor too cold.

Moderation, as an overarching concept in the study of complex systems, appears to be a relevant lens through which the data on narcissism can be seen, categorized, and potentially better understood.

THE IMPORTANCE OF THE CONTINUUM AS A CONCEPTUAL PRINCIPAL

Mathematicians make much of differences in scaling. For example, a scale that runs from zero to one is fundamentally different than a scale that runs from minus one to plus one, describing two completely different measures of influence. While this distinction may seem overly theoretical and academic, it has real-world implications.

Self-esteem is an excellent example. Viewing self-esteem as linear (i.e., an either/or assessment) has very different implications from viewing it on a continuum. If self-esteem is seen as binary, positive self-esteem is associated with positive outcomes, and lack of self-esteem is associated with negative outcomes. It follows, then, that efforts should always be directed toward building positive self-esteem. However, if self-esteem is understood on a continuum, the process is more nuanced, with both positive and negative countervailing influences. Embedded in such an orientation is the idea that there can be too little self-esteem (worthlessness) or too much self-esteem (grandiosity). Such a formulation would necessitate different, more differentiated interventions, not just the single-minded notion that "more is better."

These same problems play out in both clinical and research-oriented views of various parenting dimensions. For example, if parental love as measured by warmth is conceived of on an "either/or" scale, then love for a child is seen as valuable and lack of love for a child is seen as problematic. However, this conceptualization lacks gradation and does not reflect the nature of a continuum. A more nuanced model catches the subtleties of true psychological function. In this model, there is the potential for dysfunction from too little affection (i.e., neglect and harshness) as well as too much affection (i.e., enmeshment, grandiosity).

Shifting our understanding of parental influence to being on a continuum provides a more nuanced way of understanding effects on childhood narcissism and generating more effective forms of intervention.

THE PATH TO NARCISSISM: PARENTAL INFLUENCES UNDERSTOOD THROUGH THE LENS OF MODERATION

My study of the literature and years of clinical experience have led me to understand childhood narcissism as a disorder of the self, in large part resulting from the influence of extremes of parental behavior. Such a view understands parenting behavior on a continuum of influence and rejects binary assessments. Through this lens, narcissism is seen as born of treatment on "both ends" of a continuum, with each extreme being formative. Narcissists-to-be (N2Bs) either receive "too much" or "too little" of an essential something in the course of development. That maltreatment results in a sense of self that presents as either inflated or deflated and eventually, results in a model of relationships that is either unrealistically grandiose or functionally impoverished. From this per-spective, narcissism is best understood as a disorder of the self that grows to be accompanied by a defective model of love and relationships.

The path to narcissism is a complicated one since parental treatment works differently on each end of the continuum, and the child's experi-ence and narcissistic presentation varies accordingly. This likely accounts for the confusion among many professionals when they try to diagnose individual children or adults and explains why many professional inter-ventions are poorly formulated and often ineffective.

This new theory of narcissism may bring together contradictory findings among theorists and provide a coherent explanation of how and why such divergent parent behaviors can lead to the same dysfunctional result in the child. Equally important, this theory is less likely to be misinterpreted by the popular press. With an "either/or" (i.e., binary) understanding, parents are likely to extrapolate from the finding that if a positive sense of self can be built through doses of parental attention, then, therefore, more attention would be better than less. The conclu-sion based on this binary understanding, that is, if "some" is good then "more" must be better, is problematic. Any flavor of parental influence on any dimension taken to "either extreme" is dysfunctional.

The *binary perspective* generates a number of piecemeal directives that encourage the development of narcissism in the child. These include:

- Treating the child as special through overvaluation
- Being overindulgent

- Being neglectful
- Being harsh and critical
- Being psychologically controlling (i.e., intrusiveness, shaming)
- Being overinvolved

Similarly, a number of isolated directives encourage healthy development in the child.

- Establishment of a warm, nurturing relationship
- Age- and stage-appropriate limit setting
- Appropriate monitoring and supervision

The *continuum perspective* describes and explores the parental contributions to narcissism more fully in a broader and more conceptually coherent form.

- The child is either over- or under-nurtured.
- The child is either valued "too much" (being treated as special) or valued "too little" (being ignored and dismissed).
- The child experiences too few limits (indulged) or too many limits (too many strictures).
- The child receives too much attention or too little.
- The parent is over- or underinvested in the child.
- The parent is overly indulgent of the child's demands or overly dismissive of the child's needs.

These extremes can be mapped along two dimensions: the child's experience as shaped by the parent's *view of the child* (seen through attitudes and emotions), and the child's experience as shaped by the parent's *treatment of the child* (seen through their actions). In terms of shaping narcissistic development, the parent engages in behavior that is extreme, providing either too much or too little along a given dimension. In the process, the child experiences too much or too little of a given dimension, both shaping the same dysfunction.

In the end, the N2B child develops psychological structures that are formed by those extreme experiences and treatment. Those structures are, demonstrably, faulty. Children raised with either too little or too much develop a corresponding need for too little or too much, with either extreme satisfying the particular dysfunction. The outcome of either parental treatment is a structural defect in the child's sense of the self and, later, in deficits in the child's model of love and relationships. In contrast, the healthy child receives more moderate levels of these various dimensions. She receives, broadly speaking, "enough" attention, regard, affection, and frustration, which translate into healthy structures. These are then seen in a healthy sense of self and later, in a healthy model of love and relationships.

PARENTAL BEHAVIORS UNDERSTOOD
BY CATEGORY ON A CONTINUUM

I have conceptualized a number of parental behaviors that are most significant (considering theoretical writings, research findings, and/or my own clinical experience) and describe them on a continuum in terms of overarching categories (figure 9.1).

Two Critical Dimensions in Parenting: View of the Child (Parental Attitudes and Emotions) and Treatment of the Child (Parental Limit Setting and Involvement)

As indicated, there are a number of variables that are correlated with childhood narcissism. These include over- and under-nurture, being treated as special or unworthy, experiencing too few or too many limits, being seen as too valuable or not valuable enough, suffering unrealistic expectations or being deprived of any, being indulged or neglected, and suffering parental overinvestment or underinvestment. I have attempted to organize those observations in terms of two broad dimensions: view of the child (value and emotions/regard) and treatment of the child (limit setting and involvement). Each dimension has a cognitive component and an emotional component. Not surprisingly, parental thoughts and feelings are interwoven in predictable patterns.

The *view of the child* can be seen in both (a) the parent's attitudes about the child (i.e., assessments of the child's worth, value, and potential), and (b) the parent's feelings/emotions/regard for the child. The former is a more attitudinal construct, while the latter is a more emotional one.

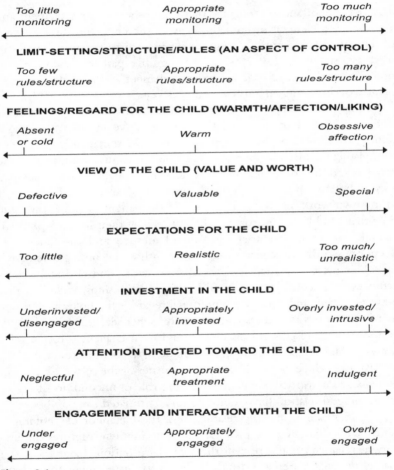

PARENTAL BEHAVIORS UNDERSTOOD ON A CONTINUUM

MONITORING OR SUPERVISION OF THE CHILD
(AN ASPECT OF CONTROL)

Too little
monitoring

Appropriate
monitoring

Too much
monitoring

LIMIT-SETTING/STRUCTURE/RULES (AN ASPECT OF CONTROL)

Too few
rules/structure

Appropriate
rules/structure

Too many
rules/structure

FEELINGS/REGARD FOR THE CHILD (WARMTH/AFFECTION/LIKING)

Absent
or cold

Warm

Obsessive
affection

VIEW OF THE CHILD (VALUE AND WORTH)

Defective

Valuable

Special

EXPECTATIONS FOR THE CHILD

Too little

Realistic

Too much/
unrealistic

INVESTMENT IN THE CHILD

Underinvested/
disengaged

Appropriately
invested

Overly invested/
intrusive

ATTENTION DIRECTED TOWARD THE CHILD

Neglectful

Appropriate
treatment

Indulgent

ENGAGEMENT AND INTERACTION WITH THE CHILD

Under
engaged

Appropriately
engaged

Overly
engaged

Figure 9.1.

The *treatment of the child* can be seen in both (a) the parent's structural efforts to manage and educate their child through the use of limits, discipline, rules, and expectations, and (b) the parent's level of engagement and involvement through shared activity and time spent together. The former is more of a cognitive construct, while the latter is a more emotional one.

It is important to recognize that there is a sustaining element and a challenging element in both the view of the child and the treatment of the child. The emotional component in each category is thought to serve as a stabilizing factor, while the cognitive part introduces frustration. The inclusion of *both* a stabilizing element and a challenging element working simultaneously together is key.

This is a concept that I borrowed from my work with graduate students. When I try to teach the most effective means of making a difficult confrontation in therapy, I describe the therapeutic alliance or trusted therapeutic relationship as the holding or sustaining part of the process, and the confrontation as the challenging part. I have developed a metaphor to capture the synergistic use of both elements. I describe it in my own work this way: "I try to hold my patient's hand at the same time that I hold up a mirror to a difficult part of their life and ask them to look carefully at what they see. When I am successful, the patient tolerates my words and reflects thoughtfully without becoming defensive."

This presents a successful therapeutic stance and also aptly characterizes an essential quality in all healthy relationships, including that between parent and child. Unconditional regard is the holding environment that allows steadiness and resolution when dealing with difficult confrontations, discussion, disruption, and even challenges to the relationship. The better the holding environment, the better stress, hardship, or tragedy—which can challenge either partner or the relationship—can be managed constructively. The stabilizing role of unconditional regard in meaningful relationships cannot be underestimated.

In maintaining healthy relationships, the metaphor of "holding a hand" while "holding a mirror" at the same moment captures the important reliance on affection in the face of frustration. In terms of the *view of the child*, parental warmth is the sustaining element that allows the child to tolerate his parent's difficult or disappointing assessments of him. Bobby must come to appreciate the limits of his athletic career if his height means he cannot be a contender, and Susie must understand that her lack of facility with auditory processing may limit her potential career as a translator.

In terms of the *treatment of the child*, the parent's warm and consistent involvement through activities and tasks is the sustaining element that allows the child to tolerate frustrating parental demands. Elliot must come to accept that he must make his bed before he goes out on Friday night. Susan must respect her father's insistence that she go to her room until she can calm down. Interestingly, the sustaining elements are all emotional in nature. The general level of involvement through shared activities and time together serves as a kind of emotional holding that calms the child when frustration and disappointment challenge them, most particularly at the hands of their own parents.

The two dimensions noted, *view* of the child and *treatment* of the child, can each be seen along a continuum. This means assessing the parent's view of the child from too negative to too positive, from too critical to too grandiose, and from coldness to excessive warmth. Similarly, this means assessing the parent's treatment of the child from excessively rule bound and disciplined to overly lax in limit setting and structure as well as limited engagement to overinvolvement.

Broad Component One: View of the Child (Parental Attitudes and Emotions).   The *view of the child* is made up of two components. The cognitive or attitude component involves the child's relative importance or value as seen through the parent's eyes. The emotional component involves feelings that extend from coldness to excessive warmth (see figure 9.2).

Any particular parent's *view of their child* through attitudes and emotions can be reflected on this axis. I remember a mother who clearly idealized her eight-year-old son. In our conversation, she enumerated his many skills and talents, his long list of awards and recognitions, and proudly announced that she believed he would be the "first Jewish president of the United States." Her view of the child would land on the far-right side of the chart's axis in terms of both affection and expectation.

I also remember a handsome, former high school football star whose seven-year-old son was standing on the soccer field near the box fiddling with his jersey and looking up at a bird while the ball whirled right past him. His head was clearly not in the game, and the father remarked to another father with a pained smile and obvious sarcasm, "Great, there's Reed standing there with his thumb up his ass. If I were

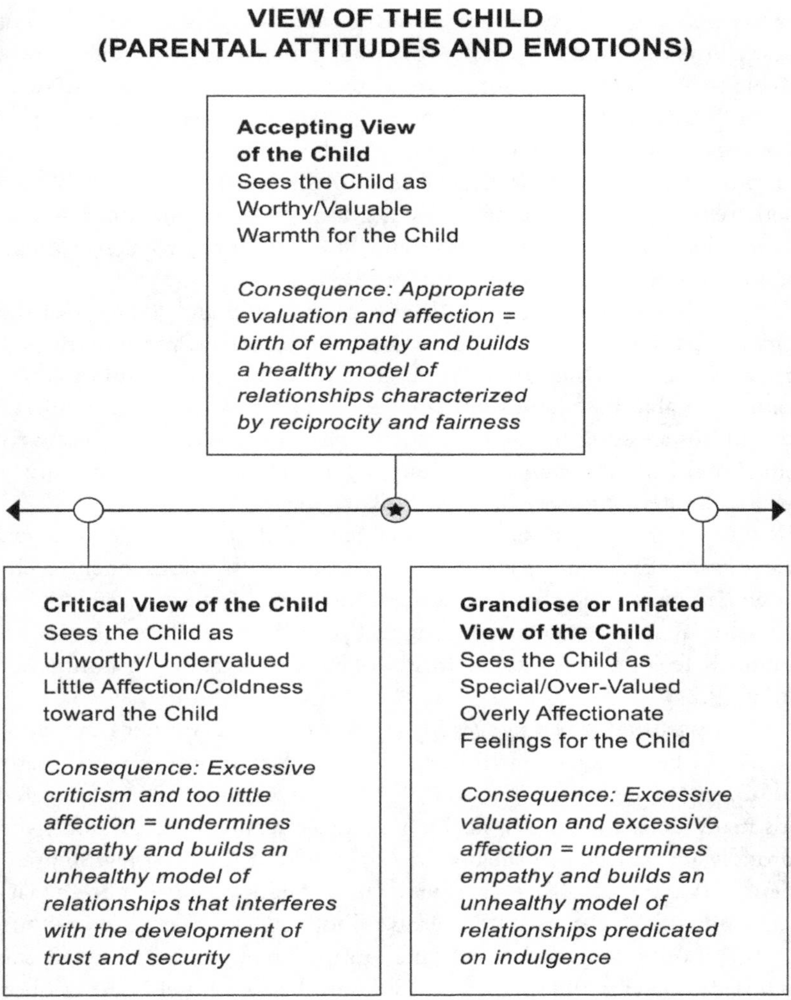

VIEW OF THE CHILD
(PARENTAL ATTITUDES AND EMOTIONS)

**Accepting View
of the Child**
Sees the Child as
Worthy/Valuable
Warmth for the Child

*Consequence: Appropriate
evaluation and affection =
birth of empathy and builds
a healthy model of
relationships characterized
by reciprocity and fairness*

Critical View of the Child
Sees the Child as
Unworthy/Undervalued
Little Affection/Coldness
toward the Child

*Consequence: Excessive
criticism and too little
affection = undermines
empathy and builds an
unhealthy model of
relationships that interferes
with the development of
trust and security*

**Grandiose or Inflated
View of the Child**
Sees the Child as
Special/Over-Valued
Overly Affectionate
Feelings for the Child

*Consequence: Excessive
valuation and excessive
affection = undermines
empathy and builds an
unhealthy model of
relationships predicated
on indulgence*

Figure 9.2.

the coach, I wouldn't keep him in the game." His view of his child would land on the far-left side of the chart's axis in terms of both regard and expectation.

Broad Component Two: Treatment of the Child (Parental Limit-Setting and Involvement). The *treatment of the child* is made up of two components. The cognitive or structural component involves parental limit setting, whether in the form of rules, discipline, or expectations. The emotional component involves engagement in the parent-child relationship through both activity and time together (see figure 9.3).

Any particular parent's *treatment of their child* through discipline/limits and level of involvement can be identified on this axis. I recall a conversation with a mother who clearly adored her eight-year-old daughter. While singing her praises in what appeared to be an accurate appraisal of exceptional skill and talent, she shared the child's rigorous schedule. She explained that she played on a select soccer team, had twice-weekly piano lessons, and worked with a regular tutor to address her mathematical genius. She explained that the school only required thirty minutes of daily reading, but she insisted her daughter read at least an hour a day. In terms of the chart, her treatment of the child would land on the far-right side of the axis for rules, structures, and expectations as well as general overinvolvement with her daughter.

I also remember a high-achieving Ivy League–educated lawyer whose nine-year-old son had performed poorly on a school history test. The father explained that he had no time to help his son with remediation. He told me, "If Russell cares about his grades, then he needs to figure it out for himself. I made it on my own. He can do the same thing *if* he decides to do the work. That's not my job or my responsibility." In terms of the chart, his treatment of the child would land on the far-left side of the axis, with limited supervision and limited involvement.

THE HEALTHY PARENT: EXAMPLES FROM CLINICAL PRACTICE

In my practice, I make assessments of parents on a regular basis. In some cases, I am making a more formal evaluation in order to make treatment recommendations in reference to a specific problem in the child. Those issues can range from a full-blown anxiety disorder to more subtle

TREATMENT OF THE CHILD
(PARENTAL LIMIT-SETTING AND INVOLVEMENT)

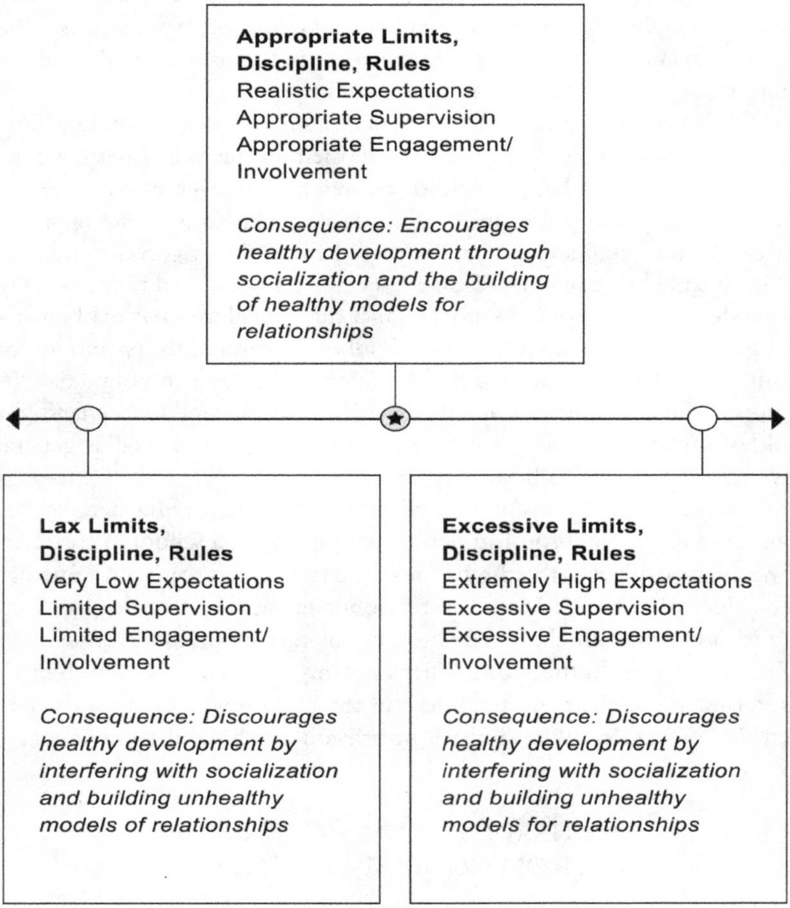

Appropriate Limits, Discipline, Rules
Realistic Expectations
Appropriate Supervision
Appropriate Engagement/
Involvement

Consequence: Encourages healthy development through socialization and the building of healthy models for relationships

Lax Limits, Discipline, Rules
Very Low Expectations
Limited Supervision
Limited Engagement/
Involvement

Consequence: Discourages healthy development by interfering with socialization and building unhealthy models of relationships

Excessive Limits, Discipline, Rules
Extremely High Expectations
Excessive Supervision
Excessive Engagement/
Involvement

Consequence: Discourages healthy development by interfering with socialization and building unhealthy models for relationships

Figure 9.3.

difficult-to-deal-with narcissistic tendencies. In other cases, I am making an informal evaluation as I work with an adult in therapy, and parenting is simply one of many areas addressed in our work together. Those informal measurements have been refined over my years of practice and now consist of a set of questions that I pose to many patients.

- To assess the parent's *view of the child*, I typically ask the parent to name three strengths in their child or, alternatively, tell me the three things they like most about their child; and name three weaknesses in their child or, alternatively, tell me the three things that worry them most about their child.
- To assess the parent's *treatment of the child*, I typically ask the parent to name several parenting strategies that they rely on in raising their child; and name other parenting strategies that they generally avoid in raising their child.
- To assess the quality of the *relationship*, which is a subset of the *treatment of the child*, I typically ask the parent to describe their relationship with their child in terms of time and engagement— that is, to tell me what they typically do together.

Parent Report of Their View and Treatment of the Child by Age

Below are a few of the things I like to hear from parents as they share their ideas about their child.

Responses of Six-Year-Old Helen's Parent
View of the Child (Strengths and Weaknesses)
She's a hard worker, and I can count on her to get things done.
She's a fantastic reader and loves to learn things from books.
She likes to play teacher and educates all her dolls in the imaginary classroom that she has concocted.
She can lose her temper and be very feisty but feels bad when she's misbehaved.
She's not always nice to her big brother and can call him some names I choose not to repeat.
She's not good at spelling and that upsets her.

Treatment of the Child (Limits, Structure, Discipline)

I set limits with Helen. She has to make her bed, feed the cat, and go to bed on time. She doesn't always like to, but she does with reminders.

I praise her when she does a good job. I also point out things that need improving.

I don't spank my kids or get mad or tell them I don't love them.

I tell them I love them, but they still have to make the bed or go to family dinner with the cousin she doesn't like.

Treatment of the Child (Engagement)

We like to spend time together. I taught her how to bake cookies and make brownies. She not only bakes but will also help with the cleanup.

I like to read to her before bed. We cuddle up and she comments at the end of each chapter about her favorite parts.

She's a good kid. I love her.

Responses of Nine-Year-Old Rick's Parent

View of the Child (Strengths and Weaknesses)

He loves to play soccer, and if I can't find him, he's in the backyard shooting goals.

He's not a very good student, but he tries hard. He's gotten better at spelling even though he hates it.

He's good with people and has several good friends. People like him because he's nice.

He is more sensitive than some boys, and I worry about that. He almost cried when he got a detention in school, but he has been getting better at handling things that don't go his way.

He can be lazy and put things off but will get it done if his father or I bring it to his attention.

Treatment of the Child (Limits, Structure, Discipline)

I believe in positive reinforcement. I try to catch him being good and say so—when he's nice to his sister or feeds the dog without being asked.

He has to put his clothes in the hamper and pick up his room—well at least clothes off the floor. He's responsible for setting the table. He doesn't like family chores but will get them done.

I send Rick to his room when he's upset—not to punish him but to give him time to settle down and think about what he's done. Then we talk about it and try to figure out how to manage better next time.

I try not to yell or say things I might regret. I don't believe that helps.

I try to give consequences that don't last too long or aren't too severe.

Treatment of the Child (Engagement)
Rick will sit in the kitchen with me and talk to me while I cook dinner. He tells me about his day and his friends.

He likes to go to the grocery store with me and we talk while we're shopping.

He likes to spend time fishing with his dad too.

Responses of Fifteen-Year-Old Rachel's Parent
View of the Child (Strengths and Weaknesses)
I love her. She's kindhearted—nice to people and animals and little kids.

She is a favorite babysitter. I sometimes think she'll grow up to be a teacher.

She is the definition of responsible. If it needs to be done, she finds a way. This has made her a school leader and a good friend. Teachers like her—so do I.

While she's generally nice she can be a pill and says some hurtful things.

It can take a while, but she always apologizes and vows to try harder next time.

She likes to get her way but can argue for a long time when crossed. She is getting better at that but is not there yet. I worry as that is a skill she will need later on.

Treatment of the Child (Limits, Structure, Discipline)
I talk to Rachel a lot—about good character, family values, right versus wrong. It's more about education than discipline.
I do give Rachel consequences for things she has done whether inappropriate or just forgotten. She doesn't like that, but she has resigned herself to accepting that's how things operate around here.
I don't believe in forcing children to talk when they're too upset for it to be successful. I wait and try to find the right time to address things I'm worried about in her behavior or just share my concerns.

Treatment of the Child (Engagement)
We like to spend time together. She lets me go shopping with her and even comment on her choices. I'm glad she wants my opinions about anything—as she *is* a teenager. We also discuss healthy habits from exercise to nutrition. She shares with me what she's thinking and reading, and she actually reads the articles I put on her desk. I'm proud to be her mom.

THE NOT-SO-HEALTHY PARENT:
EXAMPLES FROM CLINICAL PRACTICE

Not-so-healthy parent behavior can be reflected on both ends of a continuum with either unrealistic overassessment of superiority or excessive bragging or, at the other end of the spectrum, in an overly critical stance, lack of investment, or limited interaction.

Below are a few of the things I worry about when I hear them from parents as they share their ideas about their child.

Parenting Attitudes and Behaviors That Lean Toward "Too Much" through Overinvolvement and Superiority

Responses of Six-Year-Old Daniel's Parent
View of the Child (Strengths and Weaknesses)
Daniel is, without a doubt, the most talented child in his class and most likely his grade.

He's a star student. He's a great athlete. He's handsome.
Everybody loves him.
I don't believe he actually has any negative qualities, or if he does,
I haven't seen them.
I mean he can get mad but not often. There's not much for him to
be mad about. He's got it all.

Treatment of the Child (Limits, Structure, Discipline)
I believe in setting limits, but Daniel hardly ever needs any. He
does what he's told.
He doesn't really have time for chores. He's busy with his school-
work and sports.
I don't really yell at him.
I rarely scold Daniel or spank him. It doesn't really seem necessary.

Treatment of the Child (Engagement)
We spend time together at home and school. I help him with his
homework, call out spelling words, and do the nighttime reading with him.
His dad works with him around sports. They shoot hoops in the
backyard and practice soccer shots between cones.

Responses of Nine-Year-Old Betsy's Parent
View of the Child (Strengths and Weaknesses)
Betsy is an exceptional student.
She won the poetry competition for the school. She was awarded
the first-place trophy in the city-wide science fair. She was selected for the talented and gifted program in first grade.
Teachers love her and so do I.
She cries easily, particularly if I criticize her. But I think it's important that she know the mistakes she makes. How else will she
get better?
She is quiet and stays in her room a lot, but that's when she is
working. I think being quiet is just how she is, her style.

Treatment of the Child (Limits, Structure, Discipline)
I don't accept less than an A in our household. She knows that.

I don't really discipline Betsy. I point out her mistakes, tell her when she is performing under the standards we expect of her. With her talents, she should outperform her classmates.
If she underachieves, I scold her.
Betsy doesn't really have time to help around the house.
When she's not studying and has time off, we go to the store and I get her something special. High performance needs to be reinforced.

Treatment of the Child (Engagement)
We spend time together around her schoolwork.
I look over her homework and quiz her before tests.
She counts on me to provide practice before exams.

Responses of Fifteen-Year-Old Samuel's Parent
View of the Child (Strengths and Weaknesses)
Samuel is the athlete I wish I had been. He's fast and has an eye for strategy.
He's only a sophomore, but college coaches have already approached him.
He's headed for the big time.
I admit that he's not that great a student, but that doesn't really matter when you're a gifted athlete.
He doesn't need to be academic.
He's already got a ticket for success.

Treatment of the Child (Limits, Structure, Discipline)
Samuel has a full-time job as an athlete, so I don't make him help out at home.
If he slacks off with sporting events, my husband makes him run laps. He needs to learn that effort pays off.
If he's disrespectful, I tend to let it slide. My husband yells at him for it.
He needs to learn to keep his mouth shut if he's going to get along with college coaches.

Treatment of the Child (Engagement)
We spend time together around sports. I take him to soccer tournaments. I take him to soccer practice.

We talk about soccer superstars and how they got there.
He knows that I support his athletic performance. He's a super kid
and he knows I'm a super good parent.

Parenting Attitudes and Behaviors That Lean Toward "Too Little" through
Under-Involvement and Criticism

Responses of Six-Year-Old Arthur's Parent
View of the Child (Strengths and Weaknesses)
He's a good-looking kid, but he refuses to wear the clothes I put
out for him.
He has a big smile, but he doesn't show it often enough.
He's nice to his little sister.
It's hard to be Arthur. School is hard and athletics don't come easy.
I'm hoping he'll get better with time.
He doesn't like to do things he's not good at, which is why I worry
that he won't make the gains that he should.
He can be sour and demanding when he doesn't get his way.

Treatment of the Child (Limits, Structure, Discipline)
We expect a lot of Arthur. When he doesn't measure up, we let
him know. He gets a consequence.
We require Arthur to see a tutor and have a private athletic coach.
He complains, but it's necessary.
There's not much time for fun, but we take family trips to great
places.
I try not to yell, but it's hard.
He's really too big to spank at this point.

Treatment of the Child (Engagement)
We spend time together working on his schoolwork and building
his athletic skills. He doesn't always like to do it, but I believe it
will make a difference in the end.

Responses of Nine-Year-Old Christy's Parent
View of the Child (Strengths and Weaknesses)
Christy is a pretty girl. Big eyes. Big smile. Tall for her age.

She is popular on social media and has lots of friends who also like clothes.

The boys like her too because she's so pretty.

She's awfully pretty, but I worry about her weight. She's thin enough now, but she's prone to overeating. I would hate to have her eating habits spoil her good looks.

She doesn't really care about school or put in the effort. I hope that doesn't get in the way of going to a college that has all the social activities like sororities that she would want to participate in.

She's not always that nice to me, but I think it's just her age and stage. I have confidence she'll be nicer later on.

Treatment of the Child (Limits, Structure, Discipline)
I buy lots of things for Christy—things that show off her good looks. Her dad and I travel a lot and I bring home great stuff.

She likes to have friends over. We have a swimming pool and a big-screen TV, and the kids can play in the cabana.

We're not around much and don't require much from her.

We don't really have a discipline program. She knows what we expect of her.

Treatment of the Child (Engagement)
We spend time together shopping. She likes clothes, and I like clothes. That's something we have between us.

She doesn't like for me to insist on homework completion or better school performance. She's only ten but wants it to be up to her.

Responses of Fifteen-Year-Old Brett's Parent
View of the Child (Strengths and Weaknesses)
Brett is popular. He has lots of friends and not much time for us, his parents. He likes to spend time at his friends' houses and doesn't talk that much.

His mother and I believe his popularity will pay off in the end.

He's also a good athlete. Kids want to be on his basketball team because he's more likely to make it a success.

He needs to work harder on his schoolwork and the personal habits of effort and work completion.

He doesn't seem to care much what we think and has quit listening to our advice.

We both worry that he will not bounce back when things don't come easily.

Treatment of the Child (Limits, Structure, Discipline)
Brett is really too big for much discipline.

He has a curfew but that's about it. I'm not always up to enforce it.

He spends a lot of time at his best friend's house, and I expect those parents to do the parenting when he's there.

He's a good kid and doesn't require much from us.

I don't want him to drink, but I don't know how you can stop it.

Treatment of the Child (Engagement)
We don't spend that much time together.

He's busy with his sports and his friends. I think that's just how fifteen-year-old boys are.

The types of not-so-healthy parent responses differ in two ways. In the first case, the parental view of the child is based on the child's exceptionality or superiority, and parental engagement centers around that perceived strength. Whether boastful, bragging, or more understated, weaknesses are dismissed as unimportant or simply unacknowledged. In the latter case, the parental view of the child is based on the child's deficiencies or just a generally detached relationship, and parental engagement is either centered around improving the deficit or simply resigned to acceptance of the child's weakness. If the child's strengths are acknowledged, they are not perceived as particularly meaningful, and weaknesses or worry dominate the picture. In both cases, the parent-child relationship appears focused on interaction around the child's celebrated strengths or their worrisome deficits or, more generally, is characterized by disengagement. Also, there is an absence of reports of warm, affectionate, seemingly insignificant exchanges in day-to-day family life evidenced in recurring family rituals, standing jokes, daily shared habits between the two, or mutual understandings.

Identifying, explaining, and understanding the primary parenting components—the view of the child and the treatment of the child—is important in guiding parenting decisions generally and also in terms of avoiding narcissistic development. Toward that end, parents must make realistic evaluations of their own attitudes and behaviors in both areas in order to guide their parenting in the most helpful ways.

· *10* ·

Parenting Positions That Build N2B Children

Putting It All Together: The Interaction of the Parent's View of the Child and Parent's Treatment of the Child

The model of the parent's view of the child and the model of the parent's treatment of the child can form different combinations that then appear as a parental "type."

- Eileen believes that her son is special, destined to become the next Bill Gates. She has set high standards for him and is actively engaged in promoting his exceptional skill development through careful supervision of his mathematics and science homework and the engagement of tutors and advanced programming for gifted children. Focused on his achievement, she tends to cater to him.

- Edgar is frustrated with his daughter whom he sees as under-achieving. He finds her to be immature and demanding. Although he scolds her for her disappointing behavior, he does not set limits or define any achievable standards. He has little time for her, provides little encouragement, and has assumed a somewhat disengaged attitude.

- Margaret has a daughter who is the apple of her eye—prettier than she thought she would ever be. Her daughter's academic underachievement doesn't matter to Margaret. She is focused on her daughter's beauty and popularity, tending to cater to her, indulge her demands, and shower her with gifts, attention, and time.

- Robert found parenting difficult from the get-go, and his son just reinforces those negative feelings. His child is unathletic, unlike himself, and tends to be whiny and overly sensitive. Robert sets high standards, engages in harsh discipline, and sets firm boundaries, hoping to make him "more of a man." He works long hours and spends little time with his son while his elevated expectations persist.

These illustrations of parental attitude and behavior combinations can be conceptualized in a chart. If the view of the child is charted on the X-axis and the treatment of the child placed on the Y-axis, four parenting positions emerge around a conceptualized "healthy center." Figure 10.1 shows the four parenting patterns that encourage narcissistic development as derived from combinations of these two dimensions.

THE HEALTHY CENTER: FINDING THE MIDDLE GROUND IN PARENTAL ATTITUDES, EMOTIONS, LIMIT-SETTING, AND INVOLVEMENT

The middle ground (diagrammatically, the conceptual center circle) describes conditions that promote healthy development. Parental attitudes and behaviors are valued in terms of moderation. Such parents see their child as good enough and lovable as they are. They create a home environment marked by appropriate rules and structure. Discipline is established and maintained as steady and predictable. Consequences are enforced with kindness and patient explanation. Such parents require age-appropriate levels of independence and provide sufficient frustration, all in the context of adequate attention and affection. The resulting relationship between parent and child is secure and trusting.

EXPLAINING THE FOUR QUADRANTS: PARENTING POSITIONS THAT BUILD N2B CHILDREN

The four quadrants that lie outside of the healthy center describe four primary parenting positions that build N2B children. All of these extremes encourage narcissistic development and undermine the development of the healthy structures, including the child's sense of self, abilities for self-regulation, accurate perception, and expectations for relationships (see figure 10.1).

NARCISSISM UNDERSTOOD THROUGH THE VIEW OF THE CHILD (PARENTAL ATTITUDES AND EMOTIONS) AND TREATMENT OF THE CHILD (PARENTAL LIMIT-SETTING AND INVOLVEMENT)

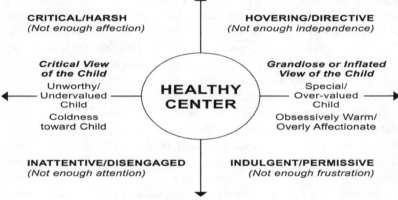

Excessive Treatment of the Child

Too Many Limits/ Discipline/Structure

Extremely High Expectations

Over-involvement

CRITICAL/HARSH
(Not enough affection)

HOVERING/DIRECTIVE
(Not enough independence)

Critical View of the Child

Unworthy/ Undervalued Child

Coldness toward Child

HEALTHY CENTER

Grandiose or Inflated View of the Child

Special/ Over-valued Child

Obsessively Warm/ Overly Affectionate

INATTENTIVE/DISENGAGED
(Not enough attention)

INDULGENT/PERMISSIVE
(Not enough frustration)

Lax Treatment of the Child

Too Few Limits/ Discipline/Structure

Very Low Expectations

Under-involvement

Healthy Treatment of the Child	**HEALTHY CENTER**	**Healthy View of the Child**
Appropriate Limits/ Discipline/Structure		Accepting view of the Child
Realistic Expectations		Worthy/Valued Child
Age-appropriate Involvement		Warmth for the Child

Figure 10.1.

Hovering/Directive Parent Position

The hovering/directive parent position is most typically identified by the parent's inflated or grandiose view of the child. The child is seen as "special," and the parent holds extremely high expectations for their superior development and ultimate success. The child is expected to walk earlier than other children, read more readily, develop precociously, and ultimately outshine classmates and peers in almost every arena. The child is overvalued, and the relationship is characterized by overinvolvement of the parents and others.

Exceedingly high parental expectations translate into excessive structure and direction, strategies that are conceived of by the parent as aids to the development of the child's perceived exceptional potential. These parents aspire to *have* the perfect child and to *be* the perfect parent. While some parents in this paradigm discipline excessively, more typically, they exercise control through excessive direction, telling the child how everything should be done and directing their behavior toward attainment of the specified goal, whether it be getting into Harvard, making a perfect score on the SAT, or receiving a college scholarship. While these may be the long-term goals, they consist of smaller day-to-day and week-to-week directives such as making perfect scores on spelling tests or winning first prize in the spelling bee or science fair. These are parents who obsessively track their children's grades, their homework, and their performance on tasks of all manner. Exceptional performance is what is expected and demanded, and every effort must be made toward the child's achievement of each goal. There is a "right way" to do almost everything.

Critical Elements in the Hovering/Directive Parenting Position: High Expectations + Seen as Special/Special Treatment = Superior/Perfectionistic/ "Better Than" Attitude (with Either High or Low Achievement). The dysfunctional behavior of hovering/directive parents, who are defined by their high expectations and involvement, coupled with both special regard for and special treatment of the child, encourages a sense of superiority in the child. The special child is, by definition, better than others and, therefore, deserves better treatment. The feelings of superiority should not be misunderstood or mistaken for confidence. Confidence in oneself or in one's abilities is not comparative; it is a strength predicated on self-knowledge and achieved through the external exercise of competence. It is actualized in the child's steady self-reliance when confronted with stress or challenge. Superiority is an exaggerated sense of one's own importance or value and is always problematic in interpersonal relationships. Successful relationships involve a mutuality of respect and contribution that reflect realistic self- and social assessments and value contributions independent of the level of performance.

Appropriate parental expectations and involvement contribute to achievement generally, but excessive expectations and overinvolvement have negative consequences for children. One type of child will strive to accommodate the parental position, becoming perfectionistic and anxious. If sufficiently skilled, they might also become a truly high achiever. These children work for parental approval and respond to the parental push for excellence through perfectionism. The child has assumed the special child/high achieving trajectory. Another type of child will resist the parental position, often resulting in underachievement. Rebelling against parental directives, these are children who claim they are unconcerned with good grades or team participation but nevertheless maintain a sense of being special and deserving of special treatment. The child has assumed the special child/low achieving trajectory. Both types of children develop in common a notion of superiority, believing that they are better than others and feeling justified in seeking special treatment.

I have treated many children and adults who were the product of a hovering/directive parent. Many proved to be out-and-out superstars, men and women who achieved remarkable success in their careers. However, the vast majority encountered extreme frustration when their interpersonal relationships did not match the experience of the earlier parent-child relationship, not affording the specialness, attentiveness, and ingratiation required, or when they suffered a major disappointment in their professional life. Failure is not managed well by children who consider themselves to be practically perfect. Still others were children who did not have the skills and capabilities to be the "special" child their parent imagined. Those children suffered with chronic feelings of unworthiness and lack of value and self-confidence. Many longed for imagined super-success, and some resorted to less-than-ethical or honest means to attain it, but all believed implicitly that exceptionality would reverse their childhood injury. The final type of child I have seen has a more mixed course. That child, or adult, thrived until parental expectation exceeded their capability, at which point, the parent turned on the child, judged the child to be deficient for having thwarted parental expectation, and withdrew their effusive affection. Sadly, those adults often maintained notions of superiority and suffered from their "fall" from achievement, success, or parental affection throughout childhood and into adulthood.

It is important to recognize that overly involved/directive parenting can have some positive outcomes. However, they are typically accompanied by a number of limitations that often go unseen, particularly during childhood, and can extend for long periods of time. The popularized "Tiger Mom" model of parenting can certainly contribute to success in certain areas in a child's life, but that success comes at a price. The associated limitations may not be evident for many years but ultimately prove costly. In my lectures, when asked about the benefits of Tiger Mom parenting, I often respond with "it depends on *when* you call the race" and "what *basis* you call it on." Pam or Paul may actually get to Harvard, take a Silicon Valley startup public, and make jillions of dollars. If success is measured by those accomplishments, then being a "Tiger Mom" might be considered an effective strategy. I have treated too many Pams and Pauls over my career and seen the associated problems in self-esteem evidenced in eating disorders or debilitating anxiety and the fallout from failed relationships all around, and I do not believe those kinds of successes outweigh the costs in adulthood. If you value contentment, connection, and the quality of relationships among family and friends, then a different type of parenting is required. The drive developed from narcissistic parenting is neither the necessary nor desired route to any measure of real-world success.

Indulgent/Permissive Parent Position

The indulgent/permissive parent position is most typically identified by the parent's outright overindulgence. The child is provided with almost everything she wants and, in some cases, with everything money can buy. She is seen as "special," prettier than other children, more likable than other children, more popular than other children, simply put, just better all around. As such, she is deserving of special treatment. She doesn't need to "worry her pretty little head" about insignificant things or the duties and obligations of daily life. The child is overly valued, and the relationship is characterized by excessive caretaking and attention accompanied by limited demands.

Indulgence has important psychological consequences. If the grandiose or inflated view of the child does not become moderated through limit setting and frustration, the child clings to a view of themselves as better than others and comes to expect special treatment in the form of effusive caring and pampering. This type of child appears spoiled and is ultimately immature, ill-equipped to engage in the mutuality of healthy relationships.

Interestingly, parental indulgence can make children look more mature than they actually are for a while, especially when younger. Parents may explain that Bobby does not tantrum much, but that seeming strength is the result of the fact that he has not been exposed to much frustration. However, as the indulged child spends more time away from the home, real-world frustrations cannot be avoided and are poorly managed. Bobby, who earlier appeared to be well mannered, evidences emotional dysregulation in the form of tantrums, harsh words, tears, or inappropriate, aggressive behavior toward others. The inability to tolerate frustration is problematic throughout life. Problems with anger management are the adult embodiment of this childhood deficiency if the root problem remains unaddressed.

Critical Elements in the Indulgent/Permissive Parenting Position: Lax Limit-Setting + Seen as Special/Special Treatment = Entitled. The critical elements in the indulgent/permissive parent position involve the parent's view of the child as special in the context of a lack of discipline and a general pattern of indulgence. The combination of this dysfunctional view of the child and this dysfunctional treatment of the child leads to a sense of entitlement. The special child feels she deserves special treatment. She has neither accepted mature limits on the self nor the realistic limits common to all healthy relationships.

Children respond to a pattern of indulgence in different ways. One type of child is less demanding of others while remaining entitled and desirous of special treatment. Another type of child is extremely demanding of others and quite disagreeable in their insistence on getting their way. Both types of children present as entitled, but one appears better socialized and more cooperative than the other. The former tends to beg their parents for the things they want and need while the latter is prone to tantrum and verbal aggression.

I have treated many children and adults who were the product of an indulgent/permissive parent. Most were generally fond of the parent, but the quality of the relationship was lacking. These children saw the parent as a source of need fulfillment as opposed to genuine affection. Superficiality, lack of reciprocity, and limited empathy characterized the parent–child relationship. Not surprisingly, these children as adults sought similar relationship qualities in a mate. They became women who "wanted to be taken care of" and men who expected a woman to "meet their needs." There was a lack of closeness in their adult relationship, a kind of need-based arrangement between the two. Prototypically, the most common marriages I have seen involved the extraordinarily beautiful woman married to the enviably wealthy man. The exchange between her beauty and his wealth appeared initially acceptable to both. Over time, with the stress of children, extended families, and the vicissitudes of life, and in the context of the relative lack of connection, such an emotionally shallow relationship became problematic, leading to marital discord and a pressing need for therapy.

Critical/Harsh Parent Position

The critical/harsh parent position is most typically identified by the parent's rigid and rule-bound discipline along with a critical view of the child. The child's weaknesses are treated as flaws and his strengths as a simple fulfillment of what was properly expected. The parenting posture is one of coldness, lack of understanding and appreciation, and is characterized by demands for compliance. The child's feelings are not typically recognized as meaningful or worthy of concern. The focus is on obedience and proper performance. Lack of compliance is treated with severe consequences and a general lack of understanding and disregard.

Exposure to harshness, criticism, and coldness have significant psychological consequences. The child struggles with insufficient affection, which is a driver in many psychological operations. Children need parental affection to fuel self-liking, to facilitate risk taking around developmentally appropriate tasks, and to restore the child's confidence in the face of inevitable disappointment and failure. Positive regard from a parent is a kind of emotional armor that insulates the child from injury and insult, both in the home and in the larger world. Without it, the child will struggle, as she lacks the mature skills and abilities to provide for herself.

Critical Elements in the Critical/Harsh Parenting Position: Strict Rules/ Harsh Discipline + Criticism/Seen as Unworthy = Manipulative. The essential elements in the critical/harsh parenting position involve high expectations that take the form of strict rules and harsh discipline and a critical attitude that finds expression in a process of ongoing correction, direction, and criticism. The parent typically sees the child as unworthy or deficient, thereby requiring parental intervention and instruction. The combination of this dysfunctional view of the child and dysfunctional treatment of the child lead to the development of manipulative behavior in the child.

Children respond to critical harsh parenting in different ways. Many, in this environment, focus on finding ways to meet their own needs. In a sense, the child is saying, "If my parent will not provide me with what I need, then I must get it for myself." Becoming manipulative, or simply becoming proficient at getting what the child needs, can be an accommodation to a barren home life. The form of accommodation in such circumstances varies. One type of child becomes mean and controlling, often the bully who flies under the radar. They can be rebellious, oppositional, and preoccupied with exercising power over others. Another type of child responds in a less socialized manner, becoming aggressive and even unlawful, with less regard for negative consequences. In either case, the child has managed the lack of affection in the home with an emotional immaturity that encourages the development of manipulative strategies that disrupt emotional closeness.

I am reminded of a couple that I treated decades ago in marital therapy. The husband embodied the caricature of a critical/harsh parent as well as that of a critical/harsh partner. In one session, he stated, without emotion, that his wife was "as fat as a pig." When I suggested that there are certain things people do not say to each other and that working to find a softer, kinder way to express an underlying concern would be a better way to communicate, he resisted. He argued that the "truth was the truth" and named his guesstimate of her likely body mass index (BMI) as support for his claim. He continued, explaining that if she "didn't like the words," she should "change her behavior." After a year and a half of therapy, he finally came to accept the general notion that words should be softened or modified out of regard for the feelings of another and to maintain the relationship. Harshness can be deeply ingrained and strongly resistant to change. It has significant psychological consequences in undermining self-esteem and setting negative models for others that drive avoidance or, paradoxically, dependence.

I have treated a number of children and adults who were the product of a critical/harsh parent. The outcomes in this area vary widely. Some children grow up to be adults who harness their well-developed skills of manipulation to succeed in business and in other professional endeavors, amassing great fortunes or power. Despite being disliked by employees and friends, such individuals are generally tolerated because of their influence, persuasiveness, and aggressive leadership. These tyrants are handled carefully by employees and underlings, since crossing them often leads to unpleasant confrontations and negative outcomes. Not every child of the harsh and critical parent grows up to be an adult who obtains a powerful position and bullies subordinates, but they nonetheless show a propensity to take risks, making them prone to white collar crime. They are known for establishing volatile, often aggressive, relationships with others. A smaller subset of adult children of the harsh/critical parent resort to a more passive kind of adaptation, sliding into a settled position of unworthiness and general lack of self-regard while falling victim to the development of depression and lack of productivity. All types suffer from interpersonal difficulties. These individuals are not inclined toward intimacy and affection, seeing people merely as a means to an end. Their lack of empathy in interpersonal relationships interferes with the establishment of meaningful connections, denying them the connection they have always needed.

Inattentive/Disengaged Parent Position

The inattentive/disengaged parent position is most typically identified by the parent's lack of involvement and ongoing critical attitude. The parental directive to be "seen and not heard" is apt. These parents want children to behave, not make demands on their time or attention, and essentially raise themselves. Such parents are described as cold and sometimes unfeeling. They place demands on the children, and they expect to be respected and obeyed.

Inattention and neglect have profound psychological consequences. Children need to be consistently loved and celebrated in their own right. They need to be seen as valuable and worthy and to be challenged with prospects for success. They need someone to play with them, invest care and concern in them, and spend time with them. The disinterested parent essentially starves the child of this needed psychological sustenance. Perhaps more importantly, the parental position establishes the child's model of love and relationships. If parents are experienced as barren, it creates an absence of drive for connection and promotes an orientation toward aloneness and a solitary emotional life.

Critical Elements in the Inattentive/Disengaged Parenting Position: Lack of Involvement + Criticism/Seen as Not Valuable = Disengaged. The critical elements in the inattentive/disengaged parenting position involve the parent's lack of involvement coupled with ongoing criticism. The child is not regarded as valuable and worthy of regard. The parental posture is cold, and there is ongoing criticism. The combination of this dysfunctional view of the child and dysfunctional treatment of the child lead to the child's emotional and physical disengagement. Relationships are not experienced as rewarding, and interpersonal contact tends to be avoided. Such children prefer being alone, and they maintain interpersonal distance when possible.

Children respond to the inattentive/disengaged parenting posture in different ways. One type of child strives to break the isolation and distance and seeks attention through either positive or negative behaviors. Another type of child resigns herself to loneliness and retreats into solitary activities. Yet another type of child accepts the barrenness in his family home and seeks relationships outside it. My clinical work suggests that the latter child makes the most successful adjustment, particularly if provided with alternate models of connection through more responsive adults.

I remember a woman who was the product of inattentive/disengaged parents. As an infant, she was adopted by a wealthy infertile couple. Both parents struggled with their own psychological issues and maintained appearances in an affectionless marriage, with both assuming socially proper roles in their wealthy community. Neither parent had emotional resources or skills to share with the child. She was raised "by the book" with emphasis on proper dress, social skills, manners, and achievement in school. A notably intelligent and naturally compliant person, she finished school with a commendable record. She attended a competitive college in New England with admirable success there. However, socially she remained isolated, lonely, and always restrained. In a stroke of good luck, she met a kind, loving man who came from a warm and engaging family. Both he and his family showed her a different way of living, being both connected and engaged. Over the years, she had a family and raised two children. Through the process of being a parent, living in a marriage that provided more support than she had ever experienced, and engaging with determination in therapy, she began to rewrite the rules of connection in her life. An old woman now, she is proud of her progress from disengagement to engagement, from restraint to risking vulnerability, and from distance to closeness. Nevertheless, she is prone to rumination, wondering about the person she might have been had she been provided adequate nurture in her childhood. Suffice it to say, insecure attachment resulting in narcissistic disengagement is a large deficit to overcome.

N2B PARENTING POSITIONS:
SUMMARY OF CHILD OUTCOMES

The identified parenting positions describe a constellation of parental attitudes, affects, and behaviors that have an impact on the child in a loosely predictable form. These general notions have been discussed generally and are described in the chart in figure 10.2.

As is apparent, each of the dysfunctional parenting positions generate narcissistic attitudes and behaviors in the child. There is, of course, overlap between symptom patterns in the child. This analysis simply attempts to correlate the most likely and predominant child outcomes with specific parenting positions. Clearly, there are numerous variables at play, and they may interact in ways still unknown.

Developmental Deficiencies: Sufficiency, Struggle, and Mastery Reconsidered

I am reminded of Charles Darwin, whose work I read in college and naively dismissed as too esoteric to be relevant. However, over the years, I have pondered his basic tenets and their implications for psychological growth and development. Adaptation is the overarching concept, but its working is predicated on the engagement in struggle—an obstacle presents itself that must be overcome, and, in this process, essential change takes place. This concept and its relevance to child development is instructive. The child must struggle against a challenge in order to grow.

THE FOUR PARENTING POSITIONS: PREDICTABLE N2B OUTCOMES IN THE CHILD

Hovering/Directive Parenting Position
High Expectations + Seen as Special/Special Treatment = **Superior/Perfectionistic/ Better-Than Attitude**
(with either high or low achievement based on the child's talents and temperament)
Developmental deficiency: Not enough independence

Indulgent/Permissive Parenting Position
Lax Limit-Setting + Seen as Special/Special Treatment = **Entitled**
Developmental deficiency: Not enough frustration

Critical/Harsh Parenting Position
Strict Rules/Harsh Discipline + Criticism/Seen as Unworthy = **Manipulative**
Developmental deficiency: Not enough affection

Inattentive/Disengaged Parenting Position
Lack of Involvement + Criticism/Seen as Not Valuable = **Disengaged**
Developmental deficiency: Not enough attention

*There is overlap between narcissistic symptom patterns in the child. The chart describes the predominant form most typically associated with the particular parenting position.

**All dysfunctional parenting positions interfere with empathy building as the child's behavior is self-focused and centered around managing self-esteem (i.e., seeking praise, achieving, manipulating, getting their way, winning, etc.). Relational concerns, specifically in terms of regard for the feelings of others, remain secondary and under-developed.

Figure 10.2.

Paradoxically, it is the obstacle that promotes growth, large enough to require new mastery but not too small to avoid structural change.

The concept of "developmental deficiency" presented in the chart fits nicely into Darwin's paradigm.

- The developmental deficiency of *not enough independence* does not challenge the child to master or develop new skills. Without sufficient opportunities for independent effort, the child is not required to find ways to problem solve and self-regulate without assistance from parents or other adults. Absent that process, the child does not build adequate confidence and self-reliance.

- The developmental deficiency of *not enough frustration* does not challenge the child to change. Without sufficient frustration, the child is not required to find new or more effective ways to calm herself in the face of difficulty, disappointment, and failure without help from parents or other adults. Absent that process, the child does not build sufficient frustration tolerance and emotional regulation skills.

- The developmental deficiency of *not enough affection* stalls growth. Without sufficient emotional sustenance and the emotional stability it provides, the child cannot sustain the normal developmental trajectory and resorts to maladaptive coping, often through manipulative and aggressive strategies.

- The developmental deficiency of *not enough attention* also stalls growth. Without enough nurturance and the trust that fuels the child through that relationship, the child diverges from a healthy developmental course when challenged and resorts to immature coping, often turning inward and away from people.

Growth is built on struggle. Positive gains are the result of successful adaptation and new mastery. Negative outcomes are the result of failed efforts to adapt due to early deprivation in the parent-child relationship.

Darwin's paradigm indirectly supports the notion of influence along the continuum. Too much struggle or too large an obstacle overwhelms the possibility of growth. Too little struggle or too small an obstacle does not require the necessary change. "Enough" struggle encourages growth through adaptation with the demand for development of new skills and abilities.

Suffice it to say, normal emotional growth is predicated on struggle. While the desire to avoid struggle is understandable, its absence is problematic. This explains the dilemma of the gifted child, the child with a hovering parent, and children born of wealth or social privilege, all of whom may not be challenged sufficiently to develop essential life skills, either because obstacles are rarely presented, or mastery comes too easily. This also explains the dilemma of the learning-disabled child or the impoverished child who has been deprived of adequate opportunities for learning and suffers the resulting developmental delays, who may be so overwhelmed by the daunting educational and social tasks ahead that growth is stalled. "Enough" challenge encourages children through providing neither too little nor too much adversity, neither too small nor too large an obstacle.

Darwin's profound insight is applicable here: "It is not the strongest of the species that survive, nor the most intelligent, but the one most responsive to change." Building the child's capacity for adaptation is key. At its core, that ability is akin to resilience. It allows children to bounce back from adversity, and, in the process, makes healthy change possible. Parents must work to provide a host of mid-range challenges that grow in complexity and demand over the developmental course. We must cheer for the child from the sidelines and offer support when they falter and fail. This is the critical balance that best serves our children and their development.

Dynamics That Drive Dysfunctional Parenting Positions

Reasons why certain parents embrace dysfunctional parenting positions are unknown. However, numerous observations and explanations have been generated in the literature and through clinical practice, which include the following:

- A parent who has been overly influenced by cultural messaging and values.
- A parent who has received misguided parenting advice.
- A parent who selfishly uses the child to meet their own emotional needs.
- A parent whose own personal ambitions have been frustrated and unfulfilled and turns to the child's performance for their own fulfillment.
- A parent who attempts to shield their child from the hardships they themselves endured.
- A parent who was coddled or indulged and replicates that pattern.
- A parent who lacks adequate role models for raising a child with warmth and limit setting and embraces dysfunctional patterns.
- A parent who was raised by a strict disciplinarian and repeats harsh rule-bound parenting.
- A parent who is overly anxious about their own security and that of the child and pushes the child to achieve without regard for the child's needs.
- A parent who is controlling generally and reenacts the need for control in parenting.
- A parent who is a narcissist and teaches narcissistic strategies and embraces narcissistic values.

There are a number of reasons why parents encourage narcissistic development in the child. Many do not understand that they are doing so. Still others are actually trying to benefit the child through misguided efforts. Whatever the reason, the parenting emphasis has shifted from attention on the needs of the child to the needs of the parents. This paradigm shift is flawed, as an overemphasis on parental needs undermines healthy emotional development in the child.

To encourage healthy development, the parent must respond to the child's needs and make their own needs secondary. The ability to put the needs of others ahead of your own is a foundational skill in the development of empathy, and one of the skills that parents most hope to instill in the child. Ironically, parents who have endorsed one of the four N2B parenting positions are failing to demonstrate a skill that they hope to teach.

The hallmark of a successful parent-child relationship consists of the child *being known*, based on accurate perception, and being *sensitively and fairly treated*, based on an accurate read of the child's needs, skills, and abilities. Overemphasis on parental needs means that the parent cannot see the child's skills and abilities realistically, the result of distorted perception. That parental distortion not only interferes with the ability to accurately assess the child's needs but also to respond to them appropriately. When parents' needs take precedence over the child's needs, parents cannot provide the kind of support that builds a secure sense of self, adequate emotional regulation, accurate perceptual skills, and a realistic model of love and relationships. The reasons for the elevation of parental needs over the child's needs are varied, but the outcome is the same: the parent cannot provide the stable, loving emotional base that secures emotional health in the child.

Problems in knowing, understanding, and accepting a child are not always ill intended. There are babies with easier and more difficult temperaments. There are children predisposed to emotional regulation and those predisposed to dysregulation. There are children who master skills with ease and those who struggle in skill development. There are more beautiful children and less attractive ones. There are more charming children and more disagreeable ones. The challenge of "good enough" parenting is to find a way to love the child you have been given, valuing them as they are.

Parenting can prove challenging on both ends of the scale. One end requires that the parent avoid transforming the child into one of their liking. On the other end, the parent must face the challenge of loving a child without overinvestment in special gifts. There are children who are extraordinarily talented, charming, beautiful, or athletic. These children present the challenge of acceptance without overinvestment, of supporting without making too much of their specialness or superiority, of loving without sharing in a kind of reflected glory. To see this child with more regard for the internal qualities of the child and less concern for the external ornamentation is a challenge.

When I lecture, I often challenge parents to accept and adapt to types of children who are outside of their range of comfort. Mismatches between parent and child are common and present both a challenge and an opportunity for growth.

A healthy response to this sort of family mismatch is well illustrated by a wonderfully bright and accomplished mother I treated who was an avid reader. Her son had a learning disability, and his deficit was in reading. She worked to find a way to relate to a child with interests far different from her own. Tall, awkward, and absolutely unathletic, she spent hours kicking a soccer ball and learning to catch his pitches. As he grew older, he came to appreciate her effort for what it was. Eventually, the difference between them became a playful joke. "Mom, I'd know you'd rather be reading a book, but how about playing catch in the backyard?" The two had bridged the gap between them and secured a loving and stable relationship.

I am similarly reminded of a Princeton-educated lawyer whose heart was set on her son following in her high-achieving footsteps. He was indeed a brilliant child but did not share her hard-driving edge. He was content to read quietly and perform adequately. When she came to see me, she was already angry with her child. This was not the child he was supposed to be, and not the child she was supposed to parent. The child had begun to withdraw from her directive control, seeming to distance himself out of self-protection. His avoidance only heightened her insistence on various performance standards. When I began to encourage her to understand his specific skills, abilities, interests, and motivations and explore her goals for him, she left my practice. It was clear that she was going to find a psychologist who would help her turn him into the child she knew he was supposed to be.

DYNAMICS UNDERLYING SPECIFIC
N2B PARENTING POSITIONS

While the broad operational explanation underlying promotion of narcissistic development appears to involve an overemphasis on parental
needs (as opposed to the child's) to the detriment of the younger person's emotional health, I offer my impressions of various dynamics that
may underlie specific N2B dysfunctional parenting positions based on
my work with patients over many years.

Dynamics: Hovering/Directive Parenting

Hovering/directive parents may be themselves high functioning narcissists. They seek to have their children adopt their own narcissistic
position. They need their children to reaffirm their superiority or, if
they have not achieved sufficiently, to assert the parent's unrecognized
superiority. Other hovering/directive parents are not narcissists but suffer low self-esteem and use the child to offset their own inadequacies
through desires to raise an exceptional child. Both sets of parents rely on
"narcissistic reflection" to manage internal deficits. The well-mannered,
high-achieving, remarkably attractive, or amazingly charming child becomes an "object" worthy of celebration and capable of reinforcing the
parent's superiority, both of which serve a deep psychological need in
the parent. The child is seen as an extension of the parent, and the child's
success is experienced as the parent's success.

Dynamics: Indulgent/Permissive Parenting

Indulgent/permissive parents are often needy and approval-seeking
individuals. They may be pleasers by nature and codependent in their
relationship patterns generally. They need approval from their child
and do not risk the child's dislike or disapproval if they set limits. Their
neediness means that they cannot discipline for fear of loss of the child's
affection. Other indulgent/permissive parents come from deprived
backgrounds where they received too little emotional or physical support. Being able to give their child the things that they did not have
growing up is an unconscious way to try and heal themselves, but, in
the end, injures the child.

Dynamics: Critical/Harsh Parenting

Harsh/critical parents are likely emotionally detached individuals who seek compliance and obedience in most relationships. They maintain military-like control (i.e., "my way or the highway") and disregard the importance of feelings or emotional connection. They see parenting as teaching the child to "obey." Some harsh/critical parents grew up with cold, unavailable parents and do not see their parenting stance as deficient. Still other harsh/critical parents believe, incorrectly, that their harshness is needed to raise a "tough" kid who can make it in the world.

Dynamics: Inattentive/Disengaged Parenting

Inattentive/neglectful parents are often selfish and preoccupied. Caught up in their own issues, whether associated with trauma, external pressures, job demands, fear of failure, or mental illness, they have little time for others. Their emotional life is constricted, and they live without connection. Some inattentive/neglectful parents grew up with inadequate nurture and do not see the limitations of their lack of engagement, understanding it inaccurately as "just the way" families operate.

The individual N2B parenting positions are to be understood as describing a constellation of influence whose direction encourages, rather than discourages, narcissism in the child. Parenting strategies that migrate toward the healthy center support the child's more fully functioning non-narcissistic development.

Moderation Parenting

Stopping N2B Development in Childhood

THE SEARCH FOR A GUIDING PRINCIPLE

$\mathcal{I}$ routinely tell parents: "The hardest job you will *ever* have is parenting." First, it is a stage-dependent process, and every time you figure out the rules for that stage, the child grows and everything changes. You must start over again and learn new operating principles. This tends to undermine confidence in your parenting skills and introduces frustration and a sense of helplessness. It's hard to build confidence when the rules change frequently, and your child is transforming before your eyes, acquiring new skills and abilities without notice. Second, more globally, questions of parenting involve the most complicated topics pondered by philosophers and theoreticians of every civilization. Most often, there are no easy answers.

Over the developmental period, parents must explain the nature of love (Why did he tell me he loved me and then kiss my best friend?), the tenets of friendship (Why did she exclude me from the party when we've been best friends since second grade?), the value of learning (Why do I have to take physics when I want to study fashion?), the benefits of empathy (How can I understand why she did something so stupid or mean or silly?), the nature of human cruelty and meanness (How can he promise to keep my secret and then post it on social media?), the burden and sting of unfairness (Why did we have to come home early from fishing because Dad said so?), and the nature of compassion (Why does it hurt so much to be hurt by someone you love?). The list is exhausting, literally.

Many questions center around events and situations in the outside world, but the hardest questions for parents are the ones directed specifically at them personally and often involve criticism. It is hard enough to give guidance when your child is upset with someone else; it's even harder when they're upset with you and their questions challenge *who* you are, *why* you do what you do, and *what* you believe. Strong emotions further complicate those exchanges.

Children need parents who at their best are able to understand, listen, and guide. Parents must answer confounding questions regarding the limits of love (You say you love me but won't let me go to the most important party of the year?), marriage (Why did you marry Dad when he can be such a jerk?), inequality (How come the Joneses have a new boat and a big house and we still have a cottage?), disappointment (You say you love me, but if you love me so much, why won't you let me get an iPhone?), morality (You yelled at me and you said you wouldn't do that again. Is that right or fair?), insecurity (Dad lost his job and now we can't go on vacation. You expect me to like that?), and the list goes on. Conflict, disappointment, and strong feelings are all part of being close, and being a parent. While rewarding and fulfilling for much of the time together, the relationship with your child is always tested by difficult moments around difficult issues.

While these are the kinds of questions that we are often asked by our children, we must also answer them for ourselves. Our answers will, in the end, guide our parenting decisions. For example, at what age do you allow your child *not* to invite every girl in the class to her birthday party? And why do you think that? This small inquiry raises much deeper, broader issues—when are you allowed to knowingly hurt another person's feelings and for what reason? When do you make exceptions—if her mother has breast cancer or if she just moved schools and has no friends? When do you bend the rules and for what reasons? Similarly, when do you prioritize your needs and allow yourself to stand up for what you want even if your actions are painful to others? It is the difficult day-to-day working through of these seemingly small but larger questions that will define who we are as parents.

These kinds of questions will challenge all of us to be our best selves, require us to overcome the pettiness born of our own experience, and to reach for the greater good in our relationships with our children. The answers we seek have baffled knowledgeable thinkers through the ages. And we must usually answer them without consulting expert philosophers, theologians, or psychologists. Responding wisely in the moment when our children encounter frustration in day-to-day and year-to-year living demands time, energy, and unyielding resolve. Parents must persevere and look beyond their immediate frustrations, disappointments, and setbacks so that they can search for meaningful answers that educate for the future.

Beyond the difficulty of answering our children's often seemingly impossible questions is the complexity of the process of parenting—that is, understanding the day-to-day steps in teaching and encouraging and ultimately identifying the guiding principles that must shape our words and parenting behavior. The questions are difficult, and the answers are hard to find.

Influence from unhealthy sources complicates matters. Modern society offers its own directives, often steering us toward winning, success, and achievement without regard for more healthy outcomes and meaningful relationships. The forces are powerful: win at all costs; don't worry about who you step on while you race to the top; get yours first; you'll be invincible once you take the lead, amass a fortune, or capture the most beautiful girl. These influences steer us wrongly away from the elements essential to achieving a healthier emotional life. They are predicated on a simplistic model. The end is assumed to justify the means, but this is a false promise. Emotional health, contentment, and happiness are, at their core, built on emotional security and meaningful relationships, concepts that are either ignored or undervalued.

What is the guiding principle? Where can we find the north star to direct our path and address our questions and concerns? What are the essential elements in the parent-child relationship, particularly in terms of discouraging narcissistic development? What we know from research, theory, and clinical experience points a clear path forward toward moderation. The importance of "some," neither "too much" nor "too little" in terms of parenting, is supported by both common sense, age-old philosophical inquiry, and emerging theory and research.

Parenting toward either end of the continuum on any number of topics, running from deficiency to excess, can contribute to narcissism in the child and unhealthy developmental outcomes generally. Parents should strive to provide neither too little nor too much in terms of both their view of the child and their treatment of the child. The *view of the child* should focus on building a sense of internal goodness and worth, not specialness, and is encouraged in the context of positive emotional regard. The *treatment of the child* should focus on the achievement of competence, not superiority, and is nurtured in the context of meaningful engagement and time spent together.

Moderation parenting is the key, but that can be difficult for parents to find and establish in a world that values winning and success above all else, goals that are embraced by too many and often reached to the exclusion of emotional health, happiness, and fulfillment. Our collective system of values has become fixated on short-term measures of success and excess, which (inadvertently perhaps) drives poor parenting.

How can parents find a way to steer toward the middle ground?

- They can resist narcissistic direction and messages, aggressive marketing, and unhealthy competition.
- They can embrace non-narcissistic values.
- They can model moderation in their own lives, balancing selfishness and generosity.
- They can raise a child with moderation parenting practices.
- They can embrace the critical values of human connection, kindness, respect, and caretaking.
- They can teach empathy—individually and socially—in family and community.
- They can live and follow the golden rule.
- They can encourage perspective-taking, listening, and learning from others.
- They can model kindness and consideration.
- They can value others for internal, not external qualities.
- They can live in the moment and appreciate small steps in making daily progress.
- They can exercise respect and consideration for their fellow man.
- They can search for the good, not the exceptional, in others and life.

Notions of moderation can be applied to all aspects of life more generally and parenting more particularly. Daily life questions appear commonplace but are predicated on the same underlying notions of balance. How little should I exercise? How much should I eat? How long should I study? How much should I work? How long should I stay with my in-laws? How much should I spend on clothes? How long should I tolerate a friend's insensitivity? How much should I give to charity? People must deal with gradations along a scale every day.

Arguably, a good life is predicated on some but not too little or too much of most activities and experiences. History would tell us that moderation has been a recurring theme through the ages. The work of Roman and Greek poets, dramatists, playwrights, and philosophers—including Hesiod, Plautus, Euripides, Plato, and Aristotle—have all extolled its virtues. Centuries later, authors too numerous to count, running from Chaucer to Ben Franklin, would echo the same sage advice.

There is a reason for old adages; they are simple statements that express a general truth. "All things in moderation," "nothing in excess," and the need to "find balance," all speak to the importance of moderation and the value of the middle ground. Not surprisingly, moderation is a concept that aligns, enhances, and explains healthy parenting positions as well.

THE PROBLEM IN LOCATING THE MIDDLE GROUND

Over the course of my work, I have found that patients and parents particularly appreciate stories about psychologists when they make mistakes. Seeing someone fall short who *should* know better humanizes the struggle. Knowing that everyone faces the same challenges and often makes the same mistakes is reassuring. I offer this story with that in mind.

When my oldest son was six years old, he was invited to join a competitive soccer team. This was clearly a compliment, as the team was made up of some of the better athletes in first grade. We discovered that the practices were on Sunday mornings, a time when our family more often went to fish at Grandpa's ranch. We threw hooks in the water, their father read chapters from *Treasure Island*, and I brought along a picnic lunch. I was unable to determine what to do. "Should we give up our Sunday ritual and give our son an opportunity to become a better player?" You might say that's an easy decision, but as a young mother who wanted the best for her child, it was not so easy for me. I did not want my son to fall behind in athletic development nor miss an opportunity to be on a winning team. I just could not figure out what to do.

Lost in my worry and indecision, I called one of my best friends, a physical therapist whom I knew understood motor development and was wise as well: "If I keep him out of soccer, will he fall so far behind that he can never catch up in later elementary school? Will he still be able to make a middle school team when it matters for self-esteem and peer relationships—I mean if I hold him back now?" She looked at me with the loving eyes of a long friendship. "You *know* the answer to this question, but I'll *remind* you." She explained that motor development was not predicated on practice of any one specific skill of course. Running, playing catch, bouncing balls, kicking rocks all contribute to eye-hand coordination and eye-foot coordination. These important maturational skills can be encouraged through all kinds of physical activities, competitive and otherwise. Why do I tell this story? Because I couldn't find the middle ground. I was not confident enough as a mother or a person to buck the cultural emphasis on getting ahead and risk losing a competitive advantage. Even with my training, it was hard to follow my own instincts.

This all happened long before I understood the fundamental notions of excess and deficiency and the inherent value of middle-ground and moderation parenting. I had not watched enough life trajectories to see the risks of pushing and overvaluing the child and ignoring a youngster's need to be engaged in ordinary family life. It seems foolish that I could not see it then, but I could not. My competitive desires blinded my vision. The same question would be asked of me for what felt like hundreds of times over the course of my children's development—whether or not to sign up for the advanced art class, accelerated math program, premier athletic trainer, summer gifted program, a community service trip that provided accelerated hours—the list went on and on. Too often, the question was focused on getting ahead, breaking out from the crowd, ensuring competitive advantage, or more generally, getting somewhere or doing something judged important, valuable, or downright essential. Too often, the question was not focused on the emotional needs of the child or considered in light of the family's values and well-being. In every case, it was difficult to buck the system and steer away from the herd and choose an alternate, independent, less traveled path.

In the end, I have written this book to build parents' confidence in "moderation parenting." I want to encourage parents to support each other and to say the things that we hesitate to say that support "good enough parenting." "Good call, it's better for your son to fish with his brothers and have a family picnic than work on competitive soccer at age six." "Good call, it's important to insist on reasonable bedtimes even though he's mad about it." "Good call, it's important for you to miss the Gala event at the Club for a game of monopoly with the kids." It is the living out of these valuable human connections that will teach and shape each of our children's futures. Specialness, excess, indulgence, and permissiveness will prove too costly in the end. Paradoxically, treating the child as ordinary, having more reasonable expectations, and providing appropriate and value-based involvement—all in the context of calm and steady affection—ensures the most healthy and successful path for the child growing up. It's an anti-excess and pro-moderation paradigm, and we would all do well to support each other in promoting it.

BLUNTING THE TRENDS TOWARD NARCISSISM

The broad goal of this book is to blunt trends toward narcissistic development in children. It has focused specifically on the contribution of parents to the development of narcissism. It must be emphasized that there are other significant contributors to narcissistic development besides parenting, including temperament and trauma, and, importantly, the complex influences of contemporary culture. Regardless of these, it is most important to reorient and reconsider the nature and origin of narcissism in childhood in order to mitigate the influences that too often—over years—lead to dysfunction.

The book offers many specific recommendations for promoting the development of healthy structures over the course of development: strengthening the child's sense of self, abilities for emotional regulation, skills in perceptual accuracy, and model of love and relationships. It has, more importantly, identified dysfunctional parenting positions that are associated with narcissistic development in each of those areas and shown strategies to reverse their impact.

Moderation is emphasized as a guiding principle in parenting. Across the major axes of influence, the collective data to date on childhood narcissism leads me to argue for parenting that steers solidly toward the middle ground. Being neither excessive nor deficient in its form and avoiding the extremes is desirable in all areas of parental influence. This landscape of influence extends from the parental "view" of the child to the parental "treatment" of the child.

The need for moderation has become an imperative, if you will, as negative societal influences have intensified over time. In an arguably profound sense, the current culture is acting much like a narcissistic parent in supporting and promoting narcissistic values, intentionally or not. Selfish, self-centered, entitled, and volatile individuals surround us. They populate businesses, organizations, and our valued institutions. The dysfunctional behavior of our peers, politicians, movie stars, clergy, professionals, and influencers of all sorts serves to normalize selfishness, insensitivity, and immature relationships. Both explicit and subliminal messages shape not only our own but also our children's values, decisions, and choices.

A tide of commercialism along with the often-unspoken goal of achieving great wealth, fame, beauty, power, or success is one we must navigate against in steering toward healthier development in our children. It is not just that commercial interests are insensitive to the needs of children and families; they are perversely aware of and intended to exploit the developmental vulnerabilities of both. In the process, "promotors" of all types are becoming ever more prolific and productive, both increasing profit and the inculcation of narcissistic values at the expense of the well-being of our children and families.

The influence of traditional print and broadcast media has exploded into the near universality of social media through the internet. The ever-widening reach of narcissistic values through more effective messaging touches all of us, pushing us in directions we might well not have ventured without those pressures.

Whether as political hyperpartisanship, social tribalism, or an economics of increasing disparity between the haves and have-nots, our current culture is losing a proper balanced sense of the inherent value of "enough." Society at large needs to appreciate and celebrate the success of being a "good enough parent" who raises a "good enough child." It is difficult to propound the significance of "enough" in a world that almost universally values "more."

Every "takeaway" written for parents applies equally to the culture generally and influencers of all types. This includes the media, from major news organizations to small social media forums, and leaders and influencers in all walks of life, from ministers to advertisers, from politicians to teachers and coaches. Cultural messaging must avoid idealizing narcissistic values and emphasizing romanticized and dysfunctional notions of love and relationships, beauty, power, wealth, weight, and sources of fulfillment. The fear-inciting politician, the profit-motivated marketeer, and others who subliminally and falsely promise happiness through product or purchase stand to hurt our children just as surely as the fourth-grade boy who lands a punch on the playground or humiliates a classmate with a cruel social media post.

Equally important is the emphasis on the need for early intervention. In order to reverse childhood tendencies and traits before they are more fully developed and set by late adolescence and early adulthood, narcissism must be addressed early—before it is too late to allow fundamental change. Intervention when the child is still young and more easily influenced is key.

I hope that the discussion of narcissism will stimulate and guide new research to validate the insights of clinical experience broadly. Understanding narcissism through the lens of moderation might be one way to influence and potentially shift research design to investigate such an orientation. Such research would be instructive and useful, both theoretically and therapeutically. The goal is to guide parents, educators, and other professionals toward parenting practices that steer away from narcissistic development incrementally and encourage parenting practices that steer toward healthy development. In the end, concern about endemic narcissism cannot be dismissed. Guiding child development away from narcissism and into healthier behavior is as worthy as the need is obvious.

Finally, it is essential that parents work to counteract negative influences, both individual and cultural, and promote healthier values in order to build steady self-esteem and the capacity for healthy relationships in children. In a world that often models, encourages, and celebrates the pathologies of excess and inconsideration, it is critical that parents offer a countervailing influence, dedicated to steering children toward a model of a healthy sense of self and relationships with others. Parents must work together to blunt not only their own negative influence on the child, but also society's contextual and more indirect influences.

We all have an investment in raising healthy children who will help create a healthier community, neighborhood, and world. The pervasive presence of narcissistic values is a threat in every sphere of human activity. My confidence is that the growth of childhood narcissism can be curbed and healthy development encouraged. Undoubtedly, this challenge matters to *all* of us; it is work that is required from *each* of us.

The Greek philosophers offer guidance in encouraging an Aristotelian emphasis on moderation. Over two thousand years later, it remains both our personal and societal challenge to embrace the middle ground in a world that increasingly values excess and disregards nuance. Along the centerline of developmental influences, the middle course offers both hope and optimism for individuals, families, and communities. If we manage to see clearly and guide bravely, we will all benefit from a world filled with more unselfish, unentitled, and empathetic children.

Notes

CHAPTER 2

1. D. Kealy and B. Rasmussen, "Veiled and Vulnerable: The Other Side of Grandiose Narcissism," *Clinical Social Work Journal* 40, no. 3 (2012): 356–65; Otto F. Kernberg, *Borderline Conditions and Pathological Narcissism* (New York: Rowman & Littlefield, 1985); James F. Masterson, *The Narcissistic and Borderline Disorders: An Integrated Developmental Approach* (New York: Brunner/Mazel, 1981). Note: Kernberg's (1985) definition emphasizes an integrated self-concept and increased capacity to love.

2. W. Keith Campbell and Carolyn Crist, *The New Science of Narcissism: Understanding One of the Greatest Psychological Challenges of Our Time—and What You Can Do about It* (Boulder, CO: Sounds True, 2020).

CHAPTER 3

1. S. Thomaes, B. J. Bushman, B. O. De Castro, and H. Stegge, "What Makes Narcissists Bloom? A Framework for Research on the Etiology and Development of Narcissism," *Development and Psychopathology* 21, no. 4 (2009): 1233–47; C. T. Barry, P. J. Frick, and A. L. Killian, "The Relation of Narcissism and Self-Esteem to Conduct Problems in Children: A Preliminary Investigation," *Journal of Clinical Child and Adolescent Psychology* 32, no. 1 (2003): 139–52.

2. P. Cramer, "Young Adult Narcissism: A 20-Year Longitudinal Study of the Contribution of Parenting Styles, Preschool Precursors of Narcissism, and Denial." *Journal of Research in Personality* 45, no. 1 (2011): 19–28; S. Akhtar and J. A. Thompson, "Overview: Narcissistic Personality Disorder," *American Journal*

of Psychiatry 139 (1982): 12–20; J. F. Masterson, *The Emerging Self: A Developmental Self and Object Relations Approach to the Treatment of the Closet Narcissistic Disorder of the Self* (New York: Brunner/Mazel, 1993).

3. R. P. Brown, K. Budzek, and M. Tamborski, "On the Meaning and Measure of Narcissism," *Personality and Social Psychology Bulletin* 35, no. 7 (2009): 951–64.

4. E. Brummelman, S. Thomaes, S. A. Nelemans, B. Orobio de Castro, G. Overbeek, and B. J. Bushman, "Origins of Narcissism in Children," *Proceedings of the National Academy of Sciences* 112, no. 12 (2015) 365–62; L. J. Otway, and V. L. Vignoles, "Narcissism and Childhood Recollections: A Quantitative Test of Psychoanalytic Predictions," *Personality and Social Psychology Bulletin* 32, no. 1 (2006): 104–16.

5. N. B. Perry, J. M. Dollar, S. D. Calkins, S. P. Keane, and L. Shanahan, "Childhood Self-Regulation as a Mechanism through Which Early Overcontrolling Parenting Is Associated with Adjustment in Preadolescence," *Developmental Psychology* 54, no. 8 (2018): 1542; Otway and Vignoles, "Narcissism and Childhood Recollections," 104–16; R. S. Horton, G. Bleau, and B. Drwecki, "Parenting Narcissus: What Are the Links between Parenting and Narcissism?," *Journal of Personality* 74, no. 2 (2006): 345–76; S. Thomaes, H. Stegge, B. J. Bushman, T. Olthof, and J. Denissen, "Development and Validation of the Childhood Narcissism Scale," *Journal Personality Assessment* 90, no. 4 (July 2008): 382–91; Robert S. Horton, "Parenting as a Cause of Narcissism: Empirical Support for Psychodynamic and Social Learning Theories," in *The Handbook of Narcissism and Narcissistic Personality Disorder: Theoretical Approaches, Empirical Findings, and Treatments*, ed. W. Keith Campbell and Joshua D. Miller (Hoboken, NJ: John Wiley and Sons, 2011), 181–90; J. D. Miller and W. K. Campbell, "Comparing Clinical and Social-Personality Conceptualizations of Narcissism," *Journal of Personality* 76, no. 3 (2008): 449–76.

6. P. J. Watson, T. Little, and M. D. Biderman, "Narcissism and Parenting Styles," *Psychoanalytic Psychology* 9, no. 2 (1992): 231; C. T. Barry, P. J. Frick, K. K. Adler, and S. J. Grafeman, "The Predictive Utility of Narcissism among Children and Adolescents: Evidence for a Distinction between Adaptive and Maladaptive Narcissism," *Journal of Child and Family Studies* 16, no. 4 (2007): 508–21; E. W. Capron, "Types of Pampering and the Narcissistic Personality Trait," *Journal of Individual Psychology* 60, no. 1 (2004).

7. K. S. Carlson and P. F. Gjerde, "Preschool Personality Antecedents of Narcissism in Adolescence and Young Adulthood: A 20-Year Longitudinal Study," *Journal of Research in Personality* 43, no. 4 (2009): 570–78.

8. P. L. Hill and B. W. Roberts, "Examining 'Developmental Me': A Review of Narcissism as a Life Span Construct," in *The Handbook of Narcissism and Narcissistic Personality Disorder: Theoretical Approaches, Empirical Findings, and*

Treatments, ed. W. Keith Campbell and Joshua D. Miller (Hoboken, NJ: John Wiley & Sons, 2011), 191–201.

9. Brummelman et al., "Origins of Narcissism in Children," 3659–62. Note: See also E. Brummelman, S. Thomaes, S. A. Nelemans, B. Orobio de Castro, and B. J. Bushman, "My Child Is God's Gift to Humanity: Development and Validation of the Parental Overvaluation Scale (POS)," *Journal of Personality and Social Psychology* 108, no. 4 (2015): 665.

10. Brummelman et al., "Origins of Narcissism in Children," 3659–62.

11. Brummelman et al., "My Child Is God's Gift to Humanity," 665.

12. B. De Clercq, K. Van Leeuwen, F. De Fruyt, A. Van Hiel, and I. Mervielde, "Maladaptive Personality Traits and Psychopathology in Childhood and Adolescence: The Moderating Effect of Parenting," *Journal of Personality* 76, no. 2 (2008): 357–83.

13. A. Khaleque, "Perceived Parental Warmth, and Children's Psychological Adjustment, and Personality Dispositions: A Meta-analysis," *Journal of Child and Family Studies* 22, no. 2 (2013): 297–306.

14. Brummelman et al., "Origins of Narcissism in Children," 3659–62; Brummelman et al., "My Child Is God's Gift to Humanity," 665.

15. E. Brummelman, J. Crocker, and B. J. Bushman, "The Praise Paradox: When and Why Praise Backfires in Children with Low Self-Esteem," *Child Development Perspectives* 10, no. 2 (2016): 111–15; E. Brummelman, S. A. Nelemans, S. Thomaes, and B. Orobio de Castro, "When Parents' Praise Inflates, Children's Self-Esteem Deflates," *Child Development* 88, no. 6 (2017): 1799–809.

16. M. R. Leary and R. F. Baumeister, "The Nature and Function of Self-Esteem: Sociometer Theory," *Advances in Experimental Social Psychology* 32 (2000): 1–62.

17. U. Orth, and R. W. Robins, "Is High Self-Esteem Beneficial? Revisiting a Classic Question," *American Psychologist* 77, no. 1 (2022): 5.

18. E. Brummelman, "How to Raise Children's Self-Esteem?" Comment on Orth and Robins, *American Psychologist* 77, no. 1 (2022): 20–22; E. Brummelman and C. Sedikides, "Raising Children with High Self-Esteem (but Not Narcissism)," *Child Development Perspectives* 14, no. 2 (2020): 83–89.

19. D. W. Winnicott, *Playing and Reality*, 2nd ed. (London: Routledge, 2005).

CHAPTER 4

1. E. Brummelman, S. Thomaes, G. M. Walton, A. M. Poorthuis, G. Overbeek, B. Orobio de Castro, and B. J. Bushman, "Unconditional Regard Buffers Children's Negative Self-Feelings," *Pediatrics* 134, no. 6 (2014): 1119–26;

S. Harter, *The Construction of the Self: Developmental and Sociocultural Foundations* (New York: Guilford Publications, 2015).

2. R. F. Baumeister, J. D. Campbell, J. I. Krueger, and K. D. Vohs, "Does High Self-Esteem Cause Better Performance, Interpersonal Success, Happiness, or Healthier Lifestyles?" *Psychological Science in the Public Interest* 4, no. 1 (2003): 1–44.

3. Baumeister, "Does High Self-Esteem Cause Better Performance," 1–44; E. Brummelman, S. A. Nelemans, S. Thomaes, and B. Orobio de Castro, "When Parents' Praise Inflates, Children's Self-Esteem Deflates," *Child Development* 88, no. 6 (2017): 1799–809; E. Brummelman, S. Thomaes, B. Orobio de Castro, G. Overbeek, and B. J. Bushman, "'That's Not Just Beautiful—That's Incredibly Beautiful!' The Adverse Impact of Inflated Praise on Children with Low Self-Esteem," *Psychological Science* 25, no. 3 (2014): 728–35.

4. M. Kowalchyk, H. Palmieri, E. Conte, and P. Wallisch, "Narcissism through the Lens of Performative Self-Elevation," *Personality and Individual Differences* 177 (2021): 110780.

5. H. Kohut, *The Restoration of the Self* (Chicago: University of Chicago Press, 2009).

6. O. F. Kernberg, *Borderline Conditions and Pathological Narcissism* (London: Rowman & Littlefield, 1985).

7. K. Horney, *New Ways in Psychoanalysis* (New York: W.W. Norton & Co., 2013).

8. A. Miller, "Depression and Grandiosity as Related Forms of Narcissistic Disturbances," *International Review of Psycho-Analysis* 6 (1979): 61–76; A. Miller and R. T. Ward, *Prisoners of Childhood: The Drama of the Gifted Child and the Search for the True Self* (Basic Books, 1981).

9. T. Millon, *Disorders of Personality*, 3rd ed. (New York: John Wiley & Sons, 1981).

10. R. S. Horton, "Parenting as a Cause of Narcissism: Empirical Support for Psychodynamic and Social Learning Theories," in *The Handbook of Narcissism and Narcissistic Personality Disorder: Theoretical Approaches, Empirical Findings, and Treatments*, eds. W. Keith Campbell and Joshua D. Miller (Hoboken, NJ: John Wiley & Sons, 2011), 181–90.

11. K. L. Mechanic and C. T. Barry, "Adolescent Grandiose and Vulnerable Narcissism: Associations with Perceived Parenting Practices," *Journal of Child and Family Studies* 24, no. 5 (2015): 1510–18.

12. Horney, *New Ways in Psychoanalysis*, 91.

13. E. Brummelman, S. Thomaes, S.A. Nelemans, B. Orobio de Castro, G. Overbeek, and B. J. Bushman, "Origins of Narcissism in Children," *Proceedings of the National Academy of Sciences* 112, no. 12 (2015): 3659–62.

14. B. K. Barber, H. E. Stolz, J. A. Olsen, W. A. Collins, and M. Burchinal, "Parental Support, Psychological Control, and Behavioral Control: Assessing

Relevance across Time, Culture, and Method," *Monographs of the Society for Research in Child Development*, (2005).

15. N. B. Perry, J. M. Dollar, S. D. Calkins, S. P. Keane, and L. Shanahan, "Childhood Self-Regulation as a Mechanism through Which Early Overcontrolling Parenting Is Associated with Adjustment in Preadolescence," *Developmental Psychology* 54, no. 8 (2018): 1542.

16. Barber, "Parental Support, Psychological Control, and Behavioral Control"; J. E. Lansford, C. Sharma, P. S. Malone, D. Woodlief, K. A. Dodge, P. Oburu, . . . and L. Di Giunta, "Corporal Punishment, Maternal Warmth, and Child Adjustment: A Longitudinal Study in Eight Countries," *Journal of Clinical Child & Adolescent Psychology* 43, no. 4 (2014): 670–85.

17. A. Morawska, C. K. Dittman, and J. C. Rusby, "Promoting Self-Regulation in Young Children: The Role of Parenting Interventions," *Clinical Child and Family Psychology Review* 22, no. 1 (2019): 43–51.

18. J. Weeland, E. Brummelman, S. R. Jaffee, R. R. Chhangur, D. Van der Giessen, W. Matthys, and G. Overbeek, "Does Caregivers' Use of Praise Reduce Children's Externalizing Behavior? A Longitudinal Observational Test in the Context of a Parenting Program," *Developmental Psychology* 58, no. 7 (2022); L. J. Otway, and V. L. Vignoles, "Narcissism and Childhood Recollections: A Quantitative Test of Psychoanalytic Predictions," *Personality and Social Psychology Bulletin* 32, no. 1 (2006): 104–16.

19. K. Sandquist, B. F. Grenyer, and P. Caputi, "The Relation of Early Environmental Experience to Shame and Self-Criticism: Psychological Pathways to Depression," Proceedings of the 44th APS Annual Conference, Darwin, Northern Territory, Australia, 30 September–4 October 2009; C. B. Carvalho, M. Sousa, C. da Motta, and J. M. Cabral, "The Role of Shame, Self-Criticism and Early Emotional Memories in Adolescents' Paranoid Ideation," *Journal of Child and Family Studies* 28, no. 5 (2019): 1337–45.

20. T. Curran and A. P. Hill, "Young People's Perceptions of Their Parents' Expectations and Criticism Are Increasing Over Time: Implications for Perfectionism," *Psychological Bulletin* 148, nos. 1–2 (2022): 107–28.

21. R. C. Loeb, L. Horst, and P. J. Horton, "Family Interaction Patterns Associated with Self-Esteem in Preadolescent Girls and Boys," *Merrill-Palmer Quarterly of Behavior and Development* 26, no. 3 (1980): 205–17; A. Khaleque "Perceived Parental Warmth, and Children's Psychological Adjustment, and Personality Dispositions: A Meta-analysis," *Journal of Child and Family Studies* 22, no. 2 (2013): 297–306.

22. Brummelman et al., "Origins of Narcissism in Children," 3659–62.

23. Curran and Hill, "Young People's Perceptions of their Parents' Expectations."

CHAPTER 5

1. E. A. Skowron, S. E. Holmes, and R. M. Sabatelli, "Deconstructing Differentiation: Self-Regulation, Interdependent Relating, and Well-Being in Adulthood, *Contemporary Family Therapy* 25, no. 1 (2003): 111–29.

2. A. Pandey, D. Hale, S. Das, A. L. Goddings, S. J. Blakemore, and R. M. Viner, "Effectiveness of Universal Self-Regulation–Based Interventions in Children and Adolescents: A Systematic Review and Meta-analysis," *JAMA Pediatrics* 172, no. 6 (2018): 566–75.

3. C. Verzeletti, V. L. Zammuner, C. Galli, and S. Agnoli, "Emotion Regulation Strategies and Psychosocial Well-Being in Adolescence, *Cogent Psychology* 3, no. 1 (2016): 1199294.

4. K. D. Vohs and R. F. Baumeister, eds., *Handbook of Self-Regulation: Research, Theory, and Applications* (New York: The Guilford Press, 2016).

5. M. M. Linehan, M. Bohus, and T. R. Lynch, "Dialectical Behavior Therapy for Pervasive Emotion Dysregulation: Theoretical and Practical Underpinnings," in *Handbook of Emotion Regulation*, ed. J. J. Gross (New York: The Guilford Press, 2007): 581–605.

6. R.F. Baumeister, "Self-Regulation, Ego Depletion, and Inhibition," *Neuropsychologia* 65 (2014): 313–19.

7. A. L. Duckworth and S. M. Carlson, "Self-Regulation and School Success. *Self-Regulation and Autonomy: Social and Developmental Dimensions of Human Conduct* 40 (2013): 208; A. L. Duckworth, E. Tsukayama, and T. A. Kirby, "Is It Really Self-Control? Examining the Predictive Power of the Delay of Gratification Task," *Personality and Social Psychology Bulletin* 39, no. 7 (2013): 843–55; W. Mischel, *The Marshmallow Test: Why Self-Control Is the Engine of Success* (New York: Little, Brown Spark, 2014).

8. Duckworth and Carlson, "Self-Regulation and School Success, 208; Duckworth, Tsukayama, and Kirby, "Is It Really Self-Control?" 843–55; Mischel, *The Marshmallow Test.*

9. A. L. Duckworth, and M. E. Seligman, "Self-Discipline Outdoes IQ in Predicting Academic Performance of Adolescents," *Psychological Science* 16, no. 12 (2005): 939–44.

10. T. E. Moffitt, L. Arseneault, D. Belsky, N. Dickson, R. J. Hancox, H. Harrington, . . . and A. Caspi, "A Gradient of Childhood Self-Control Predicts Health, Wealth, and Public Safety," *Proceedings of the National Academy of Sciences* 108, no. 7 (2011): 2693–98.

11. J. B. Li, Y. E. Willems, F. M. Stok, M. Deković, M. Bartels, and C. Finkenauer, "Parenting and Self-Control across Early to Late Adolescence: A Three-Level Meta-analysis," *Perspectives on Psychological Science* 14, no. 6 (2019): 967–1005.

12. S. Freud, *A General Introduction to Psychoanalysis* (New York: Horace Liveright, 1920), 372–87.

13. A. L Duckworth, C. Peterson, M. D. Matthews, and D. R. Kelly, "Grit: Perseverance and Passion for Long-Term Goals," *Journal of Personality and Social Psychology* 92, no. 6 (2007): 1087.

14. Sheldon, K. M., P. E. Jose, T. B. Kashdan, and A. Jarden. Personality, Effective Goal-Striving, and Enhanced Well-Being: Comparing 10 Candidate Personality Strengths. *Personality and Social Psychology Bulletin* 41, no. 4 (2015): 575–85.

15. A. Duckworth and J. J. Gross, "Self-Control and Grit: Related but Separable Determinants of Success," *Current Directions in Psychological Science* 23, no. 5 (2014): 319–25.

16. A. Caspi, B. W. Roberts, and R. L. Shiner, "Personality Development: Stability and Change," *Annual Review Psychology* 56 (2005): 453–84; C. J. Ferguson, "A Meta-analysis of Normal and Disordered Personality across the Life Span," *Journal of Personality and Social Psychology* 98, no. 4 (2010): 659; B. W. Roberts and W. F. DelVecchio, "The Rank-Order Consistency of Personality Traits from Childhood to Old Age: a Quantitative Review of Longitudinal Studies," *Psychological Bulletin* 126, no. 1 (2000): 3.

17. A. Thomaes and S. Chess, *Temperament and Development* (New York: Brunner-Routledge, 1977); A. Thomaes and S. Chess, "The New York Longitudinal Study: From Infancy to Early Adult Life," in *The Study of Temperament* (Hillsdale, NJ: Lawrence Erlbaum, 2013), 39–52; A. Thomaes and S. Chess, "Temperament and Follow-Up to Adulthood," in *Temperamental Differences in Infants and Young Children*, ed. Ruth Porter and Geralyn Lawrenson (1982), 168–75.

18. E. T. Gershoff and A. Grogan-Kaylor, "Spanking and Child Outcomes: Old Controversies and New Meta-analyses," *Journal of Family Psychology* 30, no. 4 (2016): 453; R. E. Larzelere and B. R. Kuhn, "Comparing Child Outcomes of Physical Punishment and Alternative Disciplinary Tactics: A Meta-analysis," *Clinical Child and Family Psychology Review* 8, no. 1 (2005): 1-37.

19. American Psychological Association, "Resolution on Physical Discipline of Children by Parents," press release, February 18, 2019, https://www.apa.org/news/press/releases/2019/02/physical-discipline.

20. N. B. Perry, J. M. Dollar, S. D. Calkins, S. P. Keane, and L. Shanahan, "Childhood Self-Regulation as a Mechanism through Which Early Overcontrolling Parenting Is Associated with Adjustment in Preadolescence," *Developmental Psychology* 54, no. 8 (2018): 1542.

CHAPTER 6

1. S. Bolton and J. Hattie, "Cognitive and Brain Development: Executive Function, Piaget, and the Prefrontal Cortex," *Archives of Psychology* 1, no. 3 (2017).
2. Bolton and Hattie.
3. Bolton and Hattie.
4. Jean Piaget and Barbel Inhelder, *A Child's Conception of Space*, trans. F. J. Langdon and J. L. Lunzer (New York: Humanities Press, 1956).
5. H. Borke, "Piaget's Mountains Revisited: Changes in the Egocentric Landscape," *Developmental Psychology* 11, no. 2 (1975): 240; M. Hughes and M. Donaldson, "The Use of Hiding Games for Studying the Coordination of Viewpoints," *Educational Review* 31, no. 2 (1979): 133–40.
6. M. L. Healey and M. Grossman, "Cognitive and Affective Perspective-Taking: Evidence for Shared and Dissociable Anatomical Substrates," *Frontiers in Neurology* 9 (2018): 491.
7. A. Vaish, M. Carpenter, and M. Tomasello, "Sympathy through Affective Perspective Taking and Its Relation to Prosocial Behavior in Toddlers," *Developmental Psychology* 45, no. 2 (2009): 534.
8. C. D. Batson, S. Early, and G. Salvarani, "Perspective Taking: Imagining How Another Feels versus Imagining How You Would Feel," *Personality and Social Psychology Bulletin* 23 (1997): 751–58.
9. Bolton and Hattie, "Cognitive and Brain Development."

CHAPTER 7

1. A. D. Cox, C. Puckering, A. Pound, and M. Mills, "The Impact of Maternal Depression in Young Children," *Journal of Child Psychology and Psychiatry* 28, no. 6 (1987): 917–28.
2. R. Feldman, D. Dollberg, and R. Nadam, "The Expression and Regulation of Anger in Toddlers: Relations to Maternal Behavior and Mental Representations," *Infant Behavior and Development* 34, no. 2 (2011): 310–20.
3. J. Bowlby, "The Bowlby-Ainsworth Attachment Theory," *Behavioral and Brain Sciences* 2, no. 4 (1979): 637–38.
4. Bowlby, 637–38.
5. M. S. Ainsworth, "Infant-Mother Attachment," *American Psychologist* 34, no. 10 (1979): 932.
6. M. S. Ainsworth and M. Salter, "Individual Differences in Strange-Situational Behavior of One-Year-Olds," in *The Origins of Human Social Relations*,

ed. R. Schaffer (London: Academic Press, 1969); M. S. Ainsworth, S. M. Bell, and D. J. Stayton, "Individual Differences in the Development of Some Attachment Behaviors," *Merrill-Palmer Quarterly of Behavior and Development* 18, no. 2 (1972): 123–43; D. J. Stayton, R. Hogan, and M. S. Ainsworth, "Infant Obedience and Maternal Behavior: The Origins of Socialization Reconsidered," *Child Development* (1971): 1057–69; J. Bowlby, "The Bowlby-Ainsworth Attachment Theory," *Behavioral and Brain Sciences* 2, no. 4 (1979): 637–38.

   7. Ainsworth, "Individual Differences in Strange-Situational Behavior."

   8. M. Main and J. Solomon, "Procedures for Identifying Infants as Disorganized/Disoriented during the Ainsworth Strange Situation," *Attachment in the Preschool Years: Theory, Research, and Intervention* 1 (1990): 121–60.

   9. Stayton, Hogan, and Ainsworth, "Infant Obedience and Maternal Behavior," 1057–69; M. S. Ainsworth, "The Bowlby-Ainsworth Attachment Theory," *Behavioral and Brain Sciences* 1, no. 3 (1978): 436–38.

   10. M. Main and J. Cassidy, "Categories of Response to Reunion with the Parent at Age 6: Predictable from Infant Attachment Classifications and Stable over a 1-Month Period," *Developmental Psychology* 24, no. 3 (1988): 415.

   11. Ainsworth, "Infant-Mother Attachment," 932.

   12. Ainsworth, 932.

   13. Ainsworth, 932.

   14. U. G. Wartner, K. Grossmann, E. Fremmer-Bombik, and G. Suess, "Attachment Patterns at Age Six in South Germany: Predictability from Infancy and Implications for Preschool Behavior," *Child Development* 65, no. 4 (1994): 1014–27. Note: Finding that 78 percent of children were classified in the same way at both one and six years of age.

   15. Jerome Kagan, *The Nature of the Child* (New York: Basic Books, 1984).

   16. N. A. Fox, "Psychophysiological Correlates of Emotional Reactivity during the First Year of Life," *Developmental Psychology* 25, no. 3 (1989): 364.

   17. Eric H. Erikson, *The Life Cycle Completed* (New York: W. W. Norton, 1982).

   18. L. Campbell and S. C. Stanton, "Adult Attachment and Trust in Romantic Relationships," *Current Opinion in Psychology* 25 (2019): 148–51.

   19. M. S. Ainsworth, "The Development of Infant-Mother Attachment," in *In the Beginning* (New York: Columbia University Press, 1982) 133–43; M. S. Ainsworth, "Attachments beyond Infancy," *American Psychologist* 44, no. 4 (1989): 709; J. Bowlby, "The Making and Breaking of Affectional Bonds: I. Aetiology and Psychopathology in the Light of Attachment Theory," *The British Journal of Psychiatry* 130, no. 3 (1977): 201–10; J. Bowlby, "By Ethology out of Psycho-Analysis: An Experiment in Interbreeding," *Animal Behaviour* 28, no. 3 (1980): 649–56; J. Bowlby, "Attachment and Loss: Retrospect and Prospect, *American Journal of Orthopsychiatry* 52, no. 4 (1982): 664.

20. C. George, N. Kaplan, and M. Main, "Adult Attachment Interview," Unpublished manuscript (1996).

21. K. Bartholomew, and L. M. Horowitz, "Attachment Styles among Young Adults: A Test of a Four-Category Model," *Journal of Personality and Social Psychology* 61, no. 2 (1991): 226.

22. C. Hazan, and P. R. Shaver, "Love and Work: An Attachment-Theoretical Perspective," *Journal of Personality and Social Psychology* 59, no. 2 (1990): 270.

23. K. A. Brennan and P. R. Shaver, "Dimensions of Adult Attachment, Affect Regulation, and Romantic Relationship Functioning, *Personality and Social Psychology Bulletin* 21, no. 3 (1995): 267–83.

24. Bartholomew and Horowitz, "Attachment Styles among Young Adults," 226.

25. Bartholomew and Horowitz, 226.

26. J. Cassidy, "Emotion Regulation: Influences of Attachment Relationships," *Monographs of the Society for Research in Child Development* 59, nos. 2–3, (1994): 228–49.

27. P. A. Frazier, A. L. Byer, A. R. Fischer, D. M. Wright, and K. A. DeBord, "Adult Attachment Style and Partner Choice: Correlational and Experimental Findings," *Personal Relationships* 3, no. 2 (1996): 117–36.

28. P. Shaver and C. Hazan, "Being Lonely, Falling in Love," *Journal of Social Behavior and Personality* 2, no. 2 (1987): 105.

29. M. Mikulincer and P. R. Shaver, "Attachment Theory and Emotions in Close Relationships: Exploring the Attachment-Related Dynamics of Emotional Reactions to Relational Events," *Personal Relationships* 12, no. 2 (2005): 149–68.

30. Frazier et al., "Adult Attachment Style and Partner Choice," 117–36.

31. N. Favez and H. Tissot, "Fearful-Avoidant Attachment: A Specific Impact on Sexuality?" *Journal of Sex and Marital Therapy* 45, no. 6 (2019): 510–23.

32. Favez and Tissot, 510–23.

33. E. Waters, S. Merrick, D. Treboux, J. Crowell, and L. Albersheim, "Attachment Security in Infancy and Early Adulthood: A Twenty-Year Longitudinal Study," *Child Development* 71, no. 3 (2000): 684–89.

34. C. D. Batson, S. Early, and G. Salvarani, "Perspective Taking: Imagining How Another Feels versus Imagining How You Would Feel," *Personality and Social Psychology Bulletin* 23 (1997): 751–58.

35. Leonard Bernstein, "When Asked What the Most Difficult Instrument in the Orchestra Is, Leonard Bernstein Responded," Facebook, January 6, 2016. https://www.facebook.com/LeonardBernstein/photos/a.10150211953950285/10159362309415285.

36. K. J. Rotenberg, "The Socialization of Trust: Parents' and Children's Interpersonal Trust," *International Journal of Behavioral Development* 18, no. 4 (1995): 713–26.

37. S. M. Eyberg, M. M. Nelson, and S. R. Boggs, "Evidence-Based Psychosocial Treatments for Children and Adolescents with Disruptive Behavior," *Journal of Clinical Child and Adolescent Psychology* 37, no. 1 (2008): 215–37.

CHAPTER 8

1. D. Baumrind, "Child Care Practices Anteceding Three Patterns of Preschool Behavior. *Genetic Psychology Monographs* 75, no. 1 (1967): 43–88; D. Baumrind, "Current Patterns of Parental Authority," *Developmental Psychology* 4, nos. 1–2 (1971): 1; D. Baumrind, "Rearing Competent Children," in *Child Development Today and Tomorrow,* ed. W. Damon, (Jossey-Bass/Wiley, 1988), 349–78; D. Baumrind, "The Influence of Parenting Style on Adolescent Competence and Substance Use," *The Journal of Early Adolescence* 11, no. 1 (1991): 56–95.

2. Baumrind, "The Influence of Parenting Style"; L. Steinberg, S. D. Lamborn, N. Darling, N. S. Mounts, and S. M. Dornbusch, "Over-Time Changes in Adjustment and Competence among Adolescents from Authoritative, Authoritarian, Indulgent, and Neglectful Families," *Child Development* 65, no. 3 (1994): 754–70; L. Steinberg, J. D. Elmen, and N. S. Mounts, "Authoritative Parenting, Psychosocial Maturity, and Academic Success among Adolescents," *Child Development* 60, no. 6 (1989): 1424–36.

3. Baumrind, "The Influence of Parenting Style"; Steinberg, "Over-Time Changes in Adjustment and Competence"; Steinberg, "Authoritative Parenting, Psychosocial Maturity, and Academic Success."

4. Steinberg et al., "Over-Time Changes in Adjustment and Competence," 754–70; L. Rankin Williams, K. A. Degnan, K. E. Perez-Edgar, H. A. Henderson, K. H. Rubin, D. S. Pine, and N. A. Fox, "Impact of Behavioral Inhibition and Parenting Style on Internalizing and Externalizing Problems from Early Childhood through Adolescence," *Journal of Abnormal Child Psychology* 37, no. 8 (2009): 1063–75; U. Wolfradt, S. Hempel, and J. N. Miles, "Perceived Parenting Styles, Depersonalisation, Anxiety and Coping Behaviour in Adolescents," *Personality and Individual Differences* 34, no. 3 (2003): 521–32.

5. Steinberg et al., "Over-Time Changes in Adjustment and Competence"; Williams et al., "Impact of Behavioral Inhibition and Parenting Style"; Wolfradt, "Perceived Parenting Style."

6. S. D. Lamborn, N. S. Mounts, L. Steinberg, and S. M. Dornbusch, "Patterns of Competence and Adjustment among Adolescents from Authoritative, Authoritarian, Indulgent, and Neglectful Families," *Child Development* 62, no. 5 (1991): 1049–65; Steinberg et al., "Over-Time Changes in Adjustment and Competence," 754–70; Williams et al., "Impact of Behavioral Inhibition

and Parenting Style," 1063–75; Wolfradt et al., "Perceived Parenting Styles, Depersonalisation, Anxiety and Coping Behaviour," 521–32.

7. Lamborn et al., "Patterns of Competence and Adjustment"; Steinberg et al., "Over-Time Changes in Adjustment and Competence"; Williams et al., "Impact of Behavioral Inhibition and Parenting Style"; Wolfradt et al., "Perceived Parenting Styles."

8. Baumrind, "The Influence of Parenting Style," 56–95; Lamborn et al., "Patterns of Competence and Adjustment among Adolescents," 1049–65; Steinberg et al., "Over-Time Changes in Adjustment and Competence," 754–70.

9. E. Waters and E. M. Cummings, "A Secure Base from Which to Explore Close Relationships. *Child Development* 71, no. 1 (2000): 164–72.

10. G. M. Barnes and M. P. Farrell, "Parental Support and Control as Predictors of Adolescent Drinking, Delinquency, and Related Problem Behaviors," *Journal of Marriage and the Family*, (1992): 763–76; R. A. Bean, B. K. Barber, and D. R. Crane, "Parental Support, Behavioral Control, and Psychological Control among African American Youth: The Relationships to Academic Grades, Delinquency, and Depression," *Journal of Family Issues* 27, no. 10 (2006): 1335–55; D. S. Shaw, K. Keenan, and J. I. Vondra, "Developmental Precursors of Externalizing Behavior: Ages 1 to 3. *Developmental Psychology* 30, no. 3 (1994): 355.

11. B. K. Barber and E. L. Harmon, "Violating The Self: Parental Psychological Control of Children and Adolescents" in *Intrusive Parenting: How Psychological Control Affects Children and Adolescents*, ed. B. K. Barber (Washington, DC: American Psychological Association, 2002), 15–52; E. E. Maccoby, *Social Development: Psychological Growth and the Parent-Child Relationship* (New York: Harcourt Brace Jovanovich, 1980); L. Steinberg, "Autonomy, Conflict, and Harmony in the Family Relationship," in *At the Threshold: The Developing Adolescent*, eds. S. S. Feldman and G. R. Elliott (Cambridge, MA: Harvard University Press, 1990), 255–76.

12. Barnes and Farrell, "Parental Support and Control as Predictors," 763–76; J. D. Coie and K. A. Dodge, "Aggression and Antisocial Behavior," in *Handbook of Child Psychology: Social, Emotional, and Personality Development*, eds. W. Damon and N. Eisenberg (Hoboken, NJ: John Wiley & Sons, Inc., 1998), 779–862; N. L. Galambos, E. T. Barker, and D. M. Almeida, "Parents Do Matter: Trajectories of Change in Externalizing and Internalizing Problems in Early Adolescence," *Child Development* 74, no. 2 (2003): 578–94.; G. R. Patterson, T. J. Dishion, and L. Bank, "Family Interaction: A Process Model of Deviancy Training," *Aggressive Behavior* 10, no. 3 (1984): 253–67.

13. B. K. Barber, "Parental Psychological Control: Revisiting a Neglected Construct," *Child Development* 67: (1996), 3296–319; B. K. Barber, H. E. Stolz, J. A. Olsen, W. A. Collins, and M. Burchinal, *Parental Support, Psychological Control, and Behavioral Control: Assessing Relevance across Time, Culture, and Method,*

Monographs of the Society for Research in Child Development (Malden, MA: Wiley Blackwell, 2005).

14. Barber and Harmon, "Violating the Self," 15–52; Barber et al., "Parental Support, Psychological Control, and Behavioral Control," i-147; S. Kuppens, L. Laurent, M. Heyvaert, and P. Onghena, "Associations Between Parental Psychological Control and Relational Aggression in Children and Adolescents: A Multilevel and Sequential Meta-Analysis," *Developmental Psychology* 49, no. 9 (2013): 1697.

15. B. Beebe, J. Jaffe, S. Markese, K. Buck, H. Chen, P. Cohen, L. Bahrick, H. Andrews, and S. Feldstein, "The Origins of 12-Month Attachment: A Microanalysis of 4-Month Mother-Infant Interaction," *Attachment and Human Development* 12, nos. 1–2 (2010): 3–141.

CHAPTER 9

1. T. Millon, and R. D. Davis, "An Evolutionary Theory of Personality Disorders," in *Major Theories of Personality Disorder*, eds. J. F. Clarkin and M. F. Lenzenweger (New York: Guilford Press, 1996), 221–346.

Bibliography

Ainsworth, M. S. "Attachments beyond Infancy." *American Psychologist* 44, no. 4 (1989): 709.

———. "The Bowlby-Ainsworth Attachment Theory." *Behavioral and Brain Sciences* 1, no. 3 (1978): 436–38.

———. "The Development of Infant-Mother Attachment." In *In the Beginning*, 133–43. New York: Columbia University Press, 1982.

———. "Infant–Mother Attachment." *American Psychologist*, 34 no. 10, (1979): 932.

Ainsworth, M. S., S. M. Bell, and D. J. Stayton. "Individual Differences in the Development of Some Attachment Behaviors." *Merrill-Palmer Quarterly of Behavior and Development* 18, no. 2 (1972): 123–43.

Ainsworth, M. S., and M. Salter. "Individual Differences in Strange-Situational Behavior of One-Year-Olds." In *The Origins of Human Social Relations*, edited by R. Schaffer. London: Academic Press, 1969.

Akhtar, S., and J. A. Thompson. "Overview: Narcissistic Personality Disorder." *American Journal of Psychiatry* 139 (1982): 12–20.

Alampay, L. P., J. Godwin, J. E. Lansford, A. S. Bombi, M. H. Bornstein, L. Chang, . . . and D. Bacchini. "Severity and Justness Do Not Moderate the Relation between Corporal Punishment and Negative Child Outcomes: A Multicultural and Longitudinal Study." *International Journal of Behavioral Development* 41, no. 4 (2017): 491–502.

Altschul, I., S. J., Lee, and E. T. Gershoff. "Not Hits: Warmth and Spanking as Predictors of Child Social Competence." *Journal of Marriage and Family* 78, no. 3 (2016): 695–714.

American Psychological Association. "Resolution on Physical Discipline of Children by Parents." Press release, February 18, 2019. https://www.Apa.Org/News/Press/Releases/2019/02/Physical-Discipline.

Barbin, J. N., and R. Ocampo. "Parenting Behaviors as Predictors of Narcissism." *Bedan Journal of Psychology* (2017): 34–40.

Barber, B. K. "Parental Psychological Control: Revisiting a Neglected Construct." *Child Development* 67 (1996): 3296–319.

————. *Reintroducing Parental Psychological Control.* In *Intrusive Parenting: How Psychological Control Affects Children and Adolescents,* 3–13. Washington, DC: American Psychological Association, 2002.

Barber, B. K., and E. L. Harmon. "Violating the Self: Parental Psychological Control of Children and Adolescents." In *Intrusive Parenting: How Psychological Control Affects Children and Adolescents,* edited by B. K. Barber, 15–52. Washington, DC: American Psychological Association, 2002.

Barber, B. K., J. E. Olsen, and S. C. Shagle. "Associations between Parental Psychological and Behavioral Control and Youth Internalized and Externalized Behaviors." *Child Development* 65 (1994): 1120–36.

Barber, B. K., H. E. Stolz, J. A. Olsen, W. A. Collins, and M. Burchinal. *Parental Support, Psychological Control, and Behavioral Control: Assessing Relevance across Time, Culture, and Method. Monographs of the Society for Research in Child Development.* Malden, MA: Wiley Blackwell, 2005.

Barnes, G. M., and M. P. Farrell. "Parental Support and Control as Predictors of Adolescent Drinking, Delinquency, and Related Problem Behaviors." *Journal of Marriage and the Family* (1992), 763–76.

Barry, C. T., P. J. Frick, K. K. Adler, and S. J. Grafeman. "The Predictive Utility of Narcissism among Children and Adolescents: Evidence for a Distinction between Adaptive and Maladaptive Narcissism." *Journal of Child and Family Studies* 16, no. 4 (2007): 508–21.

Barry, C. T., P. J. Frick, and A. L. Killian. "The Relation of Narcissism and Self-Esteem to Conduct Problems in Children: A Preliminary Investigation." *Journal of Clinical Child and Adolescent Psychology* 32, no. 1 (2003): 139–52.

Bartholomew, K., and L. M. Horowitz. "Attachment Styles among Young Adults: A Test of a Four-Category Model." *Journal of Personality and Social Psychology* 61, no. 2 (1991): 226.

Bates, J. E., G. S. Pettit, K. A. Dodge, and B. Ridge. "Interaction of Temperamental Resistance to Control and Restrictive Parenting in the Development of Externalizing Behavior." *Developmental Psychology* 34, no. 5 (1998): 982.

Batson, C. D., S. Early, and G. Salvarani. "Perspective Taking: Imagining How Another Feels versus Imaging How You Would Feel." *Personality and Social Psychology Bulletin* 23 (1997): 751–58.

Baumeister, R. F. "Self-Regulation, Ego Depletion, and Inhibition." *Neuropsychologia* 65 (2014): 313–19.

Baumeister, R. F., J. D. Campbell, J. I. Krueger, and K. D. Vohs. "Does High Self-Esteem Cause Better Performance, Interpersonal Success, Happiness, or Healthier Lifestyles?" *Psychological Science in the Public Interest* 4, no. 1 (2003): 1–44.

Baumeister, R. F., and M. R. Leary. "The Need to Belong: Desire for Inter-personal Attachments as a Fundamental Human Motivation." *Psychological Bulletin* 117, no. 3 (1995): 497–529.

Baumeister, R. F., K. D. Vohs, and D. M. Tice. "The Strength Model of Self-Control." *Current Directions in Psychological Science* 16, no. 6 (2007): 351–55.

Baumrind, D. "Child Care Practices Anteceding Three Patterns of Preschool Behavior." *Genetic Psychology Monographs* 75, no. 1 (1967).

———. "Current Patterns of Parental Authority." *Developmental Psychology* 4, nos. 1–2 (1971): 1.

———. "Differentiating between Confrontive and Coercive Kinds of Parental Power-Assertive Disciplinary Practices." *Human Development* 55, no. 2 (2012): 35–51.

———. "The Influence of Parenting Style on Adolescent Competence and Substance Use." *Journal of Early Adolescence* 11, no. 1 (1991): 56–95.

———. "Rearing Competent Children." In *Child Development Today and Tomorrow,* edited by W. Damon, 349–78. New York: Jossey-Bass/Wiley, 1988.

Bean, R. A., B. K. Barber, and D. R. Crane. "Parental Support, Behavioral Control, and Psychological Control among African American Youth: The Relationships to Academic Grades, Delinquency, and Depression." *Journal of Family Issues* 27, no. 10 (2006): 1335–55.

Beebe, B., J. Jaffe, S. Markese, K. Buck, H. Chen, P. Cohen, L. Bahrick, H. Andrews, and S. Feldstein. "The Origins of 12-Month Attachment: A Microanalysis of 4-Month Mother-Infant Interaction." *Attachment and Human Development* 12, nos. 1–2 (2010): 3–141.

Bolton, S., and J. Hattie. "Cognitive and Brain Development: Executive Function, Piaget, and the Prefrontal Cortex." *Archives of Psychology* 1, no. 3 (2017).

Borke, H. "Piaget's Mountains Revisited: Changes in the Egocentric Landscape." *Developmental Psychology* 11, no. 2 (1975): 240.

Bowlby, J. "Attachment and Loss: Retrospect and Prospect." *American Journal of Orthopsychiatry* 52, no. 4 (1982): 664.

———. "The Bowlby-Ainsworth Attachment Theory." *Behavioral and Brain Sciences* 2, no. 4 (1979): 637–38.

———. "By Ethology out of Psycho-Analysis: An Experiment in Interbreeding." *Animal Behaviour* 28, no. 3 (1980): 649–56.

———. "The Making and Breaking of Affectional Bonds: I. Aetiology and Psychopathology in the Light of Attachment Theory." *British Journal of Psychiatry* 130, no. 3 (1977): 201–10.

Bowlby, J., M. Fry, M. S. Ainsworth, and World Health Organization. *Child Care and the Growth of Love.* Abridged and edited by Margery Fry, 2nd ed. Harmondsworth, UK: Penguin Books, 1965.

Brennan, K. A., and P. R. Shaver. "Dimensions of Adult Attachment, Affect Regulation, and Romantic Relationship Functioning." *Personality and Social Psychology Bulletin* 21, no. 3 (1995): 267–83.

Brown, R. P., K. Budzek, and M. Tamborski. "On the Meaning and Measure of Narcissism." *Personality and Social Psychology Bulletin* 35, no. 7 (2009): 951–64.

Brummelman, E. "How to Raise Children's Self-Esteem." Comment on Orth and Robins. *American Psychologist* 77, no. 1 (2022): 20–22.

Brummelman, E., J. Crocker, and B. J. Bushman. "The Praise Paradox: When and Why Praise Backfires in Children with Low Self-Esteem." *Child Development Perspectives* 10, no. 2 (2016): 111–15.

Brummelman, E., S. Grapsas, and K. van der Kooij. "Parental Praise and Children's Exploration: A Virtual Reality Experiment." *Scientific Reports* 12, no. 1 (2022): 1–11.

Brummelman, E., S. A. Nelemans, S. Thomaes, and B. Orobio De Castro. "When Parents' Praise Inflates, Children's Self-Esteem Deflates." *Child Development* 88, no. 6 (2017): 1799–809.

Brummelman, E., M. Nikolić, B. Nevicka, and S. M. Bögels. "Early Physiological Indicators of Narcissism and Self-Esteem in Children." *Psychophysiology* (2022): E14082.

Brummelman, E., and C. Sedikides. "Raising Children with High Self-Esteem (but Not Narcissism)." *Child Development Perspectives* 14, no. 2 (2020): 83–89.

Brummelman, E., S. Thomaes, S. A. Nelemans, B. Orobio De Castro, and B. J. Bushman. "My Child Is God's Gift to Humanity: Development and Validation of the Parental Overvaluation Scale (POS)." *Journal of Personality and Social Psychology* 108, no. 4 (2015): 665.

Brummelman, E., S. Thomaes, S. A. Nelemans, B. Orobio De Castro, G. Overbeek, and B. J. Bushman. "Origins of Narcissism in Children." *Proceedings of the National Academy of Sciences* 112, no. 12 (2015): 3659–62.

Brummelman, E., S. Thomaes, B. Orobio De Castro, G. Overbeek, and B. J. Bushman. "'That's Not Just Beautiful—That's Incredibly Beautiful!' The Adverse Impact of Inflated Praise on Children with Low Self-Esteem." *Psychological Science* 25, no. 3 (2014): 728–35.

Brummelman, E., S. Thomaes, and C. Sedikides. "Separating Narcissism from Self-Esteem." *Current Directions in Psychological Science* 25, no. 1 (2016): 8–13.

Brummelman, E., S. Thomaes, M. Slagt, G. Overbeek, B. O. De Castro, and B. J. Bushman. "My Child Redeems My Broken Dreams: On Parents Transferring Their Unfulfilled Ambitions onto Their Child. *Plos One* 8, no. 6 (2013): E65360.

Brummelman, E., S. Thomaes, G. M. Walton, A. M. Poorthuis, G. Overbeek, B. Orobio De Castro, and B. Bushman. "Unconditional Regard Buffers Children's Negative Self-Feelings." *Pediatrics* 134, no. 6 (2014): 1119–26.

Bushman, B. J., and R. F. Baumeister. "Threatened Egotism, Narcissism, Self-Esteem, and Direct and Displaced Aggression: Does Self-Love or Self-Hate Lead to Violence?" *Journal of Personality and Social Psychology* 75, no. 1 (1998): 219.

Campbell, W. K., A. M. Bonacci, J. Shelton, J. J. Exline, and B. J. Bushman. "Psychological Entitlement: Interpersonal Consequences and Validation of a Self-Report Measure." *Journal of Personality Assessment* 83, no. 1 (2004): 29–45.

Campbell, W. K., and C. Crist. *The New Science of Narcissism: Understanding One of the Greatest Psychological Challenges of Our Time—and What You Can Do about It.* Boulder, CO: Sounds True, 2020.

Campbell, L., and S. C. Stanton. "Adult Attachment and Trust in Romantic Relationships." *Current Opinion in Psychology* 25 (2019): 148–51.

Capron, E. W. "Types of Pampering and the Narcissistic Personality Trait." *Journal of Individual Psychology* 60, no. 1 (2004).

Carlson, K. S., and P. F. Gjerde. "Preschool Personality Antecedents of Narcissism in Adolescence and Young Adulthood: A 20-Year Longitudinal Study." *Journal of Research in Personality* 43, no. 4 (2009): 570–78.

Carvalho, C. B., M. Sousa, C. Da Motta, and J. M. Cabral. "The Role of Shame, Self-Criticism and Early Emotional Memories in Adolescents' Paranoid Ideation." *Journal of Child and Family Studies* 28, no. 5 (2019): 1337–45.

Caspi, A., B. W. Roberts, and R. L. Shiner. "Personality Development: Stability and Change." *Annual Review Psychology* 56 (2005): 453–84.

Cassidy, J. "Emotion Regulation: Influences of Attachment Relationships." *Monographs of the Society for Research in Child Development* 59, nos. 2–3 (1994): 228–49.

Chess, S., and A. Thomas. *Goodness of Fit: Clinical Applications, from Infancy through Adult Life.* New York: Routledge, 2013.

Chess, S., A. Thomas, M. Rutter, and H. G. Birch. "Interaction of Temperament and Environment in the Production of Behavioral Disturbances in Children." *American Journal of Psychiatry* 120, no. 2 (1963): 142–48.

Clarke-Stewart, K. A. *Interactions between Mothers and Their Young Children: Characteristics and Consequences.* New Haven, CT: Yale University Press, 1972.

Coie, J. D., and K. A. Dodge. "Aggression and Antisocial Behavior." In *Handbook of Child Psychology: Social, Emotional, and Personality Development*, edited by W. Damon and N. Eisenberg, 779–862. Hoboken, NJ: John Wiley & Sons, 1998.

Cox, A. D., C. Puckering, A. Pound, and M. Mills. "The Impact of Maternal Depression in Young Children." *Journal of Child Psychology and Psychiatry* 28, no. 6 (1987): 917–28.

Cramer, P. "Narcissism and Attachment: The Importance of Early Parenting." *Journal of Nervous and Mental Disease* 207, no. 2 (2019): 69–75.

————. "Young Adult Narcissism: A 20-Year Longitudinal Study of the Contribution of Parenting Styles, Preschool Precursors of Narcissism, and Denial." *Journal of Research in Personality* 45, no. 1 (2011): 19–28.

Cummings, E. M., P. T. Davies, and S. B. Campbell. *Developmental Psychopathology and Family Process: Theory, Research, and Clinical Implications.* Guilford Publications, 2020.

Curran, T., and A. P. Hill. "Young People's Perceptions of Their Parents' Expectations and Criticism Are Increasing over Time: Implications for Perfectionism." *Psychological Bulletin* 148, no. 1–2 (2022): 107–28.

De Clercq, B., K. Van Leeuwen, F. De Fruyt, A. Van Hiel, and I. Mervielde. "Maladaptive Personality Traits and Psychopathology in Childhood and Adolescence: The Moderating Effect of Parenting." *Journal of Personality* 76, no. 2 (2008): 357–83.

Derry, K. L., J. J. Ohan, and D. M. Bayliss. "Fearing Failure: Grandiose Narcissism, Vulnerable Narcissism, and Emotional Reactivity in Children." *Child Development* 91, no. 3 (2020): E581–E596.

Duckworth, A. L., and S. M. Carlson. "Self-Regulation and School Success." *Self-Regulation and Autonomy: Social and Developmental Dimensions of Human Conduct* 40 (2013): 208.

Duckworth, A., and J. J Gross. "Self-Control and Grit: Related but Separable Determinants of Success." *Current Directions in Psychological Science* 23, no. 5 (2014): 319–25.

Duckworth, A. L., C. Peterson, M. D. Matthews, and D. R. Kelly. "Grit: Perseverance and Passion for Long-Term Goals." *Journal of Personality and Social Psychology* 92, no. 6 (2007): 1087.

Duckworth, A. L., and M. E. Seligman. "The Science and Practice of Self-Control." *Perspectives on Psychological Science* 12, no. 5 (2017): 715–18.

————. "Self-Discipline Outdoes IQ in Predicting Academic Performance of Adolescents." *Psychological Science* 16, no. 12 (2005): 939–44.

Duckworth, A. L., E. Tsukayama, and T. A. Kirby. "Is It Really Self-Control? Examining the Predictive Power of the Delay of Gratification Task." *Personality and Social Psychology Bulletin* 39, no. 7 (2013): 843–55.

Emmons, R. A. "Narcissism: Theory and Measurement." *Journal of Personality and Social Psychology* 52, no. 1 (1987): 11.

Erikson, E. H. *The Life Cycle Completed.* New York: W. W. Norton, 1982.

Eromo, T. L., and D. A. Levy. "The Rise, Fall, and Resurgence of 'Self-Esteem': A Critique, Reconceptualization, and Recommendations." *North American Journal of Psychology* 19, no. 2 (2017).

Eyberg, S. M., M. M. Nelson, and S. R. Boggs. "Evidence-Based Psychosocial Treatments for Children and Adolescents with Disruptive Behavior." *Journal of Clinical Child and Adolescent Psychology* 37, no. 1 (2008): 215–37.

Exline, J. J., R. F. Baumeister, B. J. Bushman, W. K. Campbell, and E. J. Finkel. "Too Proud to Let Go: Narcissistic Entitlement as a Barrier to Forgiveness." *Journal of Personality and Social Psychology* 87, no. 6 (2004): 894.

Favez, N., and H. Tissot. "Fearful-Avoidant Attachment: A Specific Impact on Sexuality?" *Journal of Sex and Marital Therapy* 45, no. 6 (2019): 510–23.

Feldman, R., D. Dollberg, and R. Nadam. "The Expression and Regulation of Anger in Toddlers: Relations to Maternal Behavior and Mental Representations." *Infant Behavior and Development* 34, no. 2 (2011): 310–20.

Ferguson, C. J. "A Meta-analysis of Normal and Disordered Personality across the Life Span." *Journal of Personality and Social Psychology* 98, no. 4 (2010): 659.

Flavell, J. H. "The Development of Knowledge about Visual Perception." *Nebraska Symposium on Motivation* 25 (1977): 43–76.

Fox, N. A. "Psychophysiological Correlates of Emotional Reactivity during the First Year of Life." *Developmental Psychology* 25 no. 3 (1989): 364.

Frazier, P. A., A. L. Byer, A. R. Fischer, D. M. Wright, and K. A. Debord. "Adult Attachment Style and Partner Choice: Correlational and Experimental Findings." *Personal Relationships* 3, no. 2 (1996): 117–36.

Freud, Sigmund. *A General Introduction to Psychoanalysis.* New York: Horace Liveright, 1920, 372–87.

———. "On Narcissism: An Introduction." In *The Standard Edition of the Complete Psychological Works of Sigmund Freud, Volume 14 (1914–1916): On the History of the Psycho-Analytic Movement, Papers on Metapsychology and Other Works,* 67–102. London: Hogarth Press, 1957.

Galambos, N. L., E. T. Barker, and D. M. Almeida. "Parents Do Matter: Trajectories of Change in Externalizing and Internalizing Problems in Early Adolescence." *Child Development* 74, no. 2 (2003): 578–94.

Galinsky, A. D., W. W. Maddux, D. Gilin, and J. B. White. "Why It Pays to Get Inside the Head of Your Opponent: The Differential Effects of Perspective Taking and Empathy in Negotiations. *Psychological Science* 19, no. 4 (2008): 378–84.

George, C., N. Kaplan, and M. Main. "Adult Attachment Interview." Unpublished manuscript, 1996.

Gershoff, E. T., and A. Grogan-Kaylor. "Spanking and Child Outcomes: Old Controversies and New Meta-analyses." *Journal of Family Psychology* 30, no. 4 (2016): 453.

Grapsas, S., E. Brummelman, M. D. Back, and J. J. Denissen. "The 'Why' and 'How' of Narcissism: A Process Model of Narcissistic Status Pursuit. *Perspectives on Psychological Science* 15, no. 1 (2020): 150–72.

Grapsas, S., E. Brummelman, M. Dufner, and J. J. Denissen. "Affective Contingencies of Narcissism." *Journal of Personality and Social Psychology* 123, no. 2 (2022).

Green, A., R. Maclean, and K. Charles. "Recollections of Parenting Styles in the Development of Narcissism: The Role of Gender." *Personality and Individual Differences* 167 (2020): 110246.

Grolnick, W. S. *The Psychology of Parental Control: How Well-Meant Parenting Backfires.* London: Psychology Press, 2002.

Hagger, M. S., and K. Hamilton. "Grit and Self-discipline as Predictors of Effort and Academic Attainment." *British Journal of Educational Psychology* 89, no. 2 (2019): 324–42.

Harter, S. *The Construction of the Self: Developmental and Sociocultural Foundations.* New York: Guilford Publications, 2015.

Hazan, C., and P. R. Shaver. "Love and Work: An Attachment-Theoretical Perspective." *Journal of Personality and Social Psychology* 59, no. 2 (1990): 270.

Healey, M. L., and M. Grossman. "Cognitive and Affective Perspective-Taking: Evidence for Shared and Dissociable Anatomical Substrates." *Frontiers in Neurology* 9 (2018): 491.

Hendin, H. M., and J. M. Cheek. "Assessing Hypersensitive Narcissism: A Reexamination of Murray's Narcissism Scale." *Journal of Research in Personality* 31, no. 4 (1997): 588–99.

Hennan, M. R., S. M. Dornbusch, M. C. Herron, and J. R. Herting. "The Influence of Family Regulation, Connection, and Psychological Autonomy on Six Measures of Adolescent Functioning." *Journal of Adolescent Research* 12, no. 1 (1997): 34–67.

Hill, P. L., and B. W. Roberts. "Examining 'Developmental Me' A Review of Narcissism as a Life Span Construct." In *The Handbook of Narcissism and Narcissistic Personality Disorder: Theoretical Approaches, Empirical Findings, and Treatments,* edited by W. K. Campbell and J. D. Miller, 191–201. Hoboken, NJ: John Wiley and Sons, 2011.

Horney, K. *New Ways in Psychoanalysis.* New York: W. W. Norton, 2013.

Horton, R. S. "On Environmental Sources of Child Narcissism: Are Parents Really to Blame?" In *Narcissism and Machiavellianism in Youth: Implications for the Development of Adaptive and Maladaptive Behavior,* edited by C. T. Barry, P. K. Kerig, K. K. Stellwagen, and T. D. Barry, 125–43. Washington, DC: American Psychological Association, 2011.

———. "Parenting as a Cause of Narcissism: Empirical Support for Psychodynamic and Social Learning Theories." *The Handbook of Narcissism and Narcissistic Personality Disorder: Theoretical Approaches, Empirical Findings, and Treatments,* edited by W. Keith Campbell and Joshua D. Miller, 181–90. Hoboken, NJ: John Wiley & Sons, 2011.

Horton, R. S., G. Bleau, and B. Drwecki. "Parenting Narcissus: What Are the Links between Parenting and Narcissism?" *Journal of Personality* 74, no. 2 (2006): 345–76.

Horton, R. S., and T. Tritch. "Clarifying the Links between Grandiose Narcissism and Parenting." *Journal of Psychology* 148, no. 2 (2014): 133–43.

Hughes, M., and M. Donaldson. "The Use of Hiding Games for Studying the Coordination of Viewpoints." *Educational Review* 31, no. 2 (1979): 133–40.

Hussong, A. M., J. L. Coffman, and A. G. Halberstadt. "Parenting and the Development of Children's Gratitude." *Child Development Perspectives* 15, no. 4 (2021): 235–41.

Hyler, S. E. "Personality Diagnostic Questionnaire-4." *New York: New York State Psychiatric Institute*, 1994.

Kagan, J. *The Nature of the Child*. New York: Basic Books, 1984.

Kealy, D., and B. Rasmussen. "Veiled and Vulnerable: The Other Side of Grandiose Narcissism." *Clinical Social Work Journal* 40, no. 3 (2012): 356–65.

Kernberg, O. F. *Borderline Conditions and Pathological Narcissism*. London: Rowman & Littlefield, 1985.

Khaleque, A. "Perceived Parental Warmth, and Children's Psychological Adjustment, and Personality Dispositions: A Meta-analysis." *Journal of Child and Family Studies* 22, no. 2 (2013): 297–306.

Kılıçkaya, S., N. Uçar, and M. Denizci Nazlıgül. "A Systematic Review of the Association between Parenting Styles and Narcissism in Young Adults: From Baumrind's Perspective." *Psychological Reports* 126, no. 2 (2021): 620–40.

Kohut, H. *The Restoration of the Self*. Chicago: University of Chicago Press, 2009.

Kopala–Sibley, D. C., T. Olino, E. Durbin, M. W. Dyson, and D. N. Klein. "The Stability of Temperament from Early Childhood to Early Adolescence: A Multi-method, Multi-informant Examination." *European Journal of Personality* 32, no. 2 (2018): 128–45.

Kowalchyk, M., H. Palmieri, E. Conte, and P. Wallisch. "Narcissism through the Lens of Performative Self-Elevation." *Personality and Individual Differences* 177 (2021): 110780.

Kuppens, S., and E. Ceulemans. "Parenting Styles: A Closer Look at a Well-Known Concept. *Journal of Child and Family Studies* 28, no. 1 (2019): 168–81.

Kuppens, S., L. Laurent, M. Heyvaert, and P. Onghena. "Associations between Parental Psychological Control and Relational Aggression in Children and Adolescents: A Multilevel and Sequential Meta-analysis." *Developmental Psychology* 49, no. 9 (2013): 1697.

Lamborn, S. D., N. S. Mounts, L. Steinberg, and S. M. Dornbusch. "Patterns of Competence and Adjustment among Adolescents from Authoritative, Authoritarian, Indulgent, and Neglectful Families." *Child Development* 62, no. 5 (1991): 1049–65.

Lansford, J. E., C. Sharma, P. S. Malone, D. Woodlief, K. A. Dodge, P. Oburu, . . . and L. Di Giunta. "Corporal Punishment, Maternal Warmth, and Child

Adjustment: A Longitudinal Study in Eight Countries." *Journal of Clinical Child and Adolescent Psychology* 43, no. 4 (2014): 670–85.

Larzelere, R. E., and B. R. Kuhn. "Comparing Child Outcomes of Physical Punishment and Alternative Disciplinary Tactics: A Meta-analysis." *Clinical Child and Family Psychology Review* 8, no. 1 (2005): 1–37.

Leary, M. R., and R. F. Baumeister. "The Nature and Function of Self-Esteem: Sociometer Theory." *Advances in Experimental Social Psychology* 32 (2000): 1–62.

Lerner, J. V., and J. R. Vicary. "Difficult Temperament and Drug Use: Analyses from the New York Longitudinal Study." *Journal of Drug Education* 14, no. 1 (1984): 1–8.

Li, J. B., S. S. Bi, Y. E. Willems, and C. Finkenauer. "The Association between School Discipline and Self-Control from Preschoolers to High School Students: A Three-Level Meta-Analysis." *Review of Educational Research* 91, no. 1 (2021): 73–111.

Li, J. B., Y. E. Willems, F. M. Stok, M. Deković, M. Bartels, and C. Finkenauer. "Parenting and Self-Control across Early to Late Adolescence: A Three-Level Meta-analysis." *Perspectives on Psychological Science* 14, no. 6 (2019): 967–1005.

Light, P. "Piaget and Egocentrism: A Perspective on Recent Developmental Research." *Early Child Development and Care* 12, no. 1 (1983): 7–18.

Linehan, M. M., M. Bohus, and T. R. Lynch. "Dialectical Behavior Therapy for Pervasive Emotion Dysregulation: Theoretical and Practical Underpinnings." In *Handbook of Emotion Regulation*, edited by J. J. Gross, 581–605. New York: The Guilford Press, 2007.

Loeb, R. C., L. Horst, and P. J. Horton. "Family Interaction Patterns Associated with Self-Esteem in Preadolescent Girls and Boys." *Merrill-Palmer Quarterly of Behavior and Development* 26, no. 3 (1980): 205–17.

Maccoby, E. E. *Social Development: Psychological Growth and the Parent-Child Relationship.* New York: Harcourt Brace Jovanovich, 1980.

———. "Socialization in the Context of the Family: Parent-Child Interaction." In *Handbook of Child Psychology*, vol. 4, 4th edition, edited by Paul H. Mussen, 1–101. New York: Wiley, 1983.

Main, M., and J. Cassidy. "Categories of Response to Reunion with the Parent at Age 6: Predictable from Infant Attachment Classifications and Stable over a 1-Month Period." *Developmental Psychology* 24, no. 3 (1988): 415.

Main, M., and J. Solomon. "Procedures for Identifying Infants as Disorganized/Disoriented during the Ainsworth Strange Situation." *Attachment in the Preschool Years: Theory, Research, and Intervention* 1 (1990): 121–60.

Martin, S. R., S. Côté, and T. Woodruff. "Echoes of Our Upbringing: How Growing Up Wealthy or Poor Relates to Narcissism, Leader Behavior, and Leader Effectiveness." *Academy of Management Journal* 59, no. 6 (2016): 2157–77.

Marvin, R. S., M. T. Greenberg, and D. G. Mossler. "The Early Development of Conceptual Perspective Taking: Distinguishing among Multiple Perspectives." *Child Development* 47, no. 2 (1976): 511–14.

Masterson, J. F. *The Emerging Self: A Developmental Self and Object Relations Approach to the Treatment of the Closet Narcissistic Disorder of the Self.* New York: Brunner/Mazel, 1993.

———. *The Narcissistic and Borderline Disorders: An Integrated Developmental Approach.* New York: Brunner/Mazel, 1981.

Mechanic, K. L., and C. T. Barry. "Adolescent Grandiose and Vulnerable Narcissism: Associations with Perceived Parenting Practices. *Journal of Child and Family Studies* 24, no. 5 (2015): 1510–18.

Mikulincer, M., and P. R. Shaver. "Attachment Theory and Emotions in Close Relationships: Exploring the Attachment-Related Dynamics of Emotional Reactions to Relational Events." *Personal Relationships* 12, no. 2 (2005): 149–68.

Miller, A. "Depression and Grandiosity as Related Forms of Narcissistic Disturbances." *International Review of Psycho-Analysis* 6 (1979): 61–76.

Miller, A., and R. T. Ward. *Prisoners of Childhood: The Drama of the Gifted Child and the Search for the True Self.* New York: Basic Books, 1981.

Miller, J. D., and W. K. Campbell. Comparing Clinical and Social-Personality Conceptualizations of Narcissism. *Journal of Personality* 76, no. 3 (2008): 449–76.

———, eds. *The Handbook of Narcissism and Narcissistic Personality Disorder: Theoretical Approaches, Empirical Findings, and Treatments.* Hoboken, NJ: John Wiley and Sons, 2011.

Miller, J. D., A. Dir, B. Gentile, L. Wilson, L. R. Pryor, and W. K. Campbell. "Searching for a Vulnerable Dark Triad: Comparing Factor 2 Psychopathy, Vulnerable Narcissism, and Borderline Personality Disorder." *Journal of Personality* 78, no. 5 (2010): 1529–64.

Millon, T. *Disorders of Personality.* New York: Wiley and Sons, 1981.

Millon, T., and R. D. Davis. "An Evolutionary Theory of Personality Disorders." In *Major Theories of Personality Disorder,* edited by J. F. Clarkin and M. F. Lenzenweger, 221–346. New York: Guilford Press, 1996.

Mischel, W. *The Marshmallow Test: Understanding Self-Control and How to Master It.* New York: Random House, 2014.

Moffitt, T. E., L. Arseneault, D. Belsky, N. Dickson, R. J. Hancox, H. Harrington, . . . and A. Caspi. "A Gradient of Childhood Self-Control Predicts Health, Wealth, and Public Safety." *Proceedings of the National Academy of Sciences* 108, no. 7 (2011): 2693–98.

Morawska, A., C. K. Dittman, and J. C. Rusby. "Promoting Self-Regulation in Young Children: The Role of Parenting Interventions." *Clinical Child and Family Psychology Review* 22, no. 1 (2019): 43–51.

Morf, C. C., and F. Rhodewalt. "Unraveling the Paradoxes of Narcissism: A Dynamic Self-Regulatory Processing Model." *Psychological Inquiry* 12, no. 4 (2001): 177–96.

Morris, A. S., L. Steinberg, F. M. Sessa, S. Avenevoli, J. S. Silk, and M. J. Essex. "Measuring Children's Perceptions of Psychological Control: Developmental and Conceptual Considerations." In *Intrusive Parenting: How Psychological Control Affects Children and Adolescents*, edited by B. K. Barber, 125–59. Washington, DC: American Psychological Association, 2002.

O'Brien, M. L. "Examining the Dimensionality of Pathological Narcissism: Factor Analysis and Construct Validity of the O'Brien Multiphasic Narcissism Inventory." *Psychological Reports* 61, no. 2 (1987): 499–510.

Ohio State University. "How Parents May Help Create Their Own Little Narcissists." ScienceDaily. www.sciencedaily.com/releases/2015/03/150309145019.htm (accessed February 3, 2023).

Olson, S. L., D. E. Choe, and A. J. Sameroff. "Trajectories of Child Externalizing Problems between Ages 3 and 10 Years: Contributions of Children's Early Effortful Control, Theory of Mind, and Parenting Experiences." *Development and Psychopathology* 29, no. 4 (2017): 1333–51.

Orth, U., and R. W. Robins. "Is High Self-Esteem Beneficial? Revisiting a Classic Question." *American Psychologist* 77, no. 1 (2022): 5.

Otway, L. J., and V. L. Vignoles. "Narcissism and Childhood Recollections: A Quantitative Test of Psychoanalytic Predictions. *Personality and Social Psychology Bulletin* 32, no. 1 (2006): 104–16.

Pandey, A., D. Hale, S. Das, A. L. Goddings, S. J. Blakemore, and R. M. Viner. "Effectiveness of Universal Self-Regulation–Based Interventions in Children and Adolescents: A Systematic Review and Meta-analysis." *JAMA Pediatrics* 172, no. 6 (2018): 566–75.

Paolucci, E. O., and C. Violato. "A Meta-analysis of the Published Research on the Affective, Cognitive, and Behavioral Effects of Corporal Punishment." *Journal of Psychology* 138, no. 3 (2004): 197–222.

Patterson, G. R., T. J. Dishion, and L. Bank. "Family Interaction: A Process Model of Deviancy Training." *Aggressive Behavior* 10, no. 3 (1984): 253–67.

Piaget, J., and B. Inhelder. "A Child's Conception of Space." Translated by F. J. Langdon and J. L. Lunzer. New York: Humanities Press, 1956.

Perry, N. B., J. M. Dollar, S. D. Calkins, S. P. Keane, and L. Shanahan. "Childhood Self-Regulation as a Mechanism through Which Early Overcontrolling Parenting Is Associated with Adjustment in Preadolescence. *Developmental Psychology* 54, no. 8 (2018): 1542.

Pincus, A. L., E. B. Ansell, C. A. Pimentel, N. M. Cain, A. G. Wright, and K. N. Levy. "Initial Construction and Validation of the Pathological Narcissism Inventory. *Psychological Assessment* 21, no. 3 (2009): 365.

Pinquart, M. "Associations of Parenting Dimensions and Styles with Externalizing Problems of Children and Adolescents: An Updated Meta-analysis. *Developmental Psychology* 53, no. 5 (2017): 873.

Ramsey, A., P. J. Watson, M. D. Biderman, and A. L. Reeves. "Self-Reported Narcissism and Perceived Parental Permissiveness and Authoritarianism. *Journal of Genetic Psychology* 157, no. 2 (1996): 227–38.

Raskin, R. N., and C. S. Hall. "A Narcissistic Personality Inventory." *Psychological Reports* 45, no. 2 (1979): 590.

Raskin, R., and H. Terry. "A Principal-Components Analysis of the Narcissistic Personality Inventory and Further Evidence of Its Construct Validity." *Journal of Personality and Social Psychology* 54, no. 5 (1988): 890.

Roberts, B. W., and W. F. Delvecchio. "The Rank-Order Consistency of Personality Traits from Childhood to Old Age: A Quantitative Review of Longitudinal Studies." *Psychological Bulletin* 126, no. 1 (2000): 3.

Rosenthal, S. A., J. M. Hooley, and Y. Steshenko. "Distinguishing Grandiosity from Self-Esteem: Development of the Narcissistic Grandiosity Scale." Unpublished Manuscript (2007).

Rotenberg, K. J. "The Socialisation of Trust: Parents' and Children's Interpersonal Trust." *International Journal of Behavioral Development* 18, no. 4 (1995): 713–26.

Rotenberg, K. J., M. J. Boulton, and C. L. Fox. "Cross-Sectional and Longitudinal Relations among Children's Trust Beliefs, Psychological Maladjustment and Social Relationships: Are Very High as Well as Very Low Trusting Children at Risk?" *Journal of Abnormal Child Psychology* 33, no. 5 (2005): 595–610.

Rothstein, A. "The Theory of Narcissism: An Object-Relations Perspective. *Psychoanalytic Review* 66, no. 1 (Spring 1979): 35–47.

Sandquist, K., B. F. Grenyer, and P. Caputi. "The Relation of Early Environmental Experience to Shame and Self-Criticism: Psychological Pathways to Depression." Proceedings of the 44th APS Annual Conference, Darwin, Northern Territory, Australia, September 30–October 4, 2009.

Schaefer, E. S. "Children's Reports of Parental Behavior: An Inventory." *Child Development* 36, no. 2 (1965): 413–24.

Sedikides, C., E. A. Rudich, A. P. Gregg, M. Kumashiro, and C. Rusbult. "Are Normal Narcissists Psychologically Healthy? Self-Esteem Matters." *Journal of Personality and Social Psychology* 87, no. 3 (2004): 400.

Selman, R. L. "Taking Another's Perspective: Role-Taking Development in Early Childhood." *Child Development* 42, no. 6 (December 1971): 1721–34.

Shaver, P., and C. Hazan. "Being Lonely, Falling in Love." *Journal of Social Behavior and Personality* 2, no. 2 (1987): 105.

Shaw, D. S., K. Keenan, and J. I. Vondra. "Developmental Precursors of Externalizing Behavior: Ages 1 to 3." *Developmental Psychology* 30, no. 3 (1994): 355.

Sheldon, K. M., P. E. Jose, T. B. Kashdan, and A. Jarden. "Personality, Effective Goal-Striving, and Enhanced Well-Being: Comparing 10 Candidate Personality Strengths." *Personality and Social Psychology Bulletin* 41, no. 4 (2015): 575–85.

Skowron, E. A., S. E. Holmes, and R. M. Sabatelli. "Deconstructing Differentiation: Self-Regulation, Interdependent Relating, and Well-Being in Adulthood." *Contemporary Family Therapy* 25, no. 1 (2003): 111–29.

Sorkhabi, N., and E. Middaugh. "How Variations in Parents' Use of Confrontive and Coercive Control Relate to Variations in Parent–Adolescent Conflict, Adolescent Disclosure, and Parental Knowledge: Adolescents' Perspective." *Journal of Child and Family Studies* 23, no. 7 (2014): 1227–41.

Stayton, D. J., and M. D. Ainsworth. "Individual Differences in Infant Responses to Brief, Everyday Separations as Related to Other Infant and Maternal Behaviors." *Developmental Psychology* 9, no. 2 (1973): 226.

Stayton, D. J., R. Hogan, and M. S. Ainsworth. "Infant Obedience and Maternal Behavior: The Origins of Socialization Reconsidered." *Child Development* 42, no. 4 (October 1971): 1057–69.

Steinberg, L. "Autonomy, Conflict, and Harmony in the Family Relationship." In *At the Threshold: The Developing Adolescent*, edited by S. S. Feldman and G. R. Elliott, 255–76. Cambridge, MA: Harvard University Press, 1990.

Steinberg, L., J. D. Elmen, and N. S. Mounts. "Authoritative Parenting, Psychosocial Maturity, and Academic Success among Adolescents." *Child Development* 60, no. 6 (December 1989): 1424–36.

Steinberg, L., S. D. Lamborn, N. Darling, N. S. Mounts, and S. M. Dornbusch. "Over-Time Changes in Adjustment and Competence among Adolescents from Authoritative, Authoritarian, Indulgent, and Neglectful Families." *Child Development* 65, no. 3 (1994): 754–70.

Thomaes, S., and E. Brummelman. "Parents' Socialization of Narcissism in Children." In *Handbook of Trait Narcissism*, edited by A. D. Hermann, A. B. Brunell, and J. D. Foster, 143–48. Cham, Switzerland: Springer, 2018.

Thomaes, S., E. Brummelman, A. Reijntjes, and B. J. Bushman. "When Narcissus Was a Boy: Origins, Nature, and Consequences of Childhood Narcissism." *Child Development Perspectives* 7, no. 1 (2013): 22–26.

Thomaes, S., B. J. Bushman, B. O. De Castro, and H. Stegge. "What Makes Narcissists Bloom? A Framework for Research on the Etiology and Development of Narcissism." *Development and Psychopathology* 21, no. 4 (2009): 1233–47.

Thomaes, S., A. Reijntjes, B. Orobio De Castro, B. J. Bushman, A. Poorthuis, and M. J. Telch. "I Like Me If You Like Me: On the Interpersonal Modulation and Regulation of Preadolescents' State Self-Esteem." *Child Development* 81, no. 3 (2010): 811–25.

Thomaes S., H. Stegge, B. J. Bushman, T. Olthof, and J. Denissen. "Development and Validation of the Childhood Narcissism Scale." *Journal of Personality Assessment* 90, no. 4 (July 2008): 382–91.

Thomas, A., and S. Chess. "The New York Longitudinal Study: From Infancy to Early Adult Life." In *The Study of Temperament: Changes, Continuities, and Challenges*, edited by Robert Plomin and Judith Dunn, 40–52. Hillsdale, NJ: Lawrence Erlbaum, 1986.

———. *Temperament and Development*. Brunner/Mazel, 1977.

———. "Temperament and Follow-Up to Adulthood." In *Temperamental Differences in Infants and Young Children*, edited by Ruth Porter and Geralyn Lawrenson, 168–75. London: Pitman, 1982.

Thomas, A., S. Chess, H. G. Birch, M. E. Hertzig, and S. Korn. *Behavioral Individuality in Early Childhood*. New York: New York University Press, 1963.

Thomas, A., S. Chess, and S. J. Korn. "The Reality of Difficult Temperament." *Merrill-Palmer Quarterly* 28, no. 1 (1982): 1–20.

Trumpeter, N. N., P. J. Watson, B. J. O'Leary, and B. L. Weathington. "Self-Functioning and Perceived Parenting: Relations of Parental Empathy and Love Inconsistency with Narcissism, Depression, and Self-Esteem." *The Journal of Genetic Psychology* 169, no. 1 (2008): 51-71.

Trzesniewski, K. H., and M. B. Donnellan. "Rethinking "Generation Me": A Study of Cohort Effects from 1976–2006. *Perspectives on Psychological Science* 5 no. 1 (2010): 58–75.

Twenge, J. *Generation Me: Why Today's Young Americans Are More Confident, Assertive, Entitled—And More Miserable Than Ever Before*. New York: Atria, 2006.

Twenge, J. M., S. Konrath, J. D. Foster, W. K. Campbell, and B. J. Bushman "Further Evidence of an Increase in Narcissism among College Students." *Journal of Personality* 76, no. 4 (2008): 919–28.

Vaish, A., M. Carpenter, and M. Tomasello. "Sympathy through Affective Perspective Taking and Its Relation to Prosocial Behavior in Toddlers." *Developmental Psychology* 45, no. 2 (2009): 534.

Van Schie, C. C., H. L. Jarman, E. Huxley, and B. F. Grenyer. "Narcissistic Traits in Young People: Understanding the Role of Parenting and Maltreatment." *Borderline Personality Disorder and Emotion Dysregulation* 7, no. 1 (2020): 1–10.

Vernon, P. A., V. C. Villani, L. C. Vickers, and J. A. Harris. "A Behavioral Genetic Investigation of the Dark Triad and the Big 5." *Personality and Individual Differences* 44, no. 2 (2008): 445–52.

Verzeletti, C., V. L. Zammuner, C. Galli, and S. Agnoli. "Emotion Regulation Strategies and Psychosocial Well-Being in Adolescence." *Cogent Psychology* 3, no. 1 (2016): 1199294.

Vohs, K. D., and R. F. Baumeister, eds., *Handbook of Self-Regulation: Research, Theory, and Applications.* New York: Guilford Press, 2016.

Wartner, U. G., K. Grossmann, E. Fremmer-Bombik, and G. Suess. "Attachment Patterns at Age Six in South Germany: Predictability from Infancy and Implications for Preschool Behavior." *Child Development* 65, no. 4 (1994): 1014–27.

Waters, E., and E. M. Cummings. "A Secure Base from Which to Explore Close Relationships. *Child Development* 71, no. 1 (2000): 164–72.

Waters, E., S. Merrick, D. Treboux, J. Crowell, and L. Albersheim. "Attachment Security in Infancy and Early Adulthood: A Twenty-Year Longitudinal Study." *Child Development* 71, no. 3 (2000): 68489.

Watson, P. J., and M. D. Biderman. "Narcissistic Personality Inventory Factors, Splitting, and Self-Consciousness. *Journal of Personality Assessment* 61, no. 1 (1993): 41–57.

Watson, P. J., S. E. Hickman, R. J. Morris, J. T. Milliron, and L. Whiting. "Narcissism, Self-Esteem, and Parental Nurturance." *Journal of Psychology* 129 no. 1 (1995): 61–73.

Watson, P. J., T. Little, and M. D. Biderman. "Narcissism and Parenting Styles." *Psychoanalytic Psychology* 9, no. 2 (1992): 231.

Weaver, J. M., T. J. Schofield, and L. M. Papp. "Breastfeeding Duration Predicts Greater Maternal Sensitivity over the Next Decade." *Developmental Psychology* 54, no. 2 (2018): 220.

Weeland, J., E. Brummelman, S. R. Jaffee, R. R. Chhangur, D. Van Der Giessen, W. Matthys, . . . and G. Overbeek. "Does Caregivers' Use of Praise Reduce Children's Externalizing Behavior? A Longitudinal Observational Test in the Context of a Parenting Program." *Developmental Psychology* 58, no. 7 (2022).

Willems, Y. E., J. B. Li, A. M. Hendriks, M. Bartels, and C. Finkenauer. "The Relationship between Family Violence and Self-Control in Adolescence: A Multi-level Meta-analysis." *International Journal of Environmental Research and Public Health* 15, no. 11 (2018): 2468.

Williams, L. R., K. A. Degnan, K. E. Perez-Edgar, H. A. Henderson, K. H. Rubin, D. S. Pine, . . . and N. A. Fox. "Impact of Behavioral Inhibition and Parenting Style on Internalizing and Externalizing Problems from Early Childhood through Adolescence." *Journal of Abnormal Child Psychology* 37, no. 8 (2009): 1063–75.

Winnicott, D. W. *Playing and Reality*, 2nd ed. London: Routledge, 2005.

Wolfradt, U., S. Hempel, and J. N. Miles. "Perceived Parenting Styles, Depersonalisation, Anxiety and Coping Behaviour in Adolescents." *Personality and Individual Differences* 34 no. 3 (2003): 521–32.

Acknowledgments

$\mathcal{W}$riting this book has been a personal journey—part search, part adventure, part discovery, part aspiration. Of course, every book is a team effort. Many talented people share in the credit. Their support includes everything from insight to affection, reading to reworking, editing to considering, listening to arguing, conceptualizing to recommending. Small interactions often had big impacts, and their consistent encouragement strengthened me throughout.

I want to thank many individually for their contributions and support for me and my work over a lifetime. My "girlfriends"—Nancy Bray, Sally Maxson, Diane Funk, Nancy Taylor, Nancy Mason, Sheila O'Conner, Katherine Whelan, Sunita Stewart, Reka Pole, Susan Steadman, Sheila Phaneuf, and Betty Ablon, who make life better every day. My "girls"—Laura Ramsower and Ellen Haberle, my attentive and wonderful goddaughters now raising their own children and an important part of my family.

To my "couple friends"—Lee and Sheila Simpson, Dan and Katherine Whelan, Alan and Vickye Madewell, Rex and Norma Vardeman, Bart and Mary Sue Wade, Bill and Terry Kurfess, Peter and Marguerite Vogel, Brooke and Connie McCann, Tony and Sunita Stewart, Prit and Reka Pole, Randy and Diane Milhorn, and Scott and Martha Larsen, who make life more fun. My "cousins"—Paula Sevigny, Tom Shook, and Carol Kaelson and the rest of the bunch who are ever-present reminders of the importance of family and the impact of secure attachment. To my retired editor—Susan Steadman, a successful playwright, director, and author, who graciously shared those talents with me, and who has been a writing coach, editor, and creative confidant in many projects over much of my career. To my readers—J. Martin Brown, Ted Asay, Rickye Marshall, Jennifer Phillips, Matthew Housson, James Ray, and Reka Pole, whose diligence, insight, and attention made this work more accessible, informative, and thoughtful. To the entire team at Rowman & Littlefield—but especially my editor Suzanne Staszak-Silva and my production editor Tricia Currie-Knight—who kept the process moving along with care and competence. To my agent—Joelle Delbourgo, whose smart, sharp eye for good ideas and the market and thoughtful, steady guidance have been invaluable. Much thanks to my publicity team—Dana Kaye, Angela Malamud, Jordan Brown, and Eleanor Embody—whose instincts, enthusiasm, and energy for the market are commendable. To my social media advisor—Mary Kate Bartell, who has helped immeasurably in managing a world I know little about. My photographer—Jacque Manaugh, whose magical eye turned a standard head shot into a series of images that capture a story. My website creator—Lauren Lanza Osias, a multitalented professional with a rare conceptual eye for color, design, concepts, copy, and photography, who took a few ideas and a couple pictures and turned them into so much more, creating an engaging and informative public presence on the web.

To my graduate student-researcher—Allison Gregg, whose bright mind and high energy made keeping up with the literature possible, the bibliography manageable, and article preparation easier. To my editor, assistant, and now friend—Leslie Lutz, a brilliant, highly regarded author in her own right, who has proved vital to producing this work. Like the Cat-in-the-Hat, she can synthesize complex concepts and put them onto paper with ease while simultaneously providing a tutorial in grammar and literary convention, correcting a *Chicago Manual of Style* citation, and directing me to talented publicists and designers.

To my much-missed mother—who showed me that everything important comes from the heart. My sons—who continue to fuel inspiration and sustain joy and remain the "loves" of my life. My husband—who is my best friend and whose belief in me and my projects has been unbounded. His insights, wordsmithing, and imagination are evident on every page. His love and support remain the strength beneath my work.

In the end, I am indebted to the many patients who have shared their lives with me. They have each touched my life in formative ways and taught me many of the most valuable lessons of my career.

Index

Page references for figures are italicized.

achievement, 14, 23, 29, 30; and
   authoritative parenting, 191; and
   conditional regard, 42, 82; and
   cultural messaging, xi, 35, 247; and
   emotional regulation, 89–90, 93;
   healthy attitudes toward, 77; and
   hovering/directive parenting, 228–
   30; parental overvaluation of, 77
admiration, narcissistic need for, 23,
   26, 66, 111, 203
affection, 62, 172, 172, 183,
   194, 201, 208, 210, 211, 223,
   226, 228, 229, 230, 232; on a
   continuum, 205; and critical-harsh
   parenting, 232, 233, 237, 238, 251
affective perspective-taking. See
   emotional perspective-taking
aggression: and authoritarian
   parenting, 191; in bully narcissists,
   30, 38; in grandiose narcissists, 28;
   in relation to indulgence, 231; in
   relation to parental warmth, 42
Ainsworth, Mary, 153, 156–57, 193
alcohol abuse and prevention, 192
altruism and N2B kids, motivations
   for, 51

anger, and narcissism, 9, 24, 25,
   51, 103, 172; and emotional
   regulation, 49, 108–9; and
   indulgent/permissive parenting,
   231 See also aggression; rage
antisocial behavior, and manipulative
   narcissism, 32; and neglectful
   parenting, 192; and parental
   psychological control, 193
anxiety, 12, 24, 49, 85, 100, 113,
   157, 158, 159, 163, 179, 193; in
   children of authoritarian parents,
   191; in children of hovering/
   directive parents, 230; in children
   of neglectful parents, 192; in
   children of permissive parents,
   192; and narcissism, 17, 22,
   67–68; prevention of, 42; in
   vulnerable narcissists, 28
Aristotle, 204, 249
attachment: theory, 156–64;
   fearful, 161; in infancy, 156–57;
   insecure ambivalent/resistant,
   157, 161; insecure avoidant
   and avoidant/dismissive, 157,
   161; insecure/disorganized 157;

287

self-knowledge, in relation to self-concept, 55, 57–58, 62, 105, 228
self-liking, 20, 22, 63
self-love, 20. *See also* self-esteem
Self-Regulation Theory (SRT), 90. *See also* Dialectical Behavior Theory
self-regulation, 90–91. *See also* emotional regulation
self-worth, 58, 81. *See also* self-esteem
sense of humor. *See* humor
sensorimotor stage, 120
sexual promiscuity, 30, 32, 33, 163. *See also* daredevil narcissist
shame, 24, 100; healthy toleration of, 55, 71; in N2B children, 24, 56, 55–56, 67; parental use of, 79, 83, 107, 113, 142, 145, 148
social comparison theory, 58
somatic complaints: and authoritarian parenting, 191; in children who internalize, 100; and permissive parenting, 192
SRT. *See* Self-Regulation Theory
the "Strange Situation," 157
substance abuse, 9, 24, 30, 31, 38, 89, 93, 191
success. *See* achievement
superiority, perception of, 23, 25, *237*, 56. *See also* grandiosity

talent and narcissism. *See* gifted children
tantrum, 21, 90, 91, 99, 101, 106, 109–10, 197–98, 231
temperament, 11, 18, 157–58; difficult, 11, 158; easy, 11, 158; and narcissism, 33, 34; slow to warm, 11, 158
tendencies. *See* narcissistic tendencies and traits

therapy, effect on narcissism, 33
thick-skinned, in grandiose narcissism, *28*
thin-skinned, in vulnerable narcissism, *28*
Three Mountains Task, 127
traits. *See* narcissistic tendencies and traits
trauma, effects of, 11, 12, 34, 93, 153, 155, 159, 163, 243
treatment of the child, 203–24, *214*
trust, 47; and attachment theory 156–64; in regards to love and relationships, 151–85; in relation to parental warmth, 182

unconditional love. *See* love and relationships
underachievement, and non-achieving narcissists, 30, 32, 67; and parental messaging, 77–79. *See also* achievement

values. *See* culture and narcissism
view of the child, on a continuum, 203–24, *209*, *212*
vulnerable narcissist, *28*, 29; and self-esteem, 18

warmth. *See* parental warmth
wealth, 24, 28, 33, 35, 80, 112, 172, 232, 235, 238, 252–53; and manipulative narcissism, 32. *See also* culture and narcissism
winning, concept of/values, 14, 247, 248; healthy parental attitudes toward, 77; and high-achieving narcissists, 29; need for in N2B children, 51; parental emphasis on, 79, 228. *See also* competition
the workplace, and narcissism, 24

About the Author

Mary Ann Little, PhD, is a clinical psychologist who has been in private practice for over four decades. After earning a BA from Smith College and a PhD from the University of Texas Southwestern Medical Center at Dallas, she completed postdoctoral work in Piagetian psychology at the University of Geneva at the direction of Barbel Inhelder. She is currently an adjunct professor at the University of Texas Southwestern Medical Center at Dallas and has served as an adjunct professor in the departments of psychology and special education at the University of Texas at Dallas. Little authored *Loving Your Children Better: Matching Parenting Styles to the Age and Stage of Your Children*; *Cooperation Station*, an educational toy for kids and families; and the *Competent Kids Series*. In addition, she published two picture books for children with Sonya Bemporad, MA, *James Begins Childcare* and *Beginning Childcare*, and an education aid for parents with D. Kim Reid, PhD, *Foundations for Success in the Early School Years*. She has been a consultant to numerous educational and psychiatric facilities and frequently lectures to both lay and professional audiences. When not in her Dallas office, she can be found with her husband cooking, cycling back roads in Europe, or hiking trails near Santa Fe. Visit her online at drmaryannlittle.com.

Printed in the USA
CPSIA information can be obtained
at www.ICGtesting.com
LVHW090823151123
763328LV00003B/3

9 781538 182161